Law and Justice from
Antiquity to Enlightenment

Law and Justice from Antiquity to Enlightenment

Robert W. Shaffern

ROWMAN & LITTLEFIELD PUBLISHERS, INC.
Lanham • Boulder • New York • Toronto • Plymouth, UK

ROWMAN & LITTLEFIELD PUBLISHERS, INC.

Published in the United States of America
by Rowman & Littlefield Publishers, Inc.
A wholly owned subsidary of The Rowman & Littlefield Publishing Group, Inc.
4501 Forbes Boulevard, Suite 200, Lanham, Maryland 20706
www.rowmanlittlefield.com

Estover Road
Plymouth PL6 7PY
United Kingdom

British Library Cataloguing in Publication Information Available

Library of Congress Cataloging-in-Publication Data

Shaffern, Robert W., 1963–
    Law and justice from antiquity to enlightenment / Robert W. Shaffern.
        p. cm.
    Includes bibliographical references and index.
    ISBN-13: 978-0-7425-5475-7 (cloth : alk. paper)
    ISBN-10: 0-7425-5475-9 (cloth : alk. paper)
    ISBN-13: 978-0-7425-5476-4 (pbk. : alk. paper)
    ISBN-10: 0-7425-5476-7 (pbk. : alk. paper)
    ISBN-13: 978-0-7425-5760-4 (electronic)
    ISBN-10: 0-7425-5760-X (electronic)
    1. Law—History. 2. Law, Ancient. 3. Law, Medieval. I. Title.
    K150.S52 2009
    340.09—dc22
                                                            2008028150

Printed in the United States of America

∞™ The paper used in this publication meets the minimum requirements of
American National Standard for Information Sciences—Permanence of Paper
for Printed Library Materials, ANSI/NISO Z39.48-1992.

Table of Contents

Abbreviations

CIC	Aemilius Friedberg, ed., *Corpus iuris canonici*, 2 vols. (Leipzig, Germany: B. Tauchnitz, 1879–1881).
Crisis of Church and State	Brian Tierney, *The Crisis of Church and State, 1050–1300* (Toronto, ON: University of Toronto Press, 1964).
Birks	Peter Birks and Grant McLeod, eds., *Justinian's Institutes* (Ithaca, NY: Cornell University Press, 1987).
English Constitutional History	George Burton Adams and H. Morse Stephens, eds., *Select Documents of English Constitutional History* (London, UK: MacMillan & Co., 1930).
Krueger and Mommsen	Paulus Krueger and Theodor Mommsen, eds., *Corpus iuris civilis*, 3 vols. (Berlin, Germany: Weidmann, 1899).
LCL	Loeb Classical Library (Cambridge, MA: Harvard University Press, 1911).
Pharr	Clyde Pharr, ed., *The Theodosian Code and Novels and the Sirmondian Constitutions* (Princeton, NJ: Princeton University Press, 1952).
Political Ideas	Dino Bigongiari, ed., *The Political Ideas of St. Thomas Aquinas* (New York, NY: Hafner Press, 1953).
Stein, *Roman Law*	Peter Stein, *Roman Law in European History* (Cambridge, UK: Cambridge University Press, 1999).

Tanner and   Norman P. Tanner, S. J., and G. Alberigo, eds.,
   Alberigo, Decrees   *Decrees of the Ecumenical Councils*, 2 vols. (London, UK: Sheed & Ward, 1990).

Watson   Alan Watson, ed. and trans., *The Digest of Justinian*, 4 vols. (Philadelphia, PA: University of Pennsylvania Press, 1985).

Preface

This book is essentially an introduction to the intellectual history of justice and the law in traditional European civilization. I hope that readers of this book will come to appreciate some of the most interesting and thoughtful debates and arguments in Western civilization discussed herein. The figures discussed here lived in environments very different from our own and so law—and thinking about the law—served purposes in many respects different from ours. The state and government were exceedingly weak. Most persons lived in relatively isolated, small, and mostly self-governing rural villages. The efficacy of law therefore depended oftener upon the vitality of community and culture, rather than government coercion. In addition to its inherent interest, I believe that rediscovering the jurisprudence of earlier eras might help us think more creatively and acutely about the important legal and jurisprudential problems of our day—overcrowded prisons, intergenerational welfare dependency, facile and fatuous civil suits, and the efficacy of legislation versus judicial decision—among, of course, a host of others.

I must express my gratitude to the librarians at the Weinberg Memorial Library at the University of Scranton, and the Glenn Bartle Library at Binghamton University, whose gentle guidance and aid made the writing of this book so much easier. I am also deeply grateful to the editorial staff at Rowman & Littlefield, for their generous endorsement and advocacy of my project.

Great thanks are also due to my wife, Elizabeth, who provided the moral support needed to finish this book, which is dedicated to our children, Thomas, Monica, Christina, and Caroline. May they, like the blessed, ever hunger and thirst for justice [Mt 5.6].

PART I

Law in the Fertile Crescent and Ancient Greece

While law, of course, is as old as humankind itself, the history of the law may only date from the first written references to the law and speculation about it. In some cases, like that of the ancient Fertile Crescent, law codes themselves survive from earlier civilizations. In other cases, like that of the ancient Greeks, other genres of literature may also be harvested for clues about law and jurisprudence. For Western civilization, these two civilizations established the foundations of legal history.

The *Code of Hammurabi*

The word "civilization" comes from the Latin word *civis*, meaning "citizen of a city," so the word itself refers to a way of life based on the city. In the strict sense, the Sioux tribes of the North American Great Plains were not "civilized" because their way of life—rich though it was—did not include cities. On the other hand, cities did make their first appearance in western Asia, in what is now the beleaguered nation of Iraq. Many city dwellers followed professions, such as soldiers, priests, and artisans, which did not involve the production of either food or fiber, which is to say that civilization depends on agriculture—whether arable or pastoral—which produces a surplus of necessities and makes it possible for some members of society to leave field and meadow for other endeavors. Ecological factors figured prominently in the formation of the first cities, as did human artifice. Since the end of the last Ice Age (about 12 000 BC), much of the Earth's surface has been drying out,

1

and producing the great Sahara, among other deserts. Human populations have been forced to migrate in search not only of water but also of game and habitable regions. The drying out of northern Africa and western Asia concentrated populations in river valleys, where both water and soils are capable of sustaining life, and where agriculture first probably came into being around 8000 BC. The first settlements large enough to be called cities emerged in "the Land between the Rivers," what the Greeks called Mesopotamia (from *mesos* "middle," and *potamos* "river"), and what the Arabs call *al-jazeera*, "the island", specifically, the southeast of the region bounded by the Tigris and Euphrates rivers, the ancient region of Sumer. The culture which grew up in southeast Mesopotamia eventually spread to the entire Fertile Crescent.

The cultural legacy, of which the law forms a significant part, of ancient Sumer survives even today. Although they lived among Semitic-speaking peoples, the Sumerians spoke a language unrelated to that of their neighbors. Their texts, nonetheless, survive solely in Semitic languages, chiefly Akkadian. Around 3200 BC, the Sumerians invented the first form of writing, known as cuneiform (from Latin, *cuneus*, meaning "wedge"), in which scribes pressed reeds into damp clay to form wedge-shaped characters. The first written texts were business records. Ancient Sumer was a collection of city-states, wherein each of the city-states took its turn at being hegemon of the region. The survival of the ziggurats, a kind of step-pyramid, attests to the importance of religion. The Sumerians undertook the first astronomical investigations, developed the first tables of planetary motion, and the first lunar calendars. They virtually invented geometry, developed a number system based on sixty, and derived the first tables of roots and powers (owing to the number system, which made calculations otherwise cumbersome).

The classic era of Sumerian civilization came to a close around 2200 BC, when King Sargon of Akkad (a Semite) invaded Sumer from the northwest. As a consequence of Sargon's conquest, Semites became the heirs of the Sumerians, who were culturally displaced only in their language. In all other cultural endeavors, the Semites of northwest Mesopotamia adopted the achievements of the Sumerians, and improved upon them.

After the Akkadians faded from the scene, the city of Babylon grew in power and influence. By 1800 BC, the kings of Babylon had conquered the first Mesopotamian empire. The Babylonians turned out to be exceptional students of the Sumerians. They continued the Mesopotamian tradition of mathematical excellence, and computed with both linear and quadratic equations. They improved upon the lunar calendar and tables of planetary motion.

The Babylonians likewise excelled in law. The greatest of the kings of Old Babylon was Hammurabi (1792–1750 BC), known as the "Law-Giver" because he commissioned the codification of Babylonian law, which Sumerian law must have much influenced. The *Code of Hammurabi* was carved into stone steles and erected in public, so that all could have access to the law of the land. In its epilogue, Hammurabi proclaimed the Code "in order that the strong might not oppress the weak, that justice be given the orphan and the widow"—a clause that appears time and again in later codes of law. Thus, at the very beginning of legal history, the law and the administration of justice was said to exist especially for the protection of the weak, the poor, and the humble. Hammurabi's code also established two other principles. First, that justice should be impartial and second, that, essential to the principle of impartiality, only the government made law and that law must be made public.

Hammurabi's code consisted mainly of civil, not criminal, law. The king's servants and expenditures were mostly devoted to maintaining his army and to defending the state cult, not to policing his subjects. Premodern governments were weak, and most settlements relatively isolated. Most people had to plead for and defend their own interests, property, persons, and lives in the company of their fellow villagers. Hammurabi's Code did treat murder, arson, rape, incest, robbery (in the act), kidnapping, and stealing from the temple as crimes, the penalty for which was death.[1] But not even a powerful and respected ruler like Hammurabi could maintain the institutions necessary for state investigation and prosecution of unlawful seizure of property or person. As civil law, Hammurabi's code was primarily preoccupied with the law of persons (free or servile) family law, property law, the limitation of private violence, and judicial procedure.

The *Code of Hammurabi* recognized three, unequal legal statuses—noble, common (merchants, artisans, and farmers), and slave. Legal status determined how much compensation was owed to the victim of injury. A noble was entitled to more compensation than a commoner. In the case of loss of life, compensation was owed to the relatives of the slain. Slaves had virtually no legal reality at all. When a slave had been killed, the murderer owed compensation to the slave's master, not the slave's kin. The compensatory amounts listed in the *Code of Hammurabi* were high, so as to encourage the payment of compensation rather than the undertaking of vendetta: "If a freed man strike the body of another freed man, he shall pay ten shekels in money."[2] The payment of compensation attempted to reduce violence resulting from vengeance, because "the obligation to avenge the killing of kinsmen . . . is a founding principle of all societies . . . systems of criminal law have not replaced the feud so much as diverted its energies into public forms."[3] The tensions which brought the aggrieved parties together might well last long after formal judicial procedures had been completed, and so even with the payment of compensation, and certainly in the case of vengeance-violence, the resumption of concord could be difficult. In this way should these texts from the Code be understood: "If a man put out the eye of another man, his eye shall be put out. If he break another man's bone, his bone shall be broken."[4] The point was that, once the scales had been balanced again, the dispute was closed, thereby establishing another basic tenet of jurisprudence, namely, that judicial procedures could not go on indefinitely.

In addition to settling disputes over theft, murder, and assault, much of the Code regulated family life, which also included claims to inheritances. Consummation apparently made a marriage legally valid: "If a man take a woman to wife, but have no intercourse with her, this woman is no wife to him."[5] The Code provided for divorce, and the division of property requisite to divorce: "If a man wish to separate from a . . . wife who has borne him children: then he shall give that wife her dowry, and a part of the usufruct of field, garden, and property, so that she can rear her children. If a man wishes to separate from his wife who has borne him no children, he shall give her the amount of her purchase money and the dowry which she brought from her father's house."[6]

Finally, Hammurabi's Code defined proper judicial procedure. Trial by water determined the truth of accusations:

> If any one bring an accusation against a man, and the accused go to the river and leap into the river, if he sink in the river his accuser shall take possession of his house. But if the river prove that the accused is not guilty, and he escape unhurt, then he who had brought the accusation shall be put to death, while he who leaped into the river shall take possession of the house that belonged to his accuser.[7]

Thus, false accusation would be punished at the same time that the accused was acquitted. Among the accusations subject to trial by water was adultery: "If the 'finger is pointed' at a man's wife about another man, but she is not sleeping with the other man, she shall jump into the river for her husband."[8] Hammurabi required written records of judges' decisions. If the judge should later be shown to have made an erroneous decision, "then he shall pay twelve times the fine set by him in the case, and he shall be publicly removed from the judge's bench, and never again shall he sit there to render judgement."[9]

The empire of the city of Babylon lasted until about 1100 BC, when it mysteriously collapsed, as did so many other great, eastern Mediterranean empires at the end of the Bronze Age. When civilization resumed its vitality, about 800 BC, the cultural achievements of the Babylonians had survived nonetheless, and among those achievements was the Code of the great Hammurabi; in fact, his code became a kind of Asian common law with the advent of the Persian Empire towards the end of the sixth century BC. While the Persian kings permitted local laws to continue in existence, they found that another law, applicable to the whole of their empire, was also desirable. They chose the *Code of Hammurabi* to serve this purpose, and so his law was observed from Afghanistan to Asia Minor, from Armenia to the cataracts of Egypt.

Ancient Israel

The laws of another people of the ancient Fertile Crescent may well be the most important and influential collection of legal materials in world history. The law of the Hebrews/Israelites has passed into the religio-cultural inheritance of today's Jews and Christians. Even many secularized peoples of the modern world can trace their basic legal principles to ancient Israel. Over the last century or so, scholars have pointed out the Mesopotamian inheritance of the ancient Hebrews. In particular, these scholars point to the parallel themes in the ancient Sumerian story of *The Epic of Gilgamesh* and the flood story in the book of Genesis.

The Hebrews (later Israelites) were but one of a number of peoples who inhabited the ancient Fertile Crescent. The book of Genesis, of course, preserves the memory of their national origins, located by the biblical stories in ancient Chaldea (the Semitic name for Sumer). Terah, father of the patriarch Abraham, is said to have been from "Ur of the Chaldeans" (Gn 11.28). Genesis also records the migrations of the early Hebrews northwest into Assyria, then southwest into Canaan/Palestine, and then into Egypt. The long Judaeo-Christian tradition began with the Israelites' migration out of Egypt, called the Exodus (a "going forth" from Greek, *exodos* Latin *exire*, "to go out"), and recorded in the biblical book of the same name.

According to the book of Genesis, necessity forced the ancient Hebrews to flee the land of Canaan for settlement in Egypt. Famine afflicted the land of Canaan and Egypt's agricultural abundance must have been a timely attraction. In ancient times, Egypt often served as the breadbasket for many lands and nations, owing to the regular but gentle annual floods of the Nile. Summer rains in the highlands of Abyssinia, where the great river originated, fertilized and watered the cultivatable lands downstream in Egypt.

The Hebrew migration into Egypt may well have accompanied the Hyksos invasion of that country, sometime around 1700 BC. The Hyksos, like the Hebrews, spoke a Semitic language. The invasion of the Hyksos may have benefited the Hebrews, who were their cultural and linguistic cousins, and perhaps trustworthy allies in the occupation of a hostile native population. The Genesis story of the patriarch Joseph (a Hebrew who attained high rank in Egyptian government), on the one hand, and the first chapter of Exodus (which mentions a pharaoh who knew not Joseph (Ex 1.8) and enslaved the Hebrews), on the other, may preserve dim memories of a period of prosperity and preferment, followed by generations of state servitude in Egypt. After the expulsion of the Hyksos, the Hebrews may well have been subject to reprisals as collaborators with a detested foreign regime. Even if they were not allied with the Hyksos, however, relations may still have been poor between the Hebrews and the native Egyptians. Unlike many other peoples who have settled among a wealthier and culturally more sophisticated people, the Hebrews preserved their national identity and separateness while they dwelt in Egypt. Genesis more than hints at widespread resentment of Hebrews. The Egyptians "may not eat with Hebrews; that is abhorrent to them" (Gn 43.32). When the Hyksos were out of the picture, about 1550 BC, perhaps then the Hebrews were reduced to state servitude.

Under a great national leader by the name of Moses, the Israelites, as Torah now calls them, were probably able to exploit the anarchic conditions in thirteenth-century Egypt and flee to freedom. Like their ancestors, they wandered about the deserts of Sinai and Transjordan. Sometime around 1200 BC, the Israelites crossed the Jordan River. They occupied mostly the hill country of Galilee and Judaea, while native Canaanites, to whom they were closely related in language and culture, dwelt in low-lying areas. For the next two hundred years, the Israelites were often at war with Canaanite tribes, as well as the Philistines, a people who lived on the coast of the Mediterranean, and whose origins may well have been in the islands of the Aegean Sea. All of these small nations benefited from what ancient historians have labeled a Dark Age, which began around 1100 BC (the beginning of the Iron Age), and ended sometime around 800, an era during which great empires virtually disappeared from the map of the eastern Mediterranean. In that imperial vacuum, small states could emerge, survive, and thrive.

The Israelites who crossed the Jordan under the leadership of Joshua formed a confederation of tribal groups. When confronted by a great military threat, some tribes would ally together under figures such as Samson, Jephtha, and Deborah, whom the Bible calls judges, all of whom were possessed of "the spirit of the Lord." In the tradition of Moses, their political and military authority depended upon religious leadership and prophetic charism. Against the Philistines, however, who seem to have been better organized and perhaps better equipped than the Canaanites, Israelite confederations won few military victories. Many Israelites became convinced that one national leader—a king—was necessary, in spite of the protests from some holy men, such as Samuel, who were now sometimes also called prophets. Around 1020, the Israelites acclaimed Saul as first king of Israel, whom the more able and charismatic David (around 1000) soon supplanted. David smashed the Philistines in battle and made the old Canaanite city of Jerusalem the capital of a united and relatively strong Israelite kingdom.

While David founded a dynasty that ruled until 586, his political project endured only two generations. Neither David nor Solomon, apparently, overcame the separatist tribal inclinations of the Israelites. After the death of his son Solomon in 922, the northern Israelite tribes renounced Davidic rule. These provinces, more populous and wealthier than the south, seceded from Davidic control and formed a new kingdom which came to be called Israel. The southern provinces that remained in the Davidic dynasty were known as the kingdom of Judah, after David's own tribe. Of course, this schism merely created two small, weak kingdoms, for even Israel's security soon became critical. The Dark Ages were drawing to a close, and great, new empires reemerged in the Fertile Crescent. In particular, the establishment of the powerful Assyrian Empire proved catastrophic to the kingdom of Israel. The Assyrians first reduced Israel to a tributary state, and then obliterated her altogether in 741. In keeping with Mesopotamian practices, the Assyrians marched off the entire population of the kingdom, to be resettled and assimilated elsewhere in their far-flung empire, and so Jewish tradition sometimes speaks of the "lost tribes of Israel."

The southern kingdom of Judah was poorer and less populous than her northern sister state. Judah did, however, enjoy greater political stability as a consequence of her homogeneity and Davidic inheritance. Judah's capital city remained Jerusalem, in which was the Temple of Solomon, and so continued as the cultic capital of the Israelite people. After the conquest of Israel, Judah survived as a client dependency of the Assyrians, and even outlived the great empire. In 626, a reconstituted Babylonian state attacked and destroyed the Assyrian capital of Nineveh. Judah then became a client of the Neo-Babylonian Empire, although the kings of Judah apparently believed that the fall of Assyria was their opportunity to reestablish their independence. They mistakenly relied on an alliance with the Egyptians to preserve what was left of their political autonomy. In 605, the Babylonian King Nebuchadnezzar II (605–555) destroyed the Egyptian army. In 586, he conquered

Judah and destroyed Jerusalem. The Babylonians marched high-ranking Israelites off to exile in Hammurabi's old capital city.

Return to Judah came in 536, soon after the Persian king Cyrus (559–509) destroyed the new Babylonian kingdom. The rise of the Persian Empire marked the first time that the Fertile Crescent fell under the rule of people who spoke an Indo-European language. The Persians, of course, were not Mesopotamians but rather dwelt in the Iranian plateau. Cyrus, whose regime featured religious and cultural toleration, allowed the Jews, as they were now called, to return to their native land (although by now there were large communities of Jews outside of Palestine/Judaea), and to rebuild the Temple, for which Cyrus himself provided money.

Exile from Judaea and the existence of the diaspora suggested to many Jews that national and religious survival could not be confined to one time and space. Consequently, religious texts and the authority of the scholars who expertly compiled and commented on them began to figure more and more prominently among the Jews. Many of those religious texts were compiled during the period after the exile and before the Roman conquest in 63 BC, and so come from a literary tradition nearly a millennium old.

The Spirit of the Biblical Law

The Torah contains the most sacred writings of the Jewish people, and consists of narratives and some of the most influential legal texts in world history.[10] The Torah is made up of the first five books of the Hebrew Bible (hence their name in Greek, "Pentateuch"): Genesis, Exodus, Leviticus, Numbers, and Deuteronomy (meaning "second law," in Greek (δευτερος vo μος, *deuteros nomos*), of which the last three are mostly books of law. The books of the Torah were redacted over a period of more than five hundred years. The laws in Ex 21.2–23.19, for instance, were probably redacted around 1000 BC, perhaps by priests working in King Solomon's palace school. Deuteronomy was probably redacted during the reign of King Josiah of Judah, about 621 BC, as related in 2 Kg 22.8–23.3, and was part of that king's so-called deuteronomic reform. After the compilation of Deuteronomy the righteous Josiah proceeded to destroy shrines to gods other than Yahweh in the kingdom. Other sections of Exodus, Leviticus, and Numbers probably date from the postexilic period (after 536). As their history illustrates, these texts, which were written at diverse times, also had different historical contexts. The Torah, then, consists of overlapping strata of narrative, liturgical, and legal materials.

Indeed, story and law in the Torah are mirror images of each other. The laws enumerated in the books of Exodus, Numbers, Leviticus, and Deuteronomy were handed down by priestly lawgivers, whose task was to draw meaning and instruction out of the old stories about cosmic and human origins. To derive the law of their people, the priests studied the stories about the creation, the patriarchs, and the kings of Israel and Judah. These stories reflect the interests of their writers in (1) Israelite and universal origins and (2) recurring issues. The law served as commentary on the history of the people and reinforced their sense of identity, for the patriarch Abraham was the one "who obeyed me, keeping my mandate, my commandments, my ordinances, and my instructions" (Gn 26.5). The biblical law originated with learned comparisons between Exodus and Genesis, Leviticus and Genesis, Exodus and Kings, the texts, on the one hand, and the experience of the generation wherein the laws were assembled and arranged, on the other. While the whole of the Torah cannot be dealt with here, an analysis of its most significant texts and injunctions should well illustrate the close connection between narrative and law that ancient Israelites also used to highlight their convictions and worldview.

The Decalogue

The Decalogue, or Ten Commandments, are probably the most famous laws in all human history. To this day their iconography of stone tablets decorate the exteriors and interiors of many buildings dedicated to the administration of justice. The Torah preserves two very similar versions of the Decalogue (Ex 20.2–17 and Dt 5.6–21). The Decalogue's first tablet contains the commandments to be obeyed towards God, while the second tablet governs conduct between human beings.[11] As a consequence, the first tablet of the Decalogue derived from the story of the golden calf, the tale of Israel's first national apostasy from the worship of Yahweh. The priestly lawgiver wrote that the elemental forces accompanied the giving of the law to Moses on Mount Sinai. He thus linked this first story of national apostasy to cosmic origins: "there were peals of thunder and lightning, and a heavy cloud hung over the mountain . . . Mount Sinai was all wrapped in smoke, for the Lord came down upon it in fire. The smoke rose from it as though from a furnace, and the whole mountain trembled violently" (Ex 19.16, 18). The story of the golden calf says that the Israelites tired of waiting for Moses to return after he had gone up to Mount Sinai to receive God's law. The leadership of Moses also faltered, for the Israelites "gathered around Aaron, and said to him, 'Come, make us a god who will be our leader; as for the man Moses who brought us out of the land of Egypt, we do not know what has happened to him'" (Ex 32.1). Aaron, the brother and spokesman of Moses, then ordered the people to bring their golden jewelry to him (much of which consisted of the spoils of polytheistic Egypt (see Ex 12.35–36). Aaron, who was a gold-smith, fashioned the contributions into a statue of a golden calf. Thus, the first commandment (Ex 20.2) explicitly denied this rival god: "I, the Lord (Yahweh), am your God, who brought you out of the land of Egypt, that place of slavery. You shall not have other gods besides me." Furthermore, the sin of apostasy deeply offended Yahweh, and aroused his severity: "For I, the Lord your God am a jealous God, inflicting punishment for their fathers' wickedness on the children of those who hate me, down to the third or fourth generation" (Ex 20.5). Since apostasy and idolatry went hand-in-glove, the compilers of the Decalogue also continued: "You shall not carve idols for yourselves in the shape of anything in the sky above or on the earth below or in the waters beneath the earth" (Ex 20.4).

Not only had the Israelites carved an idol but they also credited the golden calf with Israel's liberation from Egypt: "This is your God, O Israel, who brought you out of the land of Egypt! (Ex 32.5). The second command-ment (Ex 20.7) condemned this offense to Yahweh as well: "You shall not take the name of the Lord, your God, in vain." Yahweh, the God of Abra-ham, whom Moses preached and served, wrought Israel's liberation, not the god depicted in Aaron's golden calf. Furthermore, Aaron had built an altar to the golden calf, and proclaimed, "Tomorrow is a feast of the Lord." Early the next day the people offered holocausts and brought peace offerings (Ex 32.5–6). The biblical lawgiver countered with the third commandment (Ex 20.8): "Remember to keep holy the sabbath day," defiled by the veneration of the golden calf, but honored by the worship of Yahweh. In concluding the Israelites' obligations towards Yahweh, the priestly lawgiver also reminded the Israelites of His awesome creative powers, and linked the recurrent theme of apostasy to cosmic origins: "In six days the Lord made the heavens and the earth, the sea and all that is in them; but on the seventh day He rested. That is why the Lord has blessed the sabbath day and made it holy" (Ex 20.11). Other gods, whom the Israelites must reject, have no such cre-ative powers. As Moses had taught, the worship of Yahweh alone, which meant the avoidance of idols and the keeping of the Sabbath, was wrought into the order with which Yahweh created the cosmos itself. The first tablet of the Decalogue, then, also confirmed Moses's prophetic charism.

Whereas the first tablet of the Decalogue served as commentary and in-struction on the story of the golden calf, the stories of Adam and Eve, and of Cain and Abel, inspired the second tablet. The fourth commandment, "Honor your father and your mother" (Ex 20.12), completes the transition in the Decalogue from the first to the second tablets. That transition began with the account of God's creative acts as appended to the third commandment (Ex 20.11). This transition, furthermore, closes with the human experience closest to divinity, and thereby bridges human and cosmic origins. The commandment to honor father and mother ties together human obligations towards God and neighbor because in procreation men and women most nearly approach divinity. Parents bring forth other beings made in the image and likeness of God (Gn 1.27). Indeed, the first parents fell because they wanted to be godlike (Gn 3.5), for which offense God drove Adam and Eve from the Garden of Eden.

Another story of human origins inspired the priestly lawgivers to hand down the fifth commandment, "You shall not kill" (Ex 20.13), namely, the tale of Cain and Abel. Cain slew his brother (fratricide likewise being a violation of the fourth commandment because of the injury done to parents and, in these stories of human origins, all murders are fratricides) out of jealousy because "the Lord looked with favor on Abel and his offering, but on Cain and his offering he did not" (Gn 4.4–5). However, in the aftermath of that murder, Yahweh took Cain under His protection. Rather than take Cain's life, Yahweh banished him, a farmer, from the soil. Cain later complained that even this punishment was too much for him, and he complained that "anyone may kill me at sight" (Gn 4.14). God replied, however, that "if anyone kills Cain, Cain shall be avenged sevenfold" (Gn 4.15). In the wake of death, God retained His authority over life. The taking of life belongs solely to God, the author of life, as Hebrews 10.30 (also Dt 32.35) makes explicit: "vengeance is mine, says the Lord." The taking of human life could be licit, but only by the command of God, who ordered the Israelites to slay the people of Jericho, except for the family of Rahab the harlot, "because she hid the messengers we sent" (Jos 6.17).

The sixth commandment, "You shall not commit adultery" (Ex 20.14), followed the story of Cain through to its ending, for his marriage (Gn 4.17) is morally problematic, inasmuch as Eve is the only woman explicitly mentioned in Genesis up to that point. More importantly, however, Cain was the first human born of a woman to leave his parents and take a wife. Whereas the Fall set Adam against Eve, man against woman, marriage restores what the Fall had destroyed, namely, the unity of husband and wife. Adultery, which destroys that unity, Yahweh prohibits.

The last four commandments derive from the story of the Fall. God had forbidden Adam and Eve to eat the fruit of the tree of the knowledge of good and evil (Gn 2.17), so the priestly lawgivers wrote in the seventh commandment (Ex 20.15): "You shall not steal." When God confronted Adam with this transgression, Adam confessed that he had indeed eaten of the fruit, but blamed his disobedience on his wife Eve, who in turn blamed it on the serpent. The equivocations of Adam and Eve inspired the eighth commandment (Ex 20.16): "You shall not bear false witness against your neighbor."

Rarely noted in recollections of the story of the Fall of Adam and Eve is the acuity of the serpent, who told Eve that if she should eat the tree's fruit: *Your eyes will be opened and you will be like gods who know what is good and what is bad.* The original pair did possess a greater moral acumen for having taken of the fruit. God marveled at Adam and Eve, who having taken of the tree of the knowledge of good and evil, had truly become more godlike: "'See! The man has become like one of us, knowing what is good and what is bad! Therefore, he must not be allowed to put out his hand to take fruit from the tree of life also, and thus eat of it and live forever.' The Lord God therefore banished him from the garden of Eden" (Gn 3.22–23). Note that God permitted Adam and Eve to eat of the tree of life prior to the Fall. Henceforth, then, Adam and Eve were denied what they wanted, and for that matter, what they had lost—eternal life—which to the priestly lawgivers suggested the ninth and tenth commandments (Ex 20.17): "You shall not covet your neighbor's house. You shall not covet your neighbor's wife, nor his male nor female slave, nor his ox or ass, nor anything else that belongs to him."

The combination of law and narrative found in the Decalogue may also be used to understand the roots and moral significance of other ancient Israelite laws.

The *Lex Talionis*

The *lex talionis* (Ex 21.23–25, a similar version also in Dt 19.21), or law of retaliation, unique to the Bible, is one of the best-known verses in the whole book: "If injury ensues, you shall give life for life, eye for eye, tooth for tooth, hand for hand, foot for foot, burn for burn, wound for wound, stripe for stripe." The *lex talionis* is preceded in the Exodus text by a list of compensations for offenses. The gist of these texts is that full and equal restitution should be made for injuries. The priestly lawgivers were just as concerned that punishments and restitutions not be excessive as they were that they not be too lenient (Dt 25.1–3).

The roots of the *lex talionis* come from the story of Naboth's vineyard (1 Kg 21.1–29). Naboth lived in the northern kingdom of Israel, in the city of Jezreel. He owned and cultivated a vineyard adjacent to the palace of King Ahab of Israel. Ahab, who wanted to plant a garden in its place, offered Naboth another plot of land or a sum of money for that vineyard. Naboth refused to hand over "his ancestral heritage." Naboth's refusal so angered Ahab that the king took to his bed and refused to eat. Ahab's wife, Jezebel, asked what had so upset him. Ahab replied that Naboth rejected his offer. She told Ahab to stop sulking—before long Naboth's vineyard would be his.

With the elders and nobles of the kingdom of Israel, Jezebel plotted against Naboth. She ordered them to hold a feast in the city, during which they should accuse Naboth of cursing both Yahweh and the king. They did as she bade them, and Naboth was stoned to death. Upon hearing of Naboth's death, Jezebel told Ahab that he could seize Naboth's vineyard. God then ordered his prophet Elijah to confront the king with his sin, and tell him: "in the place where the dogs licked up the blood of Naboth, the dogs shall lick up your blood too" (1 Kg 21.19). God's anger towards the queen was even more aroused: "Against Jezebel, too, the Lord declared 'The dogs shall devour Jezebel in the district of Jezreel'" (1 Kg 21.23). Terrified, Ahab tore his garments and put on sackcloth. Yahweh, satisfied with his regret, decided to defer justice until the reign of Ahab's son. Ahab later fell in battle against the king of Aram, an arrow having struck him in the seams of his breastplate. In fulfillment of Elijah's prophecy, the king's bloodstained chariot was washed at the pool of Samaria and "the dogs licked up his blood" (1 Kg 22.38). The prophet Elisha, Elijah's successor and protégé, anointed Jehu, son of the king of Judah, as the new king of Israel. Jehu determined to eliminate Ahab's kin and supporters. Acting on his orders, Jehu's soldiers threw Jezebel from a window in the royal palace and left her body on the ground. They then ate, intending to bury her body later. When they returned to the corpse, however, they only found the skull, feet, and hands. Jehu's men reported back to him he said: "This is the sentence which the Lord pronounced through Elijah the Tishbite: 'In the confines of Jezreel the dogs shall eat the flesh of Jezebel'" (2 Kg 9 (2 Kg 9.36). Yet another biblical verse captures the connection between the *lex talionis* and the story of Naboth's vineyard: "a man is punished by the very things through which he sins" (Ws 11.16).

These laws and this story echo a common theme in world literature: poetic justice. The sin will be visited upon the sinner. This theme, of course, also passed into the Christian tradition, as in the words of Jesus in Gethsemane: "Put your sword back into its sheath, for all who take the sword will perish by the sword" (Mt 26.52). Poetic justice, as portrayed in the Bible, also inspired the work of Dante. In his *Inferno*, the damned are tormented through what they had sinned: hooks pierce the genitals of the lustful, tongues of fire scourge the evil counselors, and the violent are boiled in blood, for even in sin Yahweh's justice abides.

Idolatry

A number of the laws in the book of Leviticus forbid the Israelites from adopting foreign ways. The Hebrews were explicitly prohibited from adopting the customs of the Egyptians, and of the Canaanites, to whom they were closely related both culturally and linguistically: "Speak to the Israelites and tell them: I, the Lord, am your God. You shall not do as they do in the land of Egypt, where you once lived, nor shall you do in the land of Canaan, where I am bringing you; do not conform to their customs" (Lv 18.2–3). This law appears at the head of a series of sexual rules (which are discussed more later), among which is inserted: "You shall not offer any of your offspring to be immolated to Molech (a Canaanite god), thus profaning the name of your God" (Lv 18.21). Several verses later, a general injunction says: "Do not defile yourselves by any of these things by which the nations whom I am driving out of your way have defiled themselves" (Lv 18.24).

The priestly lawgivers derived these laws from stories of the patriarchs in the book of Genesis. The avoidance of foreign ways figured into the marriages of Isaac and Jacob in particular. Both of these men grew up in the midst of Canaanites, who vastly outnumbered the Hebrews. A marriage with a Canaanite woman would have created kin ties and alliances with her relations, of course, which in turn might overwhelm the lineage of the Hebrews. As surety against such a development, Abraham ordered a servant to find a wife for his son and heir, Isaac, "and I will make you swear by the Lord, the God of heaven and the God of earth, that you will not procure a wife for my son from the daughters of the Canaanites among whom I live, but that you will go to my own land and to my kindred to get a wife for my son Isaac" (Gn 24.3–4). In the next generation, Isaac's wife Rebecca feared that her son, Jacob, might take a wife from the Hittite people (Gn 27.48). Jacob was not only Isaac's son, but also heir to his property and his standing. With Rebecca's encouragement and aid, he had already deceived his old, blind father into giving him the blessing that should have been bestowed upon his older twin brother, Esau; thus, Yahweh's promise to Abraham would be handed down through Jacob's lineage, not Esau's. Isaac ordered Jacob to go to the land of Paddan-aram, for "you shall not marry a Canaanite woman! Go now to the home of your mother's father Bethuel, and there choose a wife for yourself from among the daughters of your uncle Laban" (Gn 28.1–2). Isaac thus instructed his son to take a wife in northern Mesopotamia, Rebecca's homeland, rather than Canaan, the land Yahweh promised to Abraham and his descendants.

Clearly, the priestly lawgivers forbade marriages to foreigners because their religion and worship was hateful to Yahweh. One practice of the ancient Canaanites was apparently child sacrifice, expressly forbidden in Lv 18.21: "You shall not offer any of your offspring to Molech, thus profaning the name of your God." Child sacrifice, then, was murder and blasphemy. The priestly lawgivers derived this law from the story wherein Yahweh commanded Abraham to sacrifice his only son, born in both his old age and that of his wife,

Sarah (Gn 22.1–19). God's messenger stayed Abraham's knife at the last moment, and instead Abraham offered a ram in Isaac's place.

The overall concern in the Levirate laws prohibiting marriage to foreigners, however, was idolatry. Foreign wives might turn their husbands away from the worship of Yahweh to other gods, as did the wives of King Solomon (1 Kg 11.1–3). Ethnic purity may well have been a concern of the priestly lawgivers here, yet religious purity looms even larger, for even though they were close cousins, the patriarchs esteemed Rebecca, Leah, and Rachel as desirable wives for Isaac and Jacob because these young women would not persuade their husbands to abandon the worship of Yahweh, with all the moral degradation that that apostasy would entail.

Incest
Inserted among the laws against adopting foreign ways are a series of prohibitions against incest. Such laws might be expected to be a greater concern in societies where extended families with many half-, step-, and in-law relations commonly lived in the same dwellings. However, while nearly all societies desexualize family life as much as possible through the discouragement or prohibition of incest, Abraham, Isaac, Jacob, Judah, Moses, and David all married close relatives. While the priestly lawgivers took the patriarchs as their example for their laws against idolatry and child sacrifice, they explicitly rejected incestuous marriages. At the same time, however, their laws follow the meaning of the stories about the marriages of Abraham, Isaac, and David, in particular.

While the priestly lawgivers endorsed the patriarchs' rejection of human sacrifice and marriage of foreigners, they completely rejected their marriages of close kin, for the incest laws in Leviticus begin with a general admonition not to marry close relatives: "Take no close relatives to wife" (Lv 18.6). As Gn 12.12–13 and 20.2 indicate, for instance, Sarah was Abraham's half-sister. Furthermore, when fearful for his life, Abraham prostituted his wife: "When he was about to enter Egypt, he said to his wife Sarai: 'I know well how beautiful a woman you are. When the Egyptians see you, they will say, "She is his wife;" they will kill me, but let you live. Please, say, therefore, that you are my sister, so that it may go well with me on your account and my life may be spared for your sake.' When Abram came to Egypt, the Egyptians saw how beautiful the woman was; and when Pharaoh's courtiers saw her, they praised her to Pharaoh. So she was taken into Pharaoh's palace. On her account it went very well with Abram, and he received many flocks and herds, male and female slaves, male and female asses, and camels" (Gn 12.11–13, 16).

Abraham resorted to the same humiliating ruse when he journeyed through the Negev Desert. There, King Abimelech desired Sarah, and essentially Abraham gave her to the king, saying, truthfully enough, that she was his sister (Gn 20.2). In this instance, however, God appeared to Abimelech in a dream and told the king that Sarah was Abraham's wife. Abimelech was horrified that a man should so demean his wife, and scolded Abraham for it. The king said, furthermore, that had he known the truth he would not have sent for Sarah. Indeed, he provided Abraham with animals and lands (Gn 20.3–16). Isaac likewise called Rebecca his sister when they settled in Gerar, subject to another Abimelech, king of the Philistines. This time, Abimelech himself noticed Isaac fondling Rebecca, after he had told the king she was his relation. Again, this king was mortified, and feared that his intended seduction of Rebecca would bring God's curse down upon the Philistines (Gn 26.6–11). While the text contains no hint of divine repugnance against Abraham, Abimelech feared God's retribution. Apparently, the priestly lawgivers also feared that Yahweh's punishment would be visited upon a man who married too close a relative. Just how offensive they found such marriages may be gauged from their rejection here of a patriarch's example and their endorsement of a Philistine's.

The priestly lawgivers followed their general injunction against marriage of close kin with more specific prohibitions. These rules emphasize that a father's honor ought not to be violated: "You shall not disgrace your father by having intercourse with your mother . . . you shall not have intercourse with your father's wife, for that would be a disgrace to your father" (Lv 18.7–8). Clearly, these laws had little to do with real family pathologies, in which case the law should prohibit stepfathers from committing incest with their stepdaughters, for example. Rather, the references to the father's honor suggest that the lawgivers were recalling the stories about Noah and Lot in Genesis. Noah's son Ham came upon his sleeping, naked father, who had passed out from drunkenness: "Ham, the father of Canaan, saw his father's nakedness, and he told his two brothers outside about it. Shem and Japheth, however, took a robe, and holding it on their backs, they walked backward and covered their father's nakedness; since their faces were turned the other way, they did not see their father's nakedness" (Gn 9.22–23). After Noah found Ham out, he cursed Canaan, the son of Ham, and of course, the patriarch of the Canaanites.

In another pertinent story, the daughters of Lot, the nephew of Abraham, plied him with drink so that, intoxicated, they might seduce him and become pregnant by him. They lived in the hill country, where there were few marriageable men. On two separate nights, Lot became drunk and had intercourse with his daughters. The offspring of these liaisons were Moab and Ammon, the fathers of the nations of the Moabites and the Ammonites—enemies of the early Israelites! Consequently, in addition to the laws mentioned above, in commenting on these verses the priestly lawgivers condemned sex with "your sister, your father's daughter or your mother's daughter. . . . You shall not have intercourse with your son's daughter or with your daughter's daughter. . . . You shall not have intercourse with the daughter whom your father's wife bore to him" (Lv 18.9–11).

The priestly lawgivers also explicitly prohibited liaisons with in-laws: "You shall not have intercourse with your daughter-in-law; she is your son's wife, and therefore you shall not disgrace her. You shall not have intercourse with your brother's wife. . . . You shall not have intercourse with a woman and also with her daughter, nor shall you marry and have intercourse with her son's daughter or her daughter's daughter" (Lv 18.15–17). The origins of these very specific incest prohibitions lie in the story of Judah and Tamar (Gn 38.11–26).

Judah was son of the patriarch Jacob. He found a wife, whose name was Tamar, for his eldest son, named Er. However, Er offended Yahweh and he died. Judah then urged Onan, Er's younger brother, to wed Tamar, so that Er would yet have children—the ancient Israelite custom of *levirate* or "brother-in-law" marriage that the Sadducees would later question Jesus about (Mt 22.23–33). "Onan, however, knew that the descendants would not be counted as his; so whenever he had relations with his brother's widow, he wasted his seed on the ground, to avoid contributing offspring for his brother. What he did greatly offended the Lord, and the Lord took his life also" (Gn 38.9–10). Judah then bade Tamar to dwell with him. He told her that when the youngest of his sons, Shelah, grew to adulthood, Tamar could marry him. But after Shelah reached maturity, Tamar had still not been given to him in marriage. She took off her widow's garb and put on a veil. Since her face was covered at a later encounter during Judah's travels, Judah did not recognize her and mistook her for a prostitute; Tamar played along. He propositioned Tamar, who agreed to have sex with him for the price of one kid-goat, which he would send along later. In the meantime, Judah left his cylinder seal with her as pledge for his payment. Judah impregnated Tamar. After Judah learned of her condition, he declared that she should be burned to death. When Tamar was brought before Judah, she produced the cylinder seal he had left with her as pledge of his payment for sexual intercourse. Like Laban, Isaac, and Jacob before him, Judah discovered that a member of his own household had deceived him. Judah then realized and admitted that, in not wedding Tamar to Shelah, he had wronged a woman who had had intercourse with two generations of men in the same family. The priestly lawgiver, then, sum-marized the crime and its indignity in Leviticus 18, that a liaison between father-in-law and daughter-in-law was sinful, even if her husband, his son, was dead.

Life and Death

The kosher rules against serving meat and dairy foods at the same meal are derived from a biblical law that appears three times in the Torah in virtually the same words: "You shall not boil the kid in its mother's milk" (Ex 23.19; Ex 34.26; Dt 14.21). Why should the kid not be poached its mother's milk? Would any other method of poaching be acceptable? The origin of this law may be better understood by considering several other, related laws, which also concern bodily fluids. Blood, for instance, figures in several texts: "In any of your communities you may slaughter and eat to your heart's desire as much meat as the Lord, your God, has blessed you with; and the unclean as well as the clean may eat it, as they do the gazelle or the deer. Only, you shall not partake of the blood, but must pour it out on the ground like water" (Dt 12.15–16). Another law also prohibits the consumption of the blood of ani-mals: "Everyone, whether a native or an alien, who eats of an animal that died of itself . . . shall wash his garments, bathe in water, and be unclean un-til evening, and then he shall be clean" (Lv 17.15–16). The meat from such an animal was unclean because its blood had not been poured out on the ground, as Dt 12.16 required. Menstrual blood, of course, was also unclean: "You shall not approach a woman to have intercourse with her while she is unclean from menstruation" (Lv 18.19; cf. Lv 15.19). Finally, the effusion of blood and afterbirth following the delivery of a baby likewise created un-cleanness that required ritual purification (Lv 12.1–8), as did contact with the slain in combat (Nm 31.19–20).

The law about menstrual blood, furthermore, appears in the midst of the incest prohibitions (see above), as does the condemnation of homosexual in-tercourse: "You shall not lie with a male as with a female" (Lv 18.22), later reaffirmed for the Christian tradition by St. Paul (1 Cor 6.9; Rm 1.26–27; 1 Tm 1.10). While the priestly lawgivers expressly condemned homosexual in-tercourse, they did not mention lesbian activity. Since this text appears along with the incest prohibitions derived from the story of Onan, Judah, and Tamar, the priestly lawgivers must have been recalling the spilling of the seed mentioned in that tale, for even wet-dreaming and heterosexual intercourse created uncleanness: "When a man has an emission of seed, he shall bathe his whole body in water [another life-giving fluid] and be unclean until evening. Any piece of cloth or leather with seed on it shall be washed with water and be unclean until evening. If a man lies carnally with a woman, they shall both bathe in water and be unclean until evening." (Lv 15.16–18, cf. Lv 22.4–6).

The common element in all these texts is their preoccupation with bodily fluids which either generate or preserve life—milk, blood, and semen. The kid should not be prepared for a meal in the fluid that God had ordained for its nutriment. The uncleanness of bloodshed the priestly lawgivers clearly stated: "Since the life of a living body is in its blood, I have made you put it on the altar, so that atonement may thereby be made for your own lives, because it is the blood, as the seat of life, that makes atonement. That is why I have told the Israelites: No one among you, not even a resident alien, may partake of blood" (Lv 17.11–12). Yahweh had created blood for the sustenance of life. All blood which was no longer in a living body was therefore unclean. Finally, God ordered that semen generate life through the intercourse of man and woman. Any purposeful waste of semen offended God. Another law reminded the ancient Israelites of God's life-giving creativity: "If a man guilty of a capital offense is put to death and his corpse hung on a tree, it shall not remain on the tree overnight" (Dt 21.22–23). Tradition said that only God, the author of life, could see at night. He should not, then, be offended by the sight of a dead body.

For the ancient Israelites, justice, prosperity, and life were inseparable, as in Dt 30.15–18, part of Moses's address to the Israelites just before they crossed the Jordan: "Here, then, I have today set before you life and prosperity, death and doom. If you obey the commandments of the Lord, your God, which I enjoin on you today, loving Him, and walking in His ways, and keeping His commandments, statutes and decrees, you will live and grow numerous, and the Lord, your God, will bless you in the land you are about to occupy. If, however, you turn away your hearts and will not listen, but are led astray and adore and serve other gods, I tell you now that you will certainly perish." God told his people that justice has nothing to do with injustice, that each has its own, jealously guarded domain. The chief blessings of God's justice, as revealed in the Torah, were peace and life. A just and holy people separate life from death. Both Jews and Christians preserved this reverence for life over the centuries, as for instance in the epistles of St. Paul (particularly 1 Corinthians), and the *Didache*, the first handbook of Christian catechesis, redacted around 120 AD, which began thus: "There are two ways: a Way of Life and a Way of Death, and the difference between these two ways is great."[12]

The methods of the priestly lawgivers in the Torah exemplify how traditions work. Storytelling is, of course, a primal form not only of entertainment, but of instruction and indoctrination. Ancient stories about national or religious origins or recurrent issues were handed down from generation to generation. Each generation learned and studied their meanings. These reflections on the authoritative stories are preserved, either by oral traditions, or later as written commentaries, which may take the form of other stories, poems, learned treatises, or as in the case of the Torah, laws. In turn, some of these oral traditions and literary sources themselves become almost as authoritative as the stories they aimed to clarify, such that, a great body of literature is compiled, as in the culture of ancient and modern Israel.

Furthermore, in a remarkable consistency spanning centuries, the legal traditions of ancient Israel upheld several, deeply held convictions. First, that only Yahweh deserved worship; second, that the sinner is punished by his sin; and third, that the realms of good and evil are clearly delineated. All three of these were, in turn, related to the other. When the worship of Yahweh was forgotten or perverted—as in the story of the Solomon's apostasy—the people suffered ruin. When evil was dressed up as goodness—the work of the serpent in Eden, who convinced Eve and Adam that they could be like gods—men and women suffered terrible consequences. When Jezebel shed blood to obtain what she had no claim to, her own blood was shed. The convictions from the law of ancient Israel, of course, became the foundations of Judaeo-Christian culture and civilization. Dante's poetry, for instance, serves as a testimonial to this cultural inheritance, for the souls in the *Inferno* are tormented by the sins they committed in life. Killers are boiled in blood, the genitals of the lecherous are beaten, and the sowers of division are split in two. The Torah's influence also extended to Catholic canonistic jurisprudence, which would make an indelible impression on later European civilization.

The Origins of Democratic Justice

In addition to the civilization of ancient Israel, that of ancient Athens has also exerted a profound influence on modern, Western civilization. The classical Athenians first laid down the rules used in modern Western culture to judge, investigate, and learn. Modern Americans and Europeans still aspire as a matter of course to forms of government which evolved in that place and time. The Athenians also developed basic ideas about the administration of justice that Western people still prize. First among these may well be the idea that law must be subject to reason, and that the reason for a statute should be publicly and plainly stated in its preambles.[13] That conviction was nurtured in political and judicial institutions that were also adversarial, such that cases had to be made persuasively. Thus, in ancient Athens originated that finely honed, self-critical faculty characteristic of Western civilization.

The Athenians, furthermore, were convinced that injustice resulted from intolerable levels of inequality in the *polis*, or city-state. Athenian judicial proceedings, then, depended upon *equality* among the citizens of that *polis*. They were convinced that great inequalities were the source of injustices but that "equality gives birth to friendship," which fosters concord.[14] Arguments between more-or-less gifted amateurs were foundational to the Athenians' administration of justice, which in many instances depended upon jury trials. The *ekklesia*, the assembly of all citizens, served as juries. Hence, the administration of justice, properly so-called, was exclusively committed to the *ekklesia*. Any other procedure was at best little more than blood-feud, with its threat of perpetually cyclical violence; at worst it was injustice. Consequently, for the ancient Athenians justice and its judicial institutions were inextricably tied to their democratic political institutions. Those institutions originated in the Hellenic Archaic Age (800–500 BC), during which conflict between the nobility and the commoners fostered the development of democracy.

Around 2200 BC, Indo-European speakers migrated into the Aegean region. The first dominant Greek-speaking settlements developed on the island of Crete. The Cretans exploited the riches of the Aegean Sea to make a living. By 2000 BC, they assumed cultural predominance over both islanders and mainlanders, and Greek replaced all earlier languages, although the Greeks borrowed a number of pre-Hellenic place-names, such as *Korinthos* (for the city of Corinth) and *thalassa* (sea).

Sir Arthur Evans, the great nineteenth-century archaeologist who first excavated its ruins, called this early Cretan civilization Minoan, after its legendary King Minos. The Minoans devised the first Greek alphabet. They wrote in two scripts that scholars have labeled Linear A and Linear B. While scholars have not yet deciphered Linear A, the Englishman Michael Ventris deciphered Linear B in the 1950s—one of classical scholarship's great achievements. Script and archaeology suggest that the great civilizations to the east much influenced Minoan civilization. These cultural cross-fertilizations owed much to the nature of the Cretan monarchy, whose power depended more on the control of the sea than of the land (most Cretan cities were either on the coast or very near it). Like Egyptian hieroglyphics, Linear B is a pictographic and ideographic writing system. Buildings excavated at *Knossos* suggest a Mesopotamian influence. Minoan civilization flourished until 1700 BC, when an earthquake destroyed it.

By 1500 BC, the vitality in Greek culture had passed from Crete to the mainland, to a civilization scholars call Mycenaean, after one of that civilization's important settlements, Mycenae. Like the civilization of ancient Sumer, Mycenaean civilization consisted of a confederation of city-states that took turns at hegemony. Many of the great stories of the later classical Greeks were set in the Mycenaean era, and, like the stories in the Bible, feature recurring themes. The hero Achilles, for instance, desecrated the body of the fallen Trojan hero Hector. He passed a hook into Hector's heels and dragged the corpse around the walls of Troy. Achilles later fell in combat, killed by an arrow in the heel.

Mycenaean civilization flourished until about 1100, when it too collapsed at the end of the Bronze Age. Until about 800, very few works of Greek art or literature survive. After that date, however, all signs point to a great recovery in Hellenic civilization. Greeks were migrating out of their homeland in the Peloponnese, Attica, and Boeotia, to found colonies in the Aegean islands, the Ionian coast of Asia Minor, south Italy, Sicily, even the estuary of the Rhône in the south of modern-day France. Clearly, the population was growing rapidly, which in turn suggests a productive and vibrant economy. Between 800 and 600 trade between the Greeks and the Black Sea region grew and both regions specialized in the production of certain goods. Grains were grown on the shores of the Black Sea, and sold to Greeks. Greeks produced olive oil and wine, which they could sell abroad. Indeed, the population of Attica, the plain wherein Athens lay, could no longer feed itself, and depended on economic specialization and long-distance trade for survival.

Over the course of the seventh century, epochal social changes were in motion. An agricultural depression set in during the 600s. Debt threatened the freedom and independence of many small farmers:

At that time, too, the disparity between the rich and the poor had culminated, as it were, and the city was in an altogether perilous condition; it seemed as if the only way to settle its disorders and stop its turmoils was to establish a tyranny. All the common people were in debt to the rich. For they either tilled their lands for them, paying a sixth of the increase (whence they were called *hectemorioi* and *thetes*), or else they pledged their persons for debts and could be seized by their creditors, some becoming slaves at home, and others being sold into foreign countries. Many, too, were forced to sell their own children (for there was no law against it), or to go into exile, because of the cruelty of the money-lenders.[15]

Some scholars have theorized that the increased use of money, dating from around 680, introduced new economic pressures. Indeed, writing around 700, the poet Hesiod complained that strife afflicted the land, and in so doing highlighted the *stasis* (tension between nobles and commoners) that was so prevalent a feature of politics in most Greek city-states. In the poems known as *Works and Days*, Hesiod longed for the replacement of violence by justice. He addressed his fictional brother, "You, Perses, you listen to Justice/And don't cultivate Violence . . . When it comes down to it/Justice beats out violence."[16] Conditions in Attica were deplorable. Even Zeus himself could see that a poor man could find no justice:

> The eye of Zeus sees all and knows all,
> And, if he wants, he's looking here right now,
> And the kind of justice this city harbors
> Doesn't fool him one bit.[17]

Indeed, violent men angered the gods: "For those who live for violence and vice,/Zeus, son of Kronos, broad-browed god, decrees/A just penalty."[18] For Hesiod, then, justice and violence were polar opposites; while one reigned, the other lay in abeyance.

Violence, however, was not the only threat to justice. The corruption of judges and courts was equally damaging to the establishment of justice: "There's a ruckus when the Lady Justice/Gets dragged through the streets by corrupt judges/Who swallow bribes and pervert their edicts."[19] Hesiod, of course, here indicts the rich (for only they had wealth enough to bribe judges), who exploited the troubles of the era for their own aggrandizement at the expense of poor, ordinary commoners. He warned the ruling classes that their despoliation of the poor would merit a divine vengeance: "There are, you know,/Immortal beings abroad in this world/Who do observe with what corruption and fraud/Men grind down their neighbors and destroy the state."[20] Ordinary folk, however, could also impede justice, as, for instance, they do when they commit perjury.[21] When farmers deal unfairly with each other, famine and blight are the consequence.[22]

Indeed, Hesiod was convinced that the gods troubled themselves with individual court cases. Zeus, he wrote, had thirty thousand spirits who served him as spies among men, "watching the human race,/overseeing trials for criminal acts."[23] In fact, Justice was Zeus's virgin daughter, who, when maligned by the deeds of men, complained to her father, "and speaks to him about men's unjust hearts."[24] Zeus had not given justice to brute beasts, "But to men he gave justice, and that works out/All to the good."[25] The blessings of justice, said Hesiod, were manifold:

> But when judges judge straight, for neighbors
> As well as for strangers, and never turn their backs
> On justice, their city blossoms, the people bloom.
> You'll find peace all up and down the land
> And youngsters growing tall, because broad-browed Zeus
> Hasn't marked them out for war.[26]

When the people deal fairly with each other,

> They feast on the fruits of their tended fields,
> And the earth bears them a good living too.
> Mountain oaks yield them acorns at the crown,
> Bees and honey from the trunk. Their sheep
> Are hefty with fleece, and women bear children
> Who look like their parents.[27]

Modern scholars have generally taken the great Hellenic colonizations of the coast of Asia Minor, southern Italy, and Sicily as a sign of the ending of the ancient Dark Age in the eastern Mediterranean region. Hesiod saw the emigration of numerous Hellenes from Attica, Boeotia, and the Peloponnese rather differently. The colonists left not because of prosperity, but of injustice. When justice reigned, the people "thrive/On all the good things life has to offer, and they/Never travel on ships. The soil's their whole life."[28]

By the turn of the sixth century, nobles and commoners in Attica realized that civil war threatened unless reforms could be enacted. In 593, the commoners and nobles "agreed to appoint Solon as reconciler and *archon*," or chief executive magistrate.[29] They selected Solon because he was "by birth and repute one of the leading citizens, but by wealth and position one of the middle sort."[30] Although he was one of them, Solon believed that the nobles were mostly to blame for the tensions in Attica, their love of money being their chief vice.[31] "Unrighteous are the hearts of the rulers of the people, who will one day suffer many pains for their great pride (*hubris*); for they do not know how to restrain their excesses. . . . They grow rich through unrighteous deeds, and steal for themselves right and left, respecting neither sacred nor public property."[32]

Having identified the sources of the tumult in Athens, Solon determined to reduce the intensity of *stasis* in Athens. He promulgated laws designed to protect commoners against the nobility by giving the commoners a greater share of the wealth and power; indeed, Plutarch (c. 46–c. 120 AD) says that Solon was made *archon* because he often remarked that "equality bred no war."[33] Solon cancelled farmers' debts and prohibited slavery for indebtedness. He established a council of four hundred (one hundred from each of the tribes), called the *Boulé*, whose constitutional purpose was to debate legislation before it came to the *ekklesia* for a vote. In other reforms, which Aristotle identified as the "most democratic features of Solon's constitution,"[34] Solon made justice easier to obtain for the weak:

> He gave every citizen the privilege of entering suit in behalf of one who had suffered wrong. If a man was assaulted, and suffered violence or injury, it was the privilege of any one who had the ability and the inclination to indict the wrong-doer and prosecute him. The law-giver in this way rightly accustomed the citizens, as members of one body, to feel and sympathize with one another's wrongs.[35]

Commoners then depended less on powerful patrons for justice. Since a number of cases were heard before a magistrate, Solon also granted to commoners "the right of appeal to the jury-court,"[36] which in time came to handle a great deal of judicial business, as Aristotle believed "it was inevitable that many disputes should arise and that the jury-court should decide all things both public and private."[37] Thus Solon institutionalized a distinguishing feature of the Athenian judiciary, namely, equal access to justice for all citizens. While Solon ensured that every citizen could bring suit there, in time other reformers would ensure that every citizen could serve as a juror, which is to say that every citizen could take his seat in the *ekklesia*. Even though the nobles were first angered by his cancellation of peasant debts, they eventually saw the wisdom of Solon's policies.[38] Over the next few generations, his reforms became an unquestioned feature of the Athenian way of life.

Culture and Justice in Classical Athens

Indeed, the Athenians of the fifth century took great pride in their judicial heritage. They believed that the divine protectress of their city had ordained its courts and jurisprudence. The myths featuring the royal house of Atreus, found in the Oresteian trilogy of the tragedian and patriot Aeschylus, told the story of the establishment of justice in Athens. Ancient Greek plays, like the narratives and laws in the Torah, were preoccupied with recurring issues, such as sexual morality and violence perpetrated against relatives. The two brothers, Atreus and Thyestes, were the sons of Pelops, who in turn was son of Tantalus, the king of Lydia and the mortal son of Zeus. In his scorn for the gods, who had accepted and honored him as though he were fully divine himself, Tantalus killed Pelops and served his flesh to the Olympians. Horrified, the gods punished Tantalus in Hades. He was placed there in a pool of water. Whenever he stooped to drink, the water would drain below his lips. Above that pool hung a bough of fruit which, whenever Tantalus reached for it, would jerk away from his hands. Thus, he who had prepared a wicked feast could never again slake his thirst or fill his belly.

Atreus and Thyestes inherited the evil that Tantalus had brought upon the family. Thyestes coveted his brother's wife (another sexualized family!) and seduced her. Atreus discovered that betrayal and vowed to make Thyestes pay. He killed Thyestes's sons, and, like Tantalus, served their flesh in a soup—to their own father! Atreus was king of the great city of Argos, while Thyestes held no position of power; many versions of the story hint that Atreus could have been rather more magnanimous.

The next generation avenged the murder of Thyestes's two boys. Atreus had two sons, Agamemnon, who inherited the throne of Argos, and Menelaus, who became king of Sparta when he wedded the princess Helen (whose father was Zeus himself), the legendary beauty with the "face that launched a thousand ships." Agamemnon and Menelaus involved the whole of Greece in the great Trojan War recounted chiefly in the *Iliad* and the *Odyssey*. Menelaus offered hospitality to Paris, the Trojan prince. Paris, however, lusted after Helen, kidnapped her, and took her to Troy. The Greek princes, led by Agamemnon and Menelaus, were honor-bound to rescue Helen. Her stepfather, King Tyndareus, had exacted a solemn oath from all her many suitors, wherein they pledged to champion her husband, should he be harmed because of his marriage.

The expedition, however, ran into trouble, as the Greeks had offended the goddess of nature and the hunt, Artemis (Diana), by killing one of her favorite creatures, a rabbit. She made the winds blow foul for the Greeks, until the daughter of Agamemnon, whose name was Iphigenia, should be sacrificed. Agamemnon gave up Iphigenia to be sacrificed, for his loyalty to the army and ambition for conquest exceeded his affections as a father and husband. The murder broke the heart of his wife, Clytemnestra, who vowed vengeance against Agamemnon should he return from the walls of Troy.

Agamemnon, the first play in Aeschylus's trilogy, takes place ten years later, after Troy had been defeated and destroyed. One of the few surviving Greek heroes, the returning Agamemnon is not only guilty of slaying his own daughter but of taking a lover as well—the lovely Cassandra, a prophetess and the daughter of King Priam of Troy. While Agamemnon had been away, Clytemnestra had also taken Aegisthus, the son of Thyestes, as her lover.

Aegisthus had vowed vengeance on the descendants of his uncle, Atreus. Together, Clytemnestra and Aegisthus plotted against Agamemnon, whom they murdered shortly after his return from Troy. In the play, she explains to the Chorus, who represent the Argives (citizens of Argos), that the slaying of Agamemnon was a simple exercise of justice:

> This is my husband, Agamemnon, now stone dead;
> His death the work of my right hand, whose craftsmanship
> Justice acknowledges. There lies the simple truth.[39]

The Chorus, however, refused to approve the "justice" the queen and her lover concocted, and they hope that Agamemnon's exiled son, Orestes, will avenge his father's death—even if it means killing his own mother. The play concludes with Clytemnestra, a prophetess herself, urging an end to the violence that plagues the house of Atreus.

The second play of the trilogy, *The Choephori*, or *The Libation-Bearers*, opens with Orestes's secret return to Argos. He insists that blood must be returned for blood, even though he knows that he who kills suffers the fate he has meted out to his victim. Women, says Orestes, are the source of much trouble. Helen was the cause of the Trojan War, wherein numerous Greek and Trojan heroes fell in desperate battle, and now Clytemnestra has defiled both her marriage bed and her children by taking a lover and by slaying her children's father. The idea that Paris was guilty for abducting Helen, or that Agamemnon was guilty because he had murdered his daughter and committed adultery against his wife, is ignored in the play.

Just as Aegisthus and Clymnestra resorted to ruse to kill Agamemnon, Orestes enters the royal palace disguised as a foreigner. Once there, he reveals his identity to his mother. Aware of her son's murderous intentions, Clytemnestra places the blame for his father's death on Fate, which played just as great a role in Agamemnon's death as did she. Orestes hesitates a bit—her guilt has not destroyed all affection for his mother—but he recalls that he made a pledge to Apollo to avenge his father. He drives Clytemnestra into the palace and there stabs both her and Aegisthus. Orestes then fears that the Furies, the punishers of evildoers, will pursue him. The Chorus, however, assures him that what he has done was necessary. He hoped that Apollo, who had endorsed his intentions, would grant him sanctuary:

> I will go as suppliant to Apollo's holy ground,
> Where in the temple of earth's center the lamp gleams
> With the immortal flame; and there seek refuge, exiled
> For the shedding of this kindred blood.[40]

Orestes, however, felt no need to expiate the blood of Aegisthus, his cousin.

The final play of the trilogy, *The Eumenides*, carries the story further. The gods, in particular Apollo and Athena, figure more prominently in this play than they had in the first two. As he feared, the Furies hound Orestes but Apollo, to whom Orestes has made numerous sacrifices, keeps them in check. Apollo claims that heaven despises the Furies because they deprive transgressors of the hope of redemption and compensation. Furthermore, the Furies believe that fear, rather than virtue, compels men to be good. Apollo advises Orestes to go to Athens, where he might benefit from the intervention of Athena. The Furies protest that Apollo defies

Justice for your altar's sake,
Saved a godless matricide from appointed pain, to make
Mockery of motherhood.[41]

When he arrives in Athens, Orestes admits his guilt to Athena, but claims that his wanderings and exile have expiated the sin. Athena decides to turn his case over to a jury trial of Athenian citizens, who will wield authority in her name. She appoints twelve citizens to hear the case; their decision will settle the matter once and for all. The Furies serve as prosecutors while Apollo defends Orestes. The Furies argue that while Clytemnestra did not slay kin, Orestes did, and so brought upon himself twice the moral opprobrium.[42] Apollo rejects that argument as a defilement of marriage. Clytemnestra was more despicable for slaying her husband:

You dishonor and annul the marriage-bond
Of Zeus and Hera, that confirms all marriage bonds;
And by your argument the sweetest source of joy
To mortals, Aphrodite, falls into contempt.
Marriage, that joins two persons in Fate's ordinance,
Guarded by justice, stands more sacred than an oath.[43]

Clytemnestra, argued Apollo, committed two sins that were greater than those Orestes committed. First, since Agamemnon was king, she was guilty of regicide. Secondly, since a child belongs more properly to the father than the mother, Orestes's loyalties must first have resided with Agamemnon and so he was obliged to slay his mother. Athena finds Apollo's argument more convincing, because

No mother gave me birth.[44] Therefore the father's claim
And male supremacy in all things, save to give
Myself in marriage, wins my whole heart's loyalty.

Therefore a woman's death, who killed her husband, is,
I judge, outweighed in grievousness by his.[45]

The jurors, however, were evenly split and so Athena casts the deciding vote in favor of acquittal. Athena then calms the Furies, who claim that Athens will regret Orestes's acquittal, by telling them that their honor is yet intact: "Fair trial, fair judgement, ended in an even vote,/Which brings to you neither dishonor nor defeat."[46] More importantly, the cycle of violence that had plagued three generations of Atreidae has finally been put to rest.

In the story of the Atreidae, Aeschylus presented a philosophical discussion of justice in Athens. The Furies are told that what they desire is the likeness of justice (vengeance) but not justice itself, since justice must involve the entire *polis* through its institutions of government. Apollo, the lord of justice and righteousness, and Athena, the protectress of the city, together founded the jury trial for murder, wherein the state, rather than kin, handed down justice to avoid the limitless violence that—in the stories of *Agamemnon* and *The Choephori*—often accompanied vengeance. Athena pledges to her people:

I here establish you a court inviolable,
Holy, and quick to anger, keeping faithful watch
That men may sleep in peace.[47]

She says also: "Let citizens/And jurors all in silence recognize this court/Which I ordain today in perpetuity,/That which now and always justice may be well discerned." Some men need the fear of reprisal to prevent them from doing harm. In the past, the murderer feared attack from his victim's kin. Henceforth, he will fear the decision of Athenian courts: "From your polity do not wholly banish fear./For what man living, freed from fear, will still be just?"[48] A century after Aeschylus, the philosopher Plato likewise agreed that justice effected the intentions of vengeance without its ill effects. He was convinced that the best method to rid the *polis* of evildoers "is that which effects correction by the combination of justice with vengeance, in the last instance, to the point of death or exile, usually with the result of clearing society of its most dangerous members."[49]

According to Aeschylus, then, unlike vengeance, which only the kin of the victims could pursue, justice was an enactment of the whole *polis*, which served as an extended kin group among whom concord should prevail, a sentiment Socrates upheld, even as the date of his execution drew near:

[The state] brought you into the world and reared you and educated you, and [has] given you and all your fellow citizens a share in all the good things at our disposal.[50]

The Sophist Antiphon stated similar thoughts: "Justice therefore is not to violate the laws of the city in which one is a citizen."[51] While Aeschylus assumed that war would be the state of affairs with other Greeks, to say nothing of foreign barbarians, Athenians should be at peace with each other, even though strife between her citizens would erupt now and again:

> Let war be with the stranger, at the stranger's gate;
> There let men fall in love with glory; but at home
> Let no cocks fight."[52]

In no way does it occur to Athena that what she has in mind applies to all men and women, but only to the descendants of the Athenians: "From this day forward this judicial council shall/For Aegeus' race hear every trial of homicide."[53] Indeed, she emphasizes the uniqueness of Athenian justice and government: "Guard well and reverence that form of government/Which will eschew alike licence and slavery."[54] Athens will gain a justifiable reputation as a peaceful and just state, and her fame, to say nothing of her population and prosperity, will grow. With typical Greek parochialism, Aeschylus limited justice to the plains of Attica. As Herodotus's history of the Persian Wars shows, the Athenian sense of identity depended upon this contrast with the barbarous other, degraded by despotism, fit by nature only for servitude.

The plays of Aeschylus represent earlier, archaic Athenian ideas and attitudes. In contrast, the plays of the tragedian Sophocles reflect later, classical Athenian culture. His play *Antigone* was probably first produced in 442 BC, at the height of the Athenian Empire. Whereas the plays of Aeschylus betray the great pride in Athens of a veteran of the Persian Wars, more cosmopolitanism may be discerned in Sophocles's work. One of the themes in *Antigone* is the tension between what later generations of jurists would call positive law, on the one hand, and universal law, on the other. *Antigone* is the last play in Sophocles's trilogy about the mythical, royal house of Thebes, which involved the hero Oedipus and his children. The main character in *Antigone* is no longer Oedipus, whose downfall and apotheosis have already been told in *Oedipus the King* and *Oedipus at Colonus*, but Creon, who succeeded him as king of Thebes. Oedipus had had four children by Jocasta, his wife/mother: two sons, named Eteocles and Polyneices, and two daughters, Antigone and Ismene. Oedipus had resigned the throne in the first play of the trilogy because incest cursed his immediate family; Creon was Jocasta's brother.

The two brothers, Eteocles and Polyneices, became enemies after their father had been sent into exile in Attica. Eteocles, the younger, had successfully positioned himself as heir to the city. Although he had earlier resigned his claim to the throne, Polyneices had decided to recover his claim with help he received from the city of Argos. Although the battle between the two brothers was a draw, both were slain in combat. Creon proclaimed that Eteocles should receive proper burial, but Polyneices, as he had attacked his native city, should be left for scavengers. Creon's proclamation, however, violated Hellenic law, which commanded that the dead should suffer no punishment. The Greeks believed that the souls of the unburied never found their resting place, and so burial of the dead was a pious duty; Creon had turned it into a crime, punishable by death.

The two sisters, of course, heard of the proclamation with horror. Ismene's response was to acquiesce. She and Antigone were politically dispossessed women—what could they do? Antigone, however, resolved to bury ritually her deceased brother, and cast dirt upon his body, which would satisfy the purposes of piety. The guard whom Creon had assigned to Polyneices's body confirmed what the king had heard in his palace, that Antigone had defied his orders. Creon confronted Antigone directly. She admitted everything, and more besides:

> It was not Zeus that made the proclamation;
> Nor did justice, which lives with those below, enact
> Such laws as that, for mankind. I did not believe
> Your proclamation had such power to enable
> One who will someday die to override
> God's ordinances, unwritten and secure.
> *They* are not of today and yesterday;
> They live forever.[55]

Creon denied he had done any injustice or contrary to the will of the gods. When he confronts his son Haemon, who had been betrothed to Antigone, he claims an ultimate authority: "There is nothing worse/Than disobedience to authority."[56] Little did Creon know how well he spoke, however. Convinced of his own justice, Creon orders Antigone buried alive. After that order was issued the seer Teiresias visits Creon, whom he suggests understands justice, but dangerously, imperfectly. Teiresias urges Creon away from his intended course:

> You must realize
> That you will not outlive many cycles more
> Of this swift sun before you give in exchange
> One of your own loins bred, a corpse for a corpse,
> For you have thrust one that belongs above

Below the earth, and bitterly dishonored
A living soul by lodging her in the grave;
While one that belonged indeed to the netherworld
Gods you have kept on this earth without due share
Of rites of burial, of funeral offerings,
A corpse unhallowed. With all of this you, Creon,
Have nothing to do, nor have the gods above.
These acts of yours are violence.[57]

Teiresias convinces Creon to reverse Antigone's sentence, but the king acts too late, not only to save Antigone, but his own family from disaster. Her sentence had already been executed. For despair of Antigone, however, his son Haemon had slain himself and Creon's wife, Queen Eurydice, also committed suicide when she learned that her beloved son was dead. Struck by catastrophes of his own making, Creon realizes that he has been "a vain, silly man."[58] He had indeed learned justice, says the Chorus, "but too late."[59] Like so many other characters in ancient Greek literature, Creon's undoing was *nemesis*, a just vengeance visited upon himself, which dwelt within his own being. Sophocles's discussion of justice in his trilogy of the royal house of Thebes, then, differed greatly from that of his elder contemporary Aeschylus. Whereas Aeschylus believed that justice could not be found apart from the judicial institutions of Athens, Sophocles asserted the gods themselves had woven justice into the fabric of the universe.

Sophocles's play typified a somewhat greater appreciation for foreign cultures among the classical Athenians. That appreciation came about as the result of two great wars involving almost all the Hellenic states. The Persian invasions of 490 and 480 exposed more Greeks to the cultures of ancient Mesopotamia and Egypt; indeed, despite the heroism rightly trumpeted by classical historians, most Greeks in 480 "medized," that is, submitted to an alliance with the great king, however grudgingly. A greater appreciation and admiration for the cultures of Persia and Egypt may be found in the thought of the historian of the Persian Wars himself, Herodotus. While Greeks would continue to believe themselves superior to the "barbarians," their greater knowledge of the world beyond their homeland widened their intellectual vistas.

The Peloponnesian War (431–404) likewise altered traditional points of view. That war was an unparalleled disaster for the Athenians and their empire, and prompted a good deal of criticism of long-cherished beliefs and institutions. In the funeral oration traditionally delivered at the burial of the first war-dead, the statesman Pericles described Athens as "an education to

Greece."[60] He urged his listeners: "Fix your eyes every day on the greatness of Athens as she really is and . . . fall in love with her."[61] By the war's end, however, they suffered terrible defeats such as those at Syracuse in 411, where an entire army was lost, and at Aegospotami in 406, where not only an entire navy was destroyed, but also the grain trade which Athens relied upon for food was cut off. Such events soured many Athenians on their traditional government and convictions. Such scorn may be found in the plays of Euripides, a much younger contemporary of Sophocles. In *Medea*, Jason, who has repudiated his faithful and barbarian wife Medea, tells her:

> From my deliverance, as my words shall prove—
> First, then, in Hellas dwell'st thou, in the stead
> Of land barbaric, knowest justice, learnest
> To live by law without respect of force.[62]

Jason's speech, of course, is entirely ironic. One of the great cads in all of world literature, he rejects and casts out a wife who loved him deeply. Like Clytemnestra, she had her revenge, by slaying the two boys she bore Jason, but unlike the heroine of Aeschylus, she escapes any further recrimination. The champion of Greek superiority gets his comeuppance.

This reexamination of traditional ideas preoccupied not only playwrights but also the Sophists, who were teachers of political and rhetorical effectiveness. The emergence of the Sophists was a uniquely Athenian development, for success in law and politics in that *polis* required the skillful construction of argument and oratory. The hostility of Plato meant that for a long time classical scholars had little good to say about the Sophists, but more respect has been accorded them in the last several generations, as they have received fairer consideration. Whereas Plato was sometimes hostile to democracy, the Sophists were wholehearted advocates for that form of government. Whereas the aristocrats believed themselves born to rule, the Sophists argued that political competence could be taught, and so even the humblest commoner— even, theoretically at least, a barbarian—could make a significant political contribution to the *polis*. Indeed, according to the Sophist Antiphon, Greeks treated each other much like the barbarians did:

> We reverence and honor those people who are of noble ancestry but not those of lesser households. In acting this way we treat each other like barbarians when in reality, by nature, we all have the same nature in all things, barbarians and Greeks alike. The proof of this is to be seen when we consider the things that are natural and necessary to all humankind. These things are available to

everyone in the same way, whether barbarians or Greek. Thus we all use our mouths and nostrils to breathe.[63]

For the Sophists, the very democracy which was the crowning glory of all Athens's great accomplishments suggested that all peoples could handle the business of government and justice.

The Athenian Practice of Justice

What must be borne in mind for just about any topic in premodern history is that our sources—as well as the ideas and arguments found in them—not only record past deeds, they also serve as commentaries on the "doings" of a people. Aeschylus, Sophocles, Euripides, and Plato interpreted the practices of their contemporaries. Consequently, the Athenian practice of justice must also be examined.

Although democracy has come to be conflated with "checks and balances" in modern governments, Athenian democracy had no branches of government. Virtually all sovereignty and power—whether legislative, executive, or judicial—rested in the *ekklesia*, or assembly, of all enfranchised citizens, that is, males born to citizens of Athens. Two developments of the early fifth century completed the establishment of the Athenian democracy begun in the days of Solon. The statesman Cleisthenes (c. 500 BC) sponsored reforms that conferred Athenian citizenship on both boys and girls born in Attica, regardless of their families' landed properties, such that political influence might be exerted even by citizens of the most modest means. Secondly, between the Persian Wars the statesman Themistocles persuaded the Athenians to construct a great navy, convinced as he was that the Persians would be back, and that control of the sea would be essential to the Hellenic defiance of "The Great King." The building of the navy actually complemented the reforms of Cleisthenes, as both politically empowered the poorest citizens of Athens. Landless citizens could row the triremes of the powerful Athenian navy, and so render to the *polis* military service, and claim their place in the *ekklesia*, as the Athenians had long believed that political rights should follow upon military service.[64]

Thus, the *ekklesia* which debated legislation and declarations of war also served as the principal court in Athens. The democratic spirit characteristic of the *ekklesia's* other responsibilities likewise colored its judicial business, particularly after Pericles introduced pay for jurors, making jury service possible for the poorest citizens.[65] The procedures whereby the *ekklesia* conducted its other business extended also to criminal trials. That, in turn, meant that the courts were also caught up in the highly personal politics of Athens, which may also have had a similar influence among her allies in the rest of Greece. For instance, in the Athenian ally of Corcyra, an island *polis* in the Ionian Sea, politics and justice collided in the case of Peithias, the leader of the democrats. His political enemies, friendly to Athens's enemy Corinth, accused him of subjecting Corcyra to Athenian slavery. He was acquitted and retaliated by accusing five of his richest enemies of "having procured vine-props by cutting them on the ground sacred to Zeus and to Alcinous." The jury convicted these defendants, who begged that the expensive fines be reassessed. Peithias, who was a member of the *ekklesia* in Corcyra, demanded that the original fine be paid, and *in the midst of a judicial hearing, proposed that an offensive and defensive alliance with Athens be concluded.* Supporters of the five defendants attacked the assembly. Peithias was slain; other Athenian supporters fled the city.[66] Although Thucydides here recorded a court case, Peithias's intentions were clearly political. Soon thereafter, this Corcyrean argument served as the occasion setting off the Peloponnesian War.[67]

As in many premodern societies, Athenian law recognized few crimes but all of them were considered assaults on the whole of Athens. The most common of these crimes seems to have been impiety. For instance, Solon persuaded Cylon, who was suspected of sacrilege, to submit to a trial "and to abide by the decision of three hundred jurors selected from the nobility."[68] Charges of impiety stained even the reputation of the great Pericles, who came under suspicion through association. Aspasia, a woman suspected of being Pericles's mistress, was accused of denying the gods. Her case prompted other accusations against those who "did not believe in the gods, or who taught doctrines regarding the heavens," as did Pericles's friend, the philosopher Anaxagoras. This accusation was just as much directed at Pericles as at his learned friend. Pericles was directly accused of embezzlement and was compelled to deposit his accounts of the public moneys with the *prytanes*, the auditors of the government. Pericles, however, proved the equal of his opponents: "Aspasia [Pericles] begged off, by shedding copious tears at the trial, as Aeschines says, and by entreating the jurors." On Aspasia's behalf Pericles appealed to the jurors' emotions. Fearful of what might happen to Anaxagoras, Pericles sent him abroad. As for his own case, Pericles "wagged the dog" and diverted attention from his alleged crime: "He feared a jury in his own case so [he] kindled the flame [of] the threatening and smouldering war, hoping thereby to dissipate the charges made against him and allay the people's jealousy, inasmuch as when great undertakings were on foot, and great perils threatened, the city entrusted herself to him and to him alone, by reason of his worth and power."[69] In the end, the case against Pericles seems simply to have lost procedural momentum and was dropped. Indeed, "Pericles won even greater confidence and honour among the citizens than before."[70]

Of course, the most famous Athenian trial is that found in Plato's *Apology*. The plaintiffs accused Socrates of a type of impiety, namely, corrupting the youth of Athens, which endangered the state. The charges were founded upon the hijinks of his two most famous students. Alcibiades, an Alcmaeonid and therefore related to Pericles, emerged as a military and political figure during the Peloponnesian War. He persuaded the Athenians to attack Sicily in 415. Just before the fleet was due to leave for Syracuse, sacred statues had been vandalized; many suspected Alcibiades, whom the Athenians recalled from the army.[71] Fearful of political enemies who wished to execute him, Alcibiades fled to Sparta, and aided her cause.[72] Because of Alcibiades's betrayal, the expedition ended in 413 with the destruction of the entire Athenian force. Alcibiades yet managed to rehabilitate his standing with the Athenians, and after a reconciliation and recall to the city, he was given a naval command. But, the Spartans defeated his fleet at the Battle of Noricum in 406, and his power and influence in Athens were destroyed for good.[73] Critias, another of Socrates's students, likewise collaborated with the Spartans. In 405, the Spartan general Lysander had demolished an Athenian navy at the Battle of Aegospotami, near the Hellespont. Lysander's victory interrupted the grain trade between the Black Sea and the Athenians, who were compelled to surrender to Sparta the following year.[74] Sparta demanded the replacement of Athens's democracy by an oligarchical regime known as "the Thirty," among whom Critias was one of the leaders.[75] The Thirty hunted down democrats known to have intrigued against the aristocracy during the war.[76] Critias himself had been sent into exile and showed a "lust for putting people to death."[77] In 399, a democratic coup toppled the Thirty, with the democrats eager to settle scores.

The trial of Socrates epitomizes most Athenian judicial procedures. First of all, the state brought no charges against the philosopher, nor did the state have any means by which to do so. Justice rather relied on the suits brought by private citizens, as in Plato's *Laws*: "If there is any disobedience to this law, it shall be open to anyone who pleases to lay an information [i.e., an accusation of guilt]."[78] Even in criminal cases, private citizens, such as Meletus (who entered the indictment) and Anytus (who represented angry artisans) initiated the proceedings against Socrates.[79] They also made the case for guilt. Socrates, of course, defended himself. Thus, although Socrates hinted that legal professionals worked in Athens,[80] citizen-amateurs from among the *ekklesia* generally prosecuted, defended, and sat in judgment on the accused, just like that same body heard arguments on behalf of and against proposed legislation. Thus, as Plutarch observed, the *ekklesia* also served as the main interpreter of Athenian law.[81] Athenian justice, then, prized equality over efficiency, as citizens took their turns on juries, and professional jurists and lawyers were absent, although the ability to speak well in public was invaluable. Judges and jurors were selected by lot and were paid for their trouble. The Athenians saw little difference between judges and juries; the same word was used to name both (*dikastai*, plu.). Arguments were limited by time; a water-clock was used to time them. Since trials were often used to settle personal scores, personal invective was commonplace, but the use of certain forbidden words constituted the tort of defamation. Jurors voted in secret; they dropped ballots into either a conviction or an acquittal urn.[82] The Athenians established no courts of appeal. Since the decision of juries was taken to be those of the whole *polis*, there was no other court to hear an appeal. Some penalties had been enacted in law; others were at the discretion of either the jury or the judge, as in the case of Socrates. The commonest penalties in Athenian law were ostracism (exile from the city for ten years), fines, and execution. Capital convictions were followed by a kind of sentencing hearing, where the convicted could request banishment, rather than death.[83] Socrates may have avoided a death sentence, had he not mockingly recommended to the jury that just convicted him that free maintenance by the state would be an appropriate punishment for his crimes.[84]

Most Athenian judicial procedures, however, involved torts or delicts rather than crimes. Many offenses that the modern state treats as crimes premodern polities considered torts. In Athenian jurisprudence, only an act that threatened the entire state, like impiety, qualified as a crime. According to the Athenians, theft, rape, adultery, and even sometimes murder offended private parties. The victims of these acts (or their kin) were expected to petition for compensation or restitution. For instance, in the case of murder, Athenian law was rather more preoccupied "with cleansing the city of bloodguilt rather than punishing murderers," hence blood-feud remained a prominent feature of Athenian society, although the slain's kin could bring a charge in a court of law. Murder was, however, a matter Athenian law left largely to the families involved.[85] Indeed, seeking justice for murdered kin amounted to a sacred obligation:

> If any man of the deceased's kin within the limits of cousinship, on either father's or mother's side, shall neglect his duty to institute proceedings, or to make proclamation of the excommunication first, on his own head be the pollution.[86]

Such matters were of course delicate, since the parties involved probably lived together in the same neighborhood or village, and the results of judicial procedures were felt for a long time. The two parties must reach some agreement whereby they could consider the matter closed; otherwise they risked initiating a long conflict between kin groups. For the same reason, instead of suffering the death penalty, the condemned generally went into exile, as Plato recommended.[87] Thus did Athenian law attempt to reduce tensions between the offender and offended.[88]

As for other torts, Athenian law recognized two kinds of theft. An aggravated theft was committed when the thief was caught in the act, and for which the penalty was death, perhaps because catching the thief probably meant that a fight accompanied the illicit seizure of property. All other theft the Athenians called simple theft, the punishment for which was either compensation to the victim or confinement to the stocks. Athenian law accepted double-standards with regard to rape and adultery. The law considered adultery to be a more serious problem than rape, because adultery corrupted the position of the wife within the household (*oikos*) and made uncertain the lineage of children and therefore of prospective heirs. According to their law, rape involved one victim but adultery could create a host of them. Greek misogyny also figured into the jurisprudence of sexual offenses in ancient Athens. Adultery could be committed only by wives—husbands suffered no penalties nor paid compensation for infidelity.

Like so many of their laws dealing with what modern jurisprudence would consider crimes against persons, the Athenians allowed little competence for the state in matters of marriage and child-rearing, which were left to the families of the husband and wife. The law recognized the competence of the families to negotiate marriage (*gamos*), which became legally valid only if the wife's family agreed or, in a few instances, the official recognition of the Athenian government was obtained. Dowries were expected, but not required. In the case of divorce, dowries reverted back to the wives. Marriage consisted of two stages; the first was the betrothal (*engue*), and the second a handing over (*ekdosis*) of the bride to her husband. Inheritance laws generally favored male heirs but allowed for some female inheritance of property. Newborn children could be exposed for birth defects or poor health. The property of a family served as part of its legacy that bound not only the living members of the household, but those already deceased and those yet to be born, as in the comment of Plato:

> Neither your own persons nor the estate are your own; both belong to your whole line, past and future, and still more absolutely do both lineage and estate

belong to the community. This is so surely so that I shall never, if I can help it, permit you, when shaken by age or infirmity, to be cajoled into evil testamentary dispositions by the insinuating arts of the flatterers. My law will be made with a general view to the best interests of society at large and your whole line, as I rightly hold the single person and his affairs as of minor importance.[89]

While civil war was avoided in Attica, *stasis* remained a continual factor in Athenian politics and institutions, such that the Athenians often assumed strife to be the natural condition between men: "Humanity is in a condition of public war of every man against every man."[90] That strife also encouraged excessive litigiousness, which Plato believed another serious threat to domestic tranquility:

> Little repeated torts between neighbors by their frequency engender a heavy burden of ill will and make a neighborhood a grievous and bitter hardship. Hence neighbor must take every care to do nothing exceptionable to neighbor, must keep himself strictly from all such acts, and above all from encroachment on a neighbor's lands, for whereas by no means every man can do his neighbor a service, to cause him hurt is easy enough, and any man can do it. He that disregards a boundary mark and works soil that belongs to his neighbor shall make the damage good to him, and shall, moreover, by way of medicine for his churlish insolence, pay a further sum of double the amount of damage to the sufferer.[91]

Indeed, the litigiousness of the Athenians was sometimes believed to be completely exasperating, as well as something of a waste of time:

> Athenians sit in the courts and whine throughout their lives!
> Now that's the reason why we're on the road,
> And why we've brought this basket, pot, and wreaths
> To roam in search of a land that's free from trouble:
> That's where we'd like to settle ourselves for good.[92]

In the new, utopian regime founded by the assembly-women of Aristophanes's play, courts would be superfluous:

> Chremes: I've one more question. What's the rule for fines
> incurred in law courts?
> How will they pay? It can't be right to use the common funds.
> Praxagora: There won't be any need for courts.[93]

Athenian justice was messy and imperfect, often an expression of politics, and sometimes an outlet for vendetta. A weak state had only so much to contribute to orderliness in society. Still, Athenian justice depended upon important political and legal principles, among which was equality, which the Athenians preferred to efficiency. Both sides were given an equal chance to make their arguments, and then the decision was left to third parties. The reputation of the parties involved was vital, since trustworthiness figured into the proceedings. Since the system involved virtually every Athenian male, the decisions of that system could serve as the will of the Athenian people. Although they believed that justice was the gift of the goddess Athena, the Athenians also believed that that gift was implemented by the people of their *polis*.

Notes

1. *Code of Hammurabi*, 153, 25, 155, 157, 22, 14, and 6 [All citations from www.wsu.edu/~dee/MESO/CODE.HTM (accessed December 16, 2004)].

2. *Code*, 204.

3. Alan Harding, *Medieval Law and the Foundations of the State* (Oxford, UK: Oxford University Press, 2002), p. 24.

4. *Code*, 196–197.

5. *Code*, 128.

6. *Code*, 137–138.

7. *Code*, 2. *Code*, 3 provides the same for false accusation in a murder case.

8. *Code*, 132.

9. *Code*, 5.

10. For what follows here I am indebted to Calum M. Carmichael, *The Spirit of Biblical Law* (Athens, GA: University of Georgia Press, 1996).

11. The numbering of the Ten Commandments has never been standardized, so in some reckonings the first tablet consists of one through four and the second five through ten. In others, the first through third commandments make up the first tablet and the remainder the second.

12. *Didache*, 1.1 [Maxwell Staniforth, trans., *Early Christian Writings* (New York, NY: Penguin Books, 1968), p. 191].

13. Plato, *Laws*, 723b [Edith Hamilton and Huntington Cairns, eds., *The Collected Dialogues of Plato* (Princeton, NJ: Princeton University Press, 1961), p. 1313].

14. Plato, *Laws*, 757b [Hamilton, p. 1337]. Cf. Aristotle, *Ethics*, 1137b: "The equitable is just" [Richard McKeon, ed., *The Basic Works of Aristotle* (New York, NY: Random House, 1941), p. 1020].

15. Plutarch, *Solon*, 13.1–3 [*Loeb Classical Library* (Cambridge, MA: Harvard University Press, 1911), 46:435–436].

16. Hesiod, *Works and Days*, 247–248; 252–253 [Stanley Lombardo, trans, *Hesiod: Works and Days and Theogony* (Indianapolis, IN: Hackett Publishing Co., 1993), p. 30].

17. *Works*, 307–310 [Lombardo, p. 31].

18. *Works*, 274–276 [Lombardo, p. 30].

19. *Works*, 255–257 [Lombardo, p. 30].

20. *Works*, 287–290 [Lombardo, p. 31].

21. *Works*, 324–327 [Lombardo, p. 32].

22. *Works*, 266–267 [Lombardo, p. 30].

23. *Works*, 293–294 [Lombardo, p. 31].

24. *Works*, 300 [Lombardo, p. 31].

25. *Works*, 321–322 [Lombardo, p. 32].

26. *Works*, 261–266 [Lombardo, p. 30].

27. *Works*, 268–273 [Lombardo, p. 30].

28. *Works*, 273–275 [Lombardo, p. 30].

29. Aristotle, *The Athenian Constitution*, 5.1 [P. J. Rhodes, trans., *Aristotle: The Athenian Constitution* (New York, NY: Penguin Books, 1984), p. 46].

30. Ibid.

31. Ibid.

32. M. I. Finley, *Early Greece: The Bronze and Archaic Ages* (New York, NY: W. W. Norton & Co., 1970), p. 119.

33. Plutarch, *Solon*, 14.2 [*Loeb*, 46:439].

34. Aristotle, *Ath. Cons.*, 9.1 [Rhodes, p. 50].

35. Plutarch, *Solon*, 18.5 [*Loeb*, 46:453].

36. Aristotle, *Ath. Con.*, 9.1 [Rhodes, p. 50].

37. Ibid.

38. Plutarch, *Solon*, 16.3 [*Loeb*, 46:449].

39. Aeschylus, *Agamemnon*, 1404–1406 [Philip Vellacott, trans., *Aeschylus: The Oresteian Trilogy* (New York, NY: Penguin Books, 1956), p. 91].

40. Aeschylus, *Choephori*, 1035–1038 [Vellacott, p. 142].

41. Aeschylus, *Eumenides*, 153–157 [Vellacott, p. 152].

42. Cf. Plato, *Laws*, 869b–869c [Hamilton, p. 1429], where Plato denies the right of self-defense to children attacked by murderous parents: "The law's command will be that [the son] must endure the worst rather than commit such a crime [i.e., kill one of his parents]."

43. *Eumenides*, 213–218 [Vellacott, p. 154].

44. According to myth, Athena sprang fully grown from the head of Zeus.

45. *Eumenides*, 736–740 [Vellacott, p. 172].

46. *Eumenides*, 792–793 [Vellacott, p. 174].

47. *Eumenides*, 675–677 [Vellacott, p. 170].

48. *Eumenides*, 698–699 [Vellacott, p. 171].

49. Plato, *Laws*, 735d–735e [Hamilton, p. 1321].

50. Plato, *Crito* 51c–51d [Hamilton, p. 36].

51. D. Brendan Nagle, *The Ancient World: A Social and Cultural History*, 6th ed. (Upper Saddle River, NJ: Pearson Prentice Hall, 2006) p. 148.

52. *Eumenides*, 864–866 [Vellacott, p. 176].

53. *Eumenides*, 683–685 [Vellacott, p. 170].

54. *Eumenides*, 696–697 [Vellacott, p. 171].

55. Sophocles, *Antigone*, 494–501 [David Grene and Richmond Lattimore, eds., *Greek Tragedies*, 2nd ed. (Chicago, IL: University of Chicago Press, 1991), 1:198].

56. *Antigone*, 726–727 [Grene, 1:207].

57. *Antigone*, 1132–1144 [Grene, 1:222].

58. *Antigone*, 1413 [Grene, 1:232].

59. *Antigone*, 1347 [Grene, 1:229].

60. Thucydides, *Peloponnesian War*, 2.41 [Rex Warner, trans., *Thucydides: History of the Peloponnesian War* (New York, NY: Penguin Books, 1972), p. 147].

61. Thucydides, *Peloponnesian War*, 2.43 [Warner, p. 149].

62. Euripedes, *Medea*, 534–538 [*Loeb*, 12:325].

63. Nagle, p. 148.

64. Aristotle, *Athenian Constitution*, 4.2 [P. J. Rhodes, trans., *Aristotle: The Athenian Constitution* (New York, NY: Penguin Books, 1984), p. 44]. The half-legendary tyrant Draco had enacted such a law c. 620 BC.

65. Aristotle, Ath. Cons., 27.1–3 [Rhodes, p. 70]. The Council of the Areopagus (a hill west of the Acropolis) consisted of ex-*archons*. Until the reforms of Pericles, this council had jurisdiction in religious matters, which included homicide (Ath. Cons., 3.6 [Rhodes, p. 44]).

66. Thucydides, *Peloponnesian War*, 3.70 [Warner, p. 237].

67. S. C. Todd, *The Shape of Athenian Law* (Oxford, UK: Clarendon Press, 1993), p. 158.

68. Plutarch, *Solon*, 12.1–2 [*Loeb*, 46:450].

69. Plutarch, *Pericles*, 32.3 [*Loeb*, 65:93].

70. Plutarch, *Pericles*, 33.1 [*Loeb*, 65:95].

71. Thucydides, *Peloponnesian War*, 6.28–29 [Warner, pp. 426–427].

72. Thucydides, *Peloponnesian War*, 6.91 [Warner, pp. 468–469].

73. Xenophon, *Hellenica*, 1.5.10–16 [Rex Warner, trans., *Xenophon: A History of My Times* (New York, NY: Penguin Books, 1966), pp. 75–76].

74. Xenophon, *Hellenica*, 2.3.2 [Warner, p. 109], for a list of the members of the Thirty.

75. Many Athenians believed that Socrates thought Crete and Sparta had better governments than democratic Athens. Plato, *Crito*, 52e [Hamilton, p. 38].

76. Xenophon, *Hellenica*, 2.3.12 [Warner, p. 111].

77. Xenophon, *Hellenica*, 2.3.15 [Warner, p. 112].

78. *Laws*, 745a [Hamilton, p. 1329].

79. *Apology* 19b and 23e [Hamilton, pp. 5 and 10], and *Euthyphro*, 2b [Hamilton, p. 170].

80. Plato, *Crito*, 50b [Hamilton, p. 35].

81. Plutarch, *Solon*, 18.5 [*Loeb*, 46:453–454].

82. Aristotle, Ath. Cons., 68.2–3 [Rhodes, p. 113].

83. Plato, *Crito*, 52c: "At the time of your trial you could have proposed the penalty of banishment . . . with the sanction of the state" [Hamilton, p. 37].

84. Plato, *Apology*, 37a [Hamilton, p. 22].

85. Todd, *The Shape of Athenian Law*, p. 141. For Plato, even the unintentional death of slave by his master required the "purifications required by law." Plato, *Laws*, 865d [Hamilton, p. 1426].

86. Plato, *Laws*, 871b [Hamilton, p. 1430].

87. Plato, *Laws*, 864e [Hamilton, p. 1425].

88. Todd, *Shape of Athenian Law*, p. 141.

89. Plato, *Laws* 923a–923b [Hamilton, pp. 1474–1475].

90. Plato, *Laws* 626d [Hamilton, p. 1228].

91. Plato, *Laws* 843b–843 [Hamilton, pp. 1407–1408].

92. Aristophanes, *Birds*, 40–45 [Stephen Halliwell, ed. and trans., *Aristophanes: Birds and Other Plays* (Oxford, UK: Oxford University Press, 1998), p. 54].

93. Aristophanes, *Assembly-Women*, 657–659 [Halliwell, p. 178].

PART II

The Law of the Romans

The Romans' great contribution to subsequent civilization in the West was their law. No other ancient people so rigorously applied and thought about the law. Indeed, the legal systems of most European countries today, as well as the state of Louisiana and province of Quebec, are essentially Roman law. Like their fellow Indo-Europeans the Greeks, the judicial procedures of the Romans took place within adversarial institutions. Again, the Western propensity for self-criticism surfaced in Roman legal speculation. Like the courts and law of ancient Athens, the Romans' adversarial institutions evolved out of the historical conflict between the Roman nobility, or patricians, and the commoners, or plebeians. Much of their thinking about the law was inspired by the unique Roman practice of the law. However, the Romans also added to the Western legal tradition the conception that law consisted of a rational system, which began with basic principles, from which further conclusions and insights could be reasoned—the first approach to systematic thinking about the law and justice in Western civilization. Thus, the Romans produced the first figures that can really be called jurists, who teased out of Roman legal materials universal principles of justice and jurisprudence. The jurists' speculations constitute a major contribution to Western intellectual history, for Roman law was unique in that the jurists' opinions themselves constituted a source of legislation.

Early Rome

Archaeological excavations indicate that extensive agricultural settlements on the site of the modern city date before 1000 BC. According to tradition, kings ruled Rome until 509 BC. Not all of these early kings were native-born Romans. Numa, the second of the kings and the traditional founder of the Roman state religion, was a Sabine, and the last of the kings, Tarquin, an Etruscan. Little is really known about the city during these centuries, other than that the Romans were perpetually at war with their wealthier and culturally more sophisticated neighbors like the Etruscans. The city's location, in the middle of the plain of Latium, made Rome a difficult city to defend, so the early Romans made up with aggressiveness what they lacked in natural defenses. Like their Indo-European Greek cousins, the Italians may well have come to Italy by sea, from the south, and migrated their way up the peninsula. While the Romans were in touch with Greeks from early in their history, most scholars detect little Greek influence in Roman law. According to tradition, the Roman nobles expelled their last king, Tarquin, in 509 BC. They replaced his tyrannical monarchy with an aristocratic republic, where the nobles governed on behalf of the whole people. Most historians now believe that the origins of the republic were somewhat more complicated and resulted from a conflict between two Etruscan rulers—Tarquin, the king of Rome, and Lars Porsenna, the king of the nearby city of Clusium. Lars Porsenna drove Tarquin out of Rome, which enabled the Romans to establish the republic. The earliest Roman law recognized two estates—the patrician and the plebeian. Patricians claimed descent from the nobles who had thrown out Tarquin, and as a consequence claimed a more powerful position in the city. They controlled the assemblies and magistracies that carried out the work of Roman government. The plebeians descended from everyone else; according to tradition, the plebeian estate dated from the period of the Roman monarchy. Plebeians were free-born, small farmers who provided most of the tax money and infantry for the republic. Like the Greeks, the Romans' main strike force was heavy infantry deployed in phalanx formation. At the bottom of the social scale were the free poor and slaves, neither of whom bore any military or financial responsibilities to the state. Like the Greeks, the Romans tied political rights to military obligations. Conflict between the patricians and the plebeians, on whom military obligations fell most heavily, characterize the history of the early Roman republic, the unwritten constitution of which evolved as the patrician/plebeian rivalry unfolded. The plebeians found calls for military service especially burdensome, and demanded greater legal equality with the patricians as compensation.

As the more numerous and heterogeneous estate, however, the plebeians were often led poorly and had a more difficult time identifying interests common to all of them. They realized, however, that their chief bargaining chip with the patricians and consuls was military service. Since no war could be fought without their services, they could force the patricians to give them what they wanted by refusing to answer military call-ups. A key development for plebeian prospects came in 471, with the creation of the tribunes of the plebs (two originally, later more). These officers were invested with the power to veto not only any legislation that might be passed, but also military levies. Their persons were held inviolable, and no magistrate could arrest or harm any citizen to whom they had extended protection. They could, and often did, paralyze government and military planning if they did not get what the plebeians demanded.

The Twelve Tables

The first codification of Roman law resulted from the plebeian/patrician rivalry. In addition to calls for military service, the patricians' arbitrary enforcement and interpretation of the law angered the plebeians. They insisted that a written law be compiled to curtail arbitrary practices. A board of ten (*decemviri*) was commissioned to redact the famous Twelve Tables, which the *comitia centuriata* adopted in 449.[1] These laws were engraved on bronze tablets, and erected in the Forum Romanum. No complete text of the Twelve Tables has survived to the present; they must, rather, be reconstructed from Cicero and other jurists.

The stature of the Twelve Tables in the Roman imagination lasted much longer than their efficacy. Centuries after most of them had been rendered obsolete, Cicero claimed in the first century BC that he was taught to memorize them as a schoolboy.[2] The Twelve Tables probably represent no innovations in Rome's legal traditions. Instead, they preserve the primitive law of the city; for instance, they uphold a legal distinction between patricians and plebeians that would, within a generation after their promulgation, be dispensed with: "Intermarriage shall not take place between plebeians and patricians."[3] Like the law of the ancient Athenians, the Twelve Tables mostly consisted of civil (sometimes called private), rather than criminal (sometimes called public) law. For instance, the government was not responsible for the maintenance of roads: "Persons shall mend roadways."[4] Private parties almost always initiated legal proceedings and any citizen legally accused of law-breaking was required to answer the charge in the Forum, where (after 367) a *praetor* would preside and plaintiff and defendant could present their arguments. If decisions favored the plaintiff, compensation was most often required. The Twelve Tables seem to preserve a vestige of vendetta concerning compensation for a lost limb: "If a person has maimed another limb, let there be retaliation in kind *unless* he makes agreement for composition [i.e., compensation] with him."[5] Clearly, compensation was preferred to its alternative. Some delicts, like arson, did merit capital punishment: "Any person who destroys by burning any building or heap of corn deposited alongside a house shall be bound, scourged, and put to death by burning at the stake, provided that [he] has committed the said misdeed with malice aforethought."[6] Like the law of the Athenians, the Twelve Tables recognized two kinds of theft: "If theft has been done by night, if the owner kill the thief, the thief shall be held lawfully killed . . . it is forbidden that a thief be killed by day."[7] Since about the only evidence that could be introduced into court was the testimony of witnesses, the Twelve Tables prescribed the death penalty for perjury.[8] Only three crimes are mentioned in the Twelve Tables—bribery, sedition, and defamation. The taking of bribes by judges was deemed a capital offense, as was aiding or cooperating with an enemy of the Roman people: "He who shall have roused up a public enemy, or handed over a citizen to a public enemy, must suffer capital punishment."[9] Defamation of character also merited death: "If any person has sung or composed against another person a song such as was causing slander or insult to another, he shall be clubbed to death."[10]

The Twelve Tables were also concerned with Roman family law. Many accounts of early republican law describe the authority of the male head of household (*paterfamilias*) as nearly absolute. The Twelve Tables commanded *paterfamiliae* to slay a "dreadfully deformed child," and as in ancient Athens, the *paterfamilias* possessed the authority to expose unwanted children. The authority of the *paterfamilias* was rather more restricted over the goods of the household, in that the Twelve Tables prescribed that a spendthrift was prohibited from the administration of his own goods, lest future generations have little or nothing to live on.[11] Authority over the females in the household was extensive. The law prescribed that all females should be under the authority of some male—in the case of unmarried girls and women, their father, or a brother if the father was deceased. Married women, of course, were subjected to their husbands. The only women free of such legal subjection were the Vestal Virgins.[12] Early Roman marriages were often said to be *cum manu*; that is, the father ritually handed his daughter's hand into that of her husband.[13] Divorce seems to have been rare in the early republic.

The compilation and erection of the Twelve Tables in the Forum Romanum in 449 changed little for the plebeians. The Tables themselves perpetuated the second-class status of the plebeians, and the regime of the *decemvirs* proved even more tyrannical and arbitrary than that of the consuls, who were restored to power by a coup. Still, over time the legal distinctions between patricians and plebeians dissipated and in the process the (unwritten) constitution of the mature Roman republic emerged. Roman assemblies and magistracies forged the coalition of patricians and plebeians that was in place by 300 BC, and in turn the struggle of the orders endowed those assemblies and magistracies with power. The patrician/plebeian republic conquered much of the Mediterranean world by 200 BC.

The Constitution of the Mature Roman Republic

The Roman government was an aristocratic republic. The leaders of the elites governed on behalf of the whole people. The government consisted of a number of assemblies and magistracies. Each of the three assemblies were differently structured, as well as charged with different responsibilities. Initially, the most powerful legislative assembly was the *comitia centuriata* (centuries). The centuries voted for major magistracies, constitutional laws, and declarations of war. So, for instance, in 449 the centuries passed the Valerio-Hortensian laws (named for the consuls Valerius and Hortensius, who introduced them), which made legislation passed by another assembly, the *comitia plebis* (plebiscites), binding on all Roman citizens.[14] The patricians, however, resisted the Valerio-Hortensian laws for more than a century. They continued to claim that they were not subject to plebiscites, but in 287 another plebeian refusal of military service prompted the law of a dictator, also named Hortensius, which finally made plebiscites legally binding on patricians.[15] Henceforth, the council of the plebs was the main legislative body for the republic, although elections for major magistracies continued to be held in the centuries.

The very name of the centuriate assembly probably preserves a dim memory of an era wherein Romans were classified legally according to their military obligations; like the Greeks, the Romans linked political rights to military obligations, so the very poorest had no military obligations, but neither could they exercise any sort of franchise. There were 193 centuries, each of which had one vote. The centuries were distributed, unevenly, between five classes. The first class (aristocracy) controlled 98 centuries, so no principle of "one man, one vote" was in play here.

The Roman republic had a popular assembly as well, known as the *comitia plebis* when presided over by a consul or praetor, and as the *comitia tributa* when presided over by a tribune of the people. The *comitia plebis* was divided into tribes. The tribes voted for the minor magistracies, and plebeians controlled the majority of the votes. Initially, the plebs had rather less power than the centuries, since their assembly had no legislative power, but the passage of the Valerio-Hortensian laws endowed it with much greater legal efficacy. Many of the reforms which equalized the standing of plebeians with patricians were passed in the plebs, such as the Canuleian law of 445 (introduced by the tribune Canuleius), which legalized intermarriage between patricians and plebeians.[16] Other important milestones were the Licinio-Sextian law (367), which made it legal for a plebeian to be elected consul, and required that one consul be a plebeian.[17] In 326, the Poetelian-Papirian law made it illegal for plebeians to be enslaved for debt.[18] In 300, the Ogulnian law permitted plebeians to become priests.[19]

The most prestigious assembly in the Roman republic was the Senate, which voted for most laws, and served as the chief deliberative body for the country. In the Senate sat the heads of the leading 300 families in Rome. All senators had to have already served in a number of magistracies. Bills that passed the Senate were known as *senatus consultum*, and were regarded as the most efficacious legislation recognized by the republic. The Senate's most formidable powers, however, were extra-legislative and extra-constitutional. The Senate defended Roman traditions and power, particularly with regard to conquest and religion. The Conscript Fathers (as they were affectionately known) also made most of Rome's domestic and foreign policy decisions.

While the legislative authority of the Roman republic was invested in the assemblies, a number of magistrates wielded executive powers. The magistrates were also entrusted with eliminating the abuse and corruption inherent in the concentration of power. These magistracies had their own hierarchy, so the Romans spoke of a *cursus honorum*, where the politically ambitious first ran for the lower offices, which in turn were believed to qualify them for higher positions in the government.

Almost all magistracies were elective, annual, and collegial; that is, magistrates had to win elections in either the *comitia centuriata* or the *comitia plebis*, they served for one year (no consecutive terms), and all had colleagues. For instance, the chief executive and supreme military power in the Roman republic was invested in two consuls. Essentially, they possessed many of the powers that the kings of Rome had in the days of the monarchy. The consuls were attended by twelve *lictors* each, who carried the *fasces* (axes with sticks bound around them, used to flog and behead criminals) as symbols of consular authority. A dual executive was established so that each consul could serve as a check on the other; in reality, both partners often stood for election together (akin to candidates for president and vice-president of the United States), so their policies rarely differed. Furthermore, until 367 only patricians could be elected to the office, which meant that consuls were drawn from a very exclusive and homogeneous club, in which kinship ties bound the members very closely. The pool of candidates expanded somewhat with the ratification of the Licinio-Sextian law. The primary responsibility of each consul was military command. The earliest Roman army consisted of two legions (about four thousand heavy infantry, plus cavalry and light infantry auxiliaries). Each consul commanded one legion. Even in her early days, Rome often fought more than one war at the same time, in which case each of the consuls was conducting his own campaign. If both consuls should be campaigning together, each commanded on alternate days—like the Athenians, the republican Romans often prized equality over efficiency. A few years after the promulgation of the Twelve Tables, the office of military tribune with consular powers was created to take the place of the consuls when relations between the patricians and plebeians were especially bad. The patricians' determination to retain the office of consul prompted the plebeians to demand this office. Since these officers were tribunes, some could be selected from the plebeians, and since they wielded consular power, others could be selected from the patricians.[20] A college of military tribunes replaced election of consuls about two-thirds of the years between the publication of the Twelve Tables and the promulgation of the Licinio-Sextian law, which rendered the office of military tribune obsolete.

Three other, early magistracies were the *quaestors*, the *censors*, and the tribunes of the people. The office of *quaestor* (two initially, later raised to four) dates from the earliest days of the republic, and may even have preceded it. *Quaestors* administered the state treasury. In the early days of the republic they were appointed by the consuls, but the office was made elective (in the *concilium plebis*) probably by the reforms of the Valerio-Hortensian laws of 447.[21]

Initially, the consuls were responsible for public order and the census. The census took account of the number of Roman citizens and also assigned them their legal status. Often, the demands of military command prevented the consuls from attending to this task, as they were away on campaign. Thus, in 443 these tasks were entrusted to two *censors*, who were elected every five years for a term of eighteen months. They also were charged with enforcing republican moral sentiments. Membership in the Senate demanded a minimum pool of wealth as well as moral fitness, meaning that the candidate in question had been innocent of any publicly scandalous behavior. The censors had the authority to evaluate senators according to these criteria, and so they possessed the important power of removing members of the Senate. Censors also supervised the administration of the *ager publicus*, the land owned by the Roman government.[22]

Around 471, the plebeians demanded the creation of a magistracy to protect their interests. The patricians then conceded the creation of the office of tribunes of the people (initially two, eventually a college of ten). Their very name invokes the common people, who were traditionally organized into tribes. The tribunes, elected in the *concilium plebis*, possessed great power. The sacred law itself protected their persons; anyone who harmed them could be killed without reprisal. Tribunes could grant protection (*auxilium*) to whomever they wished and could veto (*intercessio*) any prospective legislation or act of the consuls.

Several other important magistracies were established in the fourth century. Again, initially consuls served as the chief judges for the Roman people but their military responsibilities kept them away from the city for extended periods of time. In 366, the Romans created the office of *praetor*,[23] who supervised the administration of justice in the city. They presided over civil court cases. The praetor resembled the attorney general of the United States more than any American judge. Early in their history, when a praetor entered office he customarily issued an edict which promulgated the basic rules of procedure pertaining to his jurisdiction. The Praetor's Edict would in time become an important concept in Roman law. In 367, the Romans formally made the *curule aedileship* a magistracy. These four officers, which date from the earliest republic, were initially filled by patricians but soon after 367 became a plebeian magistracy. *Aediles* supervised the temples wherein plebiscites were registered, had oversight of markets and Rome's food supply, and held the customary games.[24]

Three magistrates, however, were not elected but appointed in time of national emergency. The consuls, at the direction of the Senate, could appoint a dictator; indeed, the protocol for a dictator stated that the Senate should order the consuls that "the state take no harm." He served for six months and his decisions were final. He chose the Master of Horse, who was his cavalry commander.[25] The dictator was attended by all 24 *lictors*, who thus represented the investiture of full executive authority in the dictator. In the case of the death or resignation of both consuls prior to an election, the senators named an *interrex* to administer the government until special elections for consul could take place (by law a period of five days).

The Imperial Republic

Despite the tensions between plebeian infantrymen and their patrician commanders, and in spite of an unenviable defensive position, the Roman army eventually bested all its Italian enemies. That Rome was in the plain of

Latium made her hard to defend; furthermore, warlike enemies surrounded the Romans. Only twelve miles to the northeast was the wealthy and large Etruscan city of Veii, and to the south lay the cities of Latium, related to the Romans by blood and language, but enemies nonetheless. In the Po valley lived Celtic tribes, who in 386 marched south and sacked Rome. Although traumatized by the sack, the Romans quickly recovered and resumed their position as the most powerful city in central Italy. Unlike the Greeks, the Romans decided that retaining territories and cities often required that they give the conquered a stake in the Roman republic. To that end, the Romans sometimes offered limited citizenship to subdued Italian cities and enlisted their military units alongside the legions. The Romans thereby gave their allies (*auxilia*, as they came to be known) a share in the glory and the spoils. The Romans rarely gave allies full citizenship, but rather *civitas sine suffragio*, citizenship without the right to vote. The denial of the franchise rarely caused friction with allies, since most of them were too far away from Rome to travel for elections. When they visited the city, however, they were Romans in law. Thus, one of the fundamental principles of imperial administration—which in time would form a commonwealth of diverse nations—dated from the early history of the Roman republic.

With central Italy having been pacified by 350 BC, the Romans spent the next half-century waging war in the south. Three costly wars were fought with the Samnite people (341, 327–304, and 298–291), who dwelt in the southern Apennine Mountains. Before this round of wars, the Romans had actually had very good relations with these rugged shepherds. The occasion for the wars was conflict between the Samnites and the coastal-dwelling Campanians, with whom the Romans had valuable commercial ties, as well as friendly relations. In the end, the Romans decided that their interests lay primarily with the Campanians. In each of these three wars, the Samnites often manhandled the legions. They humiliated the Romans at the Battle of the Claudine Forks (327), where a surrounded Roman army surrendered without a fight. Still, the Romans persisted, and refused to accept any outcome but victory. They learned to outmaneuver the Samnites. The Romans enjoyed internal lines of communication and controlled the coastal roads, which they used to deny Samnite shepherds their summer pasturage in the valleys. With their victory in the Third Samnite War, Rome was in control of almost all Italy south of the Po River by 291, and had also won toeholds in Greece and Sicily.

By 272, when the last southern Italian city fell to the Romans, another dangerous enemy had emerged, the Carthaginians of North Africa. The Romans had long had good relations with the Carthaginians. The Etruscans threatened the interests of both cities, and so an ancient alliance, rooted in a common enemy, bound Rome and Carthage. The imperial expansion of the two cities—Rome in Italy; Carthage in Sicily—created antagonisms. Furthermore, the Romans and Carthaginians had little in common. The Romans were Indo-Europeans; the Carthaginians were Semites, emigrants from Phoenicia (Levant). The Romans farmed the land; the Carthaginians sailed the entire Mediterranean and acquired most of their wealth through commerce. They possessed an impressive navy while the Romans were landlubbers.

The two great powers clashed in the three Punic Wars (264–241, 218–202, and 146 BC). During these bloody conflicts, the Senate emerged as the most important assembly in the Roman government. Although the Romans suffered a number of catastrophic defeats in the first two wars, the Senate prevented panic and rallied the people to carry on the struggle to victory. In the first war, the Romans overcame their naval inexperience. They built their first fleets based on captured Carthaginian models. Since most ancient naval battles resembled land actions, wherein the Romans excelled, the Romans instantly became a formidable naval power, defeated the Carthaginians, and added Sicily to their possessions. In the Second Punic War, the genius of the Carthaginian general Hannibal inflicted two defeats that for any other enemy would have been fatal. In one of the most spectacular and risky campaigns ever undertaken in world military history, Hannibal marched overland to Gibraltar, crossed into Spain, and invaded Italy. He annihilated vast Roman armies at Lake Trasimene (217), and Cannae (216). Between these two battles, Carthaginian forces slaughtered about 60 000 legionnaries. When news of these defeats reached Rome, leading senators calmed the people, and supervised the preparation of defenses and the training of new troops. Convinced thereby that an attack on Rome was too risky, Hannibal remained in southern Italy for the next thirteen years, and tried to foment disloyalty to Rome in Campania and Samnia. In 210, a new Roman commander came on the scene. The young and brash Scipio hailed from an old and revered patrician family. He determined to take the fight to the Carthaginians. With Hannibal still in southern Italy, he first attacked the Carthaginian empire in Spain. Having defeated the Carthaginians there, he invaded Africa. Hannibal abandoned Italy to defend his home city. The two great generals collided at the Battle of Zama (202), where Scipio conquered and Carthaginian imperial ambitions collapsed. Carthage relinquished her Spanish empire to Rome, along with some North African territories. Only one great power now remained in the western Mediterranean.

Conquest had by now, however, gotten under the Roman skin—something in which the Romans took great pride. Furthermore, as the great power of the Mediterranean, many smaller, eastern kingdoms states now asked the Romans for help in fighting their battles—a policy dangerous for the independence of the weaker power. After 200 BC, the Romans waged a number of wars of conquest in Greece and Asia Minor. In 146, the Romans finally obliterated Carthage, as well as Corinth, by then the most powerful city in Greece. During the second half of the second century BC, Rome fielded about 47 000 legionnaries each year, usually in long campaigns far from home. The lands of men who died without heirs reverted to the Roman state, and often then passed into the control or ownership of the politically well-connected. Senators, who had displayed such great leadership and patriotism during the dangerous era of the Punic Wars, now shamefully despoiled men who had served the republic with honor and courage. The Italian allies, too, wondered what benefits they enjoyed for fighting alongside Romans.

Empire had cost the Romans dearly. Small Italian farmers had been the economic and military foundations of the republic but combat deaths, long absences from home, crippling war wounds, and the intimidations of the wealthy had ruined the old socio-economic network. Between 133 and 28 BC, reform movements, civil wars, and more wars of conquest fill the pages of Roman history. Faction divided the Romans. Tensions escalated with the Italian allies, who tired of the endless call-ups for military service. Spokesmen for the aristocracy and free peasants (many of them now landless, and living in the city of Rome) took turns at political celebrity. Generals conquered at least as much for their own political ambitions as for the glory or defense of the Roman people. The republic's most prestigious assembly, the Senate, no longer provided the leadership that gave Rome victory over Hannibal; instead, leading senators advanced their own interests. After conquering the region of Gaul, an aristocrat named Julius Caesar (100–43 BC) seemed to have quieted the tumult but at the expense of the republic itself. His assassination merely delayed the republic's collapse.

Rome's provinces shared in the disorder and mismanagement of the late republic. Too often provincial governors believed that their authority had been granted to make themselves rich, rather than govern competently. Cries for justice reached Rome from her conquered territories. In only one example, the orator, jurist, and statesman Cicero accused Verres, who had been governor of Sicily (73–71), of extracting 2 000 000 *sesterces* from the inhabitants of that island! In a letter written to his brother Quintus, the *propraetor* of Asia, Cicero, who fully realized that the potential for corruption and self-aggrandizement was plentiful, laid out principles for just provincial government. Cicero's birth in the southern Italian town of Arpinum may have made him more sympathetic to the plight of provincials. He was by no means naïve and knew well that more was needed than good men: "In these matters, however, experience itself has by this time taught you that it is by no means sufficient to possess these virtues yourself, but that you must keep diligent watch around you."[26] Governors must desire the good of the provincials more than wealth or power. Above all, provincial governors must realize that they are accountable to allies, citizens, and the state for the behavior of all provincial officials.

The traditional patron/client relationship inspired Cicero's vision for Roman provincial government. Patrons, the more powerful partner, defended their clients, the weaker partners, and were expected to support their efforts to obtain jobs and preferment. In turn, clients were expected to support their patrons' political ambitions—a loud, unruly crowd of supporters could influence the decisions of important magistrates. Cicero counseled Quintus to extend the patron/client relationship to the province as a whole. He recommended that Quintus appoint his own freedmen (former slaves), who as his clients would be more accountable to him, to positions in the administration. He also encouraged making alliances with local, non-Roman aristocrats, who were accustomed to influencing regional affairs. This coalition of supporters and provincials should serve the cause of good provincial government. Cicero seemed to think that wealthy men made better governors than men of middling wealth, who would be more tempted by bribes.

Cicero's letter to his brother Quintus also highlighted the growing significance of the equestrian order in the late republic—the order to which Cicero himself belonged, although his whole career (as well as his first marriage) aimed at social and legal advancement to the highest nobility. As the name suggests, the equestrian order originated with those Romans wealthy enough to serve in the legions as cavalry—they could afford their own battle horses, which the state did not provide. Thus, they were a subset of the *nobiles*, ranking below senators but above the small landowners who served as legionary infantrymen. The ambition of such men, of course, was to rise in the social hierarchy; the administrative needs of the imperial republic provided numerous opportunities for advancement in wealth and rank, and at the same time required men with experience in the keeping of accounts and collection of revenues. Rome's increasing reliance on publicans (tax farmers, usually from the equestrian order) troubled Cicero.[27] While the equestrians' administrative skills had undeniably served the imperial republic well, as "new men" of ambition, they were inclined to plunder rather than govern the provinces.

Finally, Cicero recommended to Quintus that new duties and taxes were to be avoided, as provincials especially resented them. In the end, Cicero wrote, attending to justice was the best policy, for if justice was done the provincials, all other problems could be worked out.[28] Cicero thus argued that the policies long followed by the Romans in Italy should also be extended to her conquests. As in Italy, governors should cultivate the loyalty and expertise of local magnates. Governors could best control their subordinates by nominating them from their clients, or perhaps reducing those subordinates to clientage.

Cicero's Jurisprudence

Along with his laudable efforts to improve Roman provincial administration, Marcus Tullius Cicero (106–43 BC) stands as one of the most influential and formidable Roman intellectuals of the first century BC. He was also revered as one of the greatest Latin prose stylists. Even today, teachers assign his works to students just beginning their study of the Latin language. Born to a wealthy although not particularly well-connected family in Arpinum in 104 BC, Cicero was educated in Rome and Greece, where he studied with Epicurean, Stoic, and Academic philosophers. He quickly made a reputation for himself as a defense attorney, and also served the republic as *quaestor* in Sicily (75), consul (63), and governor of the province of Cilicia (57). As consul, Cicero foiled the conspiracy of Catiline to overthrow his beloved republic. Other political endeavors enjoyed much less success, as Cicero overestimated the abilities and loyalties of his allies, gained the bitter enmity of his enemies, and failed to appreciate just how weak the republican government had become. He cultivated relations with Pompey, the enemy of Julius Caesar, whom he believed was the best chance to save the republic. Of course, Julius Caesar defeated Pompey at the Battle of Pharsalus in 48; Pompey was murdered shortly thereafter. Cicero then laid low until Caesar's assassination in 44, after which he believed Marc Antony to be the great threat to a republic which was now moribund in all but name. Cicero hoped that Caesar's adopted heir Octavian might be used against Antony, but when the two younger men, along with Lepidus, formed another triumvirate, Cicero's fate was sealed. Octavian agreed to hand Cicero over to the executioners, who ended his life on December 7, 43. His head and hands were nailed to the Rostrum in the Forum.

Cicero influenced literature and jurisprudence far longer and more deeply than he did the politics of the first century. He wrote hundreds of speeches for delivery in court, as well as a great many letters to friends and family. He also wrote a number of treatises wherein he claimed no originality, but rather the application of Greek philosophy, in which he was deeply interested his whole life. Two of his treatises, *De legibus* (*On laws*) and *De republica* (*On the*

commonwealth) were written during a short period of tranquility for the republic, as Caesar was away from Rome conquering Gaul, and Pompey, the favorite of the Senate, was in control of Italy. Both treatises, written in the
form of the Platonic dialogue, long influenced Roman jurisprudence, and
would be quoted by students of the Roman law into the early modern period.

Traditionalist that he was, Cicero was convinced that government and law
must be examined in the light of history, a genre that he believed was regret-
tably scarce in Latin literature.[29] Rome's laws and government excelled pre-
cisely because they arose from the historical experience of her people: "Our
own constitution . . . had been established not by one man's ability but by that
of many, not in the course of one man's life but over several ages and generations . . . there had to be practical experience over a long period of history."[30]
Many great historical figures had contributed to the constitution. Romulus,
for instance, had wisely decided not to found a coastal city because the sea exposed such cities to numerous dangers and strange peoples like the Greeks and
Carthaginians. He likewise arranged for commoners to have aristocratic patrons (patron/client relationship), which morally enriched the peasants.[31]
Numa (d. c. 673 BC), the Sabine who ruled as the second king of Rome, established the traditional religion, which, even after the cultural influence of
the Greeks infiltrated Rome, still served as the foundation of the republic's
culture and morality.[32] King Tarquin (traditionally dated 616–579 BC)
founded the equestrian order, and King Servius (traditionally dated 578–535
BC) the *comitia centuriata*, a body which brilliantly balanced the interests in
Rome: "Servius's system ensured that the mass of the people was neither excluded from the right to vote (for that would have been high-handed), nor
given too much power, which would have been dangerous."[33] The history of
law in Rome was a story of legal guarantees safeguarded by precedent. Indeed,
the first legislation passed by the centuries after the expulsion of the kings was
the *lex Valeria*, which prohibited the flogging or execution of a Roman citizen
without appeal. A generation later, the establishment of tribunes of the plebs
served to check the ambitions and tyranny of the consuls.[34] The Twelve Tables provided for appeals "against every verdict and sentence." "Though the
people were free, not much was done through them; most things were done
on the authority of the Senate *according to custom and precedent*."[35] In days
long gone by, the traditions of the Roman people themselves served as the law
of the republic.[36] Thus, Cicero's jurisprudence was decidedly conservative.
The old must be adapted to serve the new, and no radical changes with the
past were in the interests of the people of Rome.

Like Plato, Aristotle, and Polybius, Cicero argued that in every state a determined succession of regimes follows one upon the other. Monarchy de-

generates into tyranny, against which the nobles rebel; they then establish an aristocracy. After several generations, power corrupts the aristocracy, which then collapses into an oligarchy. In time, oligarchies fall to the rebellion of the commoners, and a democracy emerges. That government will corrode over time as well. A strong ruler will replace it, and a new monarchy begins the cycle all over again.[37] Like Plato, Cicero believed that the purest form of government was monarchy, but in an all too messy reality, a mixed constitution, like the Roman republic, with its monarchical, aristocratic, and democratic elements, best served the commonwealth.[38] Governments that lacked a mixed constitution degraded because "unless a state maintains a fair balance of rights, duties, and functions (the magistrates having adequate power, the aristocratic council adequate influence, and the people adequate freedom) its constitutional organization cannot be preserved from change."[39] Rome enjoyed that constitutional balance because "a republic is the property of the public. But a public is not every kind of human gathering, congregating in any manner, but a numerous gathering brought together by legal consent and community of interest." No republic existed where tyrants, self-interested cliques, or the masses dominated.[40] Human nature itself, rather than some concession to evil, ordains republican government: "The primary reason for its coming together is not so much weakness as a sort of innate desire on the part of human beings to form community."[41]

In addition to his understanding of history, Stoicism influenced Cicero's jurisprudence. He had studied at the Stoic Academy in Athens as a youngster. He believed that Stoic jurisprudence argued that statute law should mirror the equilibrium of the cosmos. Laws, he wrote, "which have been formulated in various terms to meet the temporary needs of communities, enjoy the name of laws thanks to popular approval rather than actual fact."[42] Instead, rational reflection on the equilibrium of the cosmos suggested "the principles of right living," which "make everyone a better person."[43] In drafting legislation, then, human nature—which calls all human beings to their rational, best selves—served as the best criterion: "We can distinguish a good law from a bad one solely by the criterion of nature . . . for nature has created perceptions which we have in common, and has sketched them in our minds in such a way that we classify honorable things as virtues and dishonorable things as vices."[44] Of course, the science of right living was philosophy; consequently, in jurisprudence philosophy should be anterior to either the Twelve Tables or the Praetor's Edict, because they were specific to time and place, whereas philosophy probed the eternal verities of reality.[45]

For the jurist, justice is the most important inquiry in philosophy. Cicero insisted that the study of law must involve reflection upon justice; otherwise litigation is the only purpose of the courts: "What is so majestic as the law of the land? Yet what is more petty than the function of those who answer queries?"[46] He was convinced that the law should serve the purpose of right living, and that the law, properly so-called, mirrored transcendent Justice, since "we are born for justice, and that what is just is based, not on opinion, but on nature."[47] Since there are no essential differences among men and women, justice is the same for every human being.[48] Because of human sociability, the citizens of the commonwealth share justice with each other: "We have been made by nature to share justice amongst ourselves and to impart it to one another."[49]

Of course, Cicero also reflected on the nature and attributes of law itself. He insisted that the law was rational, arguable, and universal:

> *Law in the proper sense is right reason in harmony with nature.* It is spread through the whole human community, unchanging and eternal, calling people to their duty by its commands and deterring them from wrongdoing by its prohibitions. When it addresses a good man, its commands and prohibitions are never in vain; but those same commands and prohibitions have no effect on the wicked . . . we cannot be exempted from this law by any decree of the Senate or the people; nor do we need anyone else to expound or explain it. There will not be one such law in Rome and another in Athens, one now and another in the future, but all peoples at all times will be embraced by a single and eternal and unchangeable law . . . whoever refuses to obey it will be turning his back on himself. Because he has denied his nature as a human being.[50]

Justice accompanies law, indeed, is almost indistinguishable from it: "There is one, single justice. It binds together human society and has been established by one, single law. That law is right reason in commanding and forbidding. A man who does not acknowledge this law is unjust."[51] The law, furthermore, agrees with the intention and plan of God for the cosmos: "Law was not thought up by the intelligence of human beings, nor is it some kind of resolution passed by communities, but rather an eternal force which rules the world by the wisdom of its commands and prohibitions . . . the original and final law is the intelligence of God."[52] Cicero illustrated his thinking with the story of the son of Tarquin Superbus, the last king of Rome, who violated no written law when he raped Lucretia, but broke the eternal law.[53] Thus, a fundamental element in Cicero's jurisprudence distinguished between statute law—law actually enacted by government—and the law inherent in the cosmos, in which human nature participates. Finally, justice compensated for human frailty and, as in Hammurabi's code, protected the weak: "The mother of justice is not nature, nor good intentions, but weak-

ness . . . for justice . . . teaches us to spare all men, take thought for the interests of mankind, give everyone his due, and not lay hands on the things
belonging to the gods, the state, or somebody else."[54]

Laws that merely expressed the will of the people could not guarantee justice, for "many harmful and pernicious measures are passed in human communities . . . in a community a law of just any kind will not be a law, even if
the people (in spite of its harmful character) have accepted it."[55] Indeed, Cicero knew well that injustices routinely passed for statute law: "It's a foolish-
ness to believe that all laws proclaimed by governments are just, for some are
tyrannical."[56] The mere ratification of law, even if constitutional, assures no
establishment of justice: "If . . . laws were validated by the orders of peoples,
the enactments of politicians, and the verdicts of judges, then it would be just
to rob, just to commit adultery, just to introduce forged wills, provided those
things were approved by the votes or decrees of the populace."[57] In addition,
argued Cicero, because men hold a great number of contradictory opinions,
jurists and legislators must refer to a transcendant standard of truth.[58]

Despite what Cicero has said about universal human nature, he did not
mean that everyone was equal to the task of the jurist, legislator, or magistrate; in the words he put into the mouth of his good friend Laelius: "It was
right that a talk about the state should be given, preferably, by a statesman."[59]
Like Plato, Cicero believed that an elite trained in the virtues was best suited
to administer governments. In keeping with the intensely personal nature of
Roman politics, Cicero was convinced that a government of morally out-
standing men best served the common good.[60] The condition of states rested
upon the public-spiritedness of its best citizens: "I believe that changes in the
conduct of states mirror changes in the lives and life-style of the aristocracy."[61] Their principal job was to safeguard the liberty of all the citizens, for
"nothing can be sweeter than liberty."[62] Equality, for instance, Cicero argued,
was impossible to maintain over the generations, because "the people themselves, even when free from all restraint, give many special privileges to many
persons." Political equality could have but a brief duration; economic equality briefer still.[63]

A formal education and a suitable temperament were indispensable to any
who aspired to serving in government. The proper educations for a statesman
were available only to the privileged, such as the Scipios, the conquerors of
Carthage and Greece, who could boast an ancient heritage of care for the Roman state. Scipio imagined statesmanship as a form of craftsmanship: "I am
aware that every craftsman in his own work, if he is any good, thinks, ponders,
and strives for nothing except to improve in that field. *I have inherited this task
from my parents and ancestors, that is, the supervision and management of the*

country."[64] The Scipios had also been taught from boyhood the temperament a servant of the state needed. Indeed, Scipio believed that he had learned more about law and government from his family than books.[65] While education was important, temperament, which included affection for homeland, mattered more.[66]

Cicero did believe that intellectual and temperamental preparation for rule reinforced one another; that is, that education was also moral formation. He insisted that the study of the liberal arts was the only education for aspirants to authority, since the liberal arts (even astronomy) freed their students from superstition: "When an eclipse of the sun brought sudden darkness, and the Athenians' minds were in the grip of panic, the great Pericles is said to have told his fellow-citizens a fact which he had heard from his former tutor Anaxagoras, namely that this thing invariably happened at fixed intervals when the entire moon passed in front of the sun's orb . . . by pointing out this fact and backing it up with an explanation he released the people from their fear."[67] The liberal arts also cultivated dispositions and virtues appropriate to legislators and magistrates. Students of the liberal arts become more humane, less disposed to severity or excess.[68] The result was a good man, possessed of the virtues and living in accordance with nature: "The highest good is either to live according to nature (i.e., to enjoy a life of moderation governed by moral excellence) or to follow nature and live . . . by her law."[69] The tradition of liberal arts education was just then maturing. Most educational theorists enumerated seven liberal arts—rhetoric, dialectic, logic, arithmetic, astronomy, music, and geometry. The Roman educational regime of the liberal arts long survived the Roman state, and deeply influenced the educational program of both the Middle Ages and the Renaissance.

Only the true statesman, reared from childhood in service to kith and kin, and liberally educated, could draft laws that could educate his countrymen to moral excellence, for "there is no doubt that, as the law should correct wickedness and promote goodness, a code of conduct may be derived from it."[70] As George Will's book title stated, statecraft was soulcraft.[71] The statesman, properly so-called, "will indeed have taken trouble to find out about justice and laws and will certainly have studied their foundations . . . he will be well-versed in the fundamental principles of law."[72] The cultivation of moral excellence depended not only on rational discourse but also on doing right again and again, so that right conduct became habitual. In this way, over time, citizens internalize what the law prescribes.[73] The code of conduct which the law taught made man generous and eager to serve their fellow-citizens, indeed, a friend to all. "A person who is called generous and open-handed has duty in mind, not gain."[74] Cicero asked rhetorically, "Where is that holy thing, friendship, if no one loves a friend wholeheartedly, as they say, for his own sake?"[75] Friendship, in turn, was the fruit of wisdom, which displayed goodwill: "When a wise man shows this goodwill, which ranges so far and wide, to someone endowed with equal moral excellence, an effect is produced which some people think incredible, *though it is actually inevitable*, namely, that he loves the other person as much as he loves himself."[76] In short, a life lived in accordance with law (properly so-called) created individuals who no longer did the right out of fear but did the right for its own sake. Ultimately, the law cultivates the virtues, "since, then, there is nothing better than reason, and reason is present in both man and God, there is a primordial partnership in reason between man and God. But those who share reason also share right reason; and since that is law, we men must also be thought of as *partners with the gods in law*;"[77] indeed, God Himself was a kind of magistrate over the cosmos.[78] The fairness which the law teaches makes men good since "all good men love what is fair *in itself and what is right in itself*."[79]

For Cicero, the magistrate educates his fellow-citizens: "A magistrate's function is to take charge and to issue directives which are right, beneficial, and in accordance with the laws . . . in fact it is true to say that a magistrate is a speaking law, and law a silent magistrate."[80] Indeed, magistrates define the state itself.[81] As a consequence, his "commands shall be just, and citizens shall obey them quietly and without protest. [He] shall punish the guilty and unruly citizen by fine, prison, or flogging."[82] Thus, the magistrate had a solemn duty to provide for family and religion: "For the purposes of life and its practical conduct a system has been devised, consisting of legal marriages, legitimate children, and sacred shrines belonging to the domestic gods of Roman families."[83] His responsibilities likewise extended to the proper worship of the gods, since right order in the state depended upon religion, and "people cannot adequately attend to religion in the home without the guidance of the officials who are in charge of public ceremonies."[84] He must see to it that the people "approach the gods in purity [and] . . . adopt a spirit of holiness." Since the whole of the Roman people's welfare depended upon the gods' kindness, "No one shall have gods of his own . . . they shall worship those gods whose worship has been handed down in its proper form by their forefathers." Consequently, the magistrate must see to it that the Romans "preserve the rituals of their family and friends." No litigation may take place on important religious festivals.[85]

Finally, like Aeschylus, Cicero maintained that the procedure of government, which must be held sacrosanct, best safeguarded justice: "Every republic

. . . must be governed by some decision-making process if it is to last."[86] Of all decision-making ordinances of the constitution, none could be as significant as an election or a verdict.[87] Violence perpetrated upon the workings of the government is the surest enemy of justice: "Nothing is more damaging to a state, nothing so contrary to justice and law, nothing less appropriate to a civilized community, than to force through a measure by violence where a country has a settled and established constitution."[88] Radical alterations in government amplified, rather than diminished, injustice.

The Establishment of the Principate

Empire offered ambitious Romans various ways to circumvent the republic's constitutionally weak checks on political power. For instance, the need for provincial government augmented the power of the consuls. After their year in office terminated, they were sent to govern provinces as proconsuls. Once in their new jurisdictions, former consuls continued to wield military authority, with which they confiscated great casks of wealth from subject peoples. Contrary to republican traditions, the demands of imperial administration and wars of conquest privileged efficiency at the expense of equality. Despite conservative grumblings at home, for instance, Scipio Africanus wielded the consulship for several years because he was Rome's ablest general. Roman survival and victory in the Second Punic War depended more upon having the best commanders in charge of the legions than the traditional consular turn-taking. Marius (157–86), who had much wealth but little pedigree, rose to power in much the same way. In the year 105, the German tribes of the Cimbri and Teutones had obliterated the Roman army (commanded by a consul of a senatorial family) sent to drive them from the Po valley. The Romans desperately needed a brilliant military leader. Furthermore, the bellicose republic, already fighting several wars, lacked troops. Senators grudgingly asked Marius, who had already made his reputation as a military commander in North Africa, to take command of a new army. As a "new man," Marius despised the privileges of the senators, broke with tradition, and enrolled great numbers of landless Italians in his legions. So long as he led these men to victory, they owed their livelihoods to him and he could, therefore, count on their loyalty. Marius reorganized the Roman forces and defeated the Cimbri in 102. The following year he won a great victory over the Teutones. The German threat was over but Marius had been consul for five consecutive years, and, though an equestrian, emerged as the most powerful man in Rome. Over the next generation, ambitious characters followed the same plot, and grew in power through conquest, cleverness, and terror.

By the middle of the first century before Christ, the old constitution of Rome lay in shambles, as powerful figures had mass-murdered their rivals, and violated the law when it suited their purposes. Most understood that popular support outweighed respect for tradition. Doles of grain and money maintained the loyalty of thousands of dispossessed and alienated poor citizens in Rome. The support of soldiers, however, trumped all other considerations. Able generals who shared the spoils with their men (many of whom would otherwise be without an income) could pretty well do as they pleased. Julius Caesar was just such a figure. He had served as a military commander under the murderous Sulla (dictator from 82 to 79 BC), and was the only senator who supported the grant of the *imperium infinitum* (unlimited power) to another general, Pompey, who used that authority to destroy pirates in the Mediterranean. With the support of both Pompey and Crassus (another maniacally ambitious noble), Caesar was elected consul in 59. The following year, Caesar went to his proconsulate in Gaul, which at the time consisted mostly of the southernmost valley of the Rhone River. Various Celtic and Germanic peoples then threatened the security of Roman Gaul, and of course Caesar's duty was to secure the province. He went much farther, however, and spent the next seven years (58–52 BC) conquering an area the size of modern Texas, fighting some of the most creative and daring military campaigns in history. Caesar's spectacular victories, as well as his philanthropy, had made him powerful enough to be feared by important senators, who turned to Pompey for support against him. Convinced that he would be arrested in Rome, Caesar marched into Italy with his battle-hardened legions. Uncertain of the best moves against Caesar, Pompey fled to Greece and there organized his resistance and mulled over his strategy. Pompey's absence, of course, meant that Caesar entered Rome as its lord and master. In 48 BC, Caesar crossed over to Greece, and convincingly defeated Pompey's army at the Battle of Pharsalus. Pompey fled to Egypt, where he was beheaded.

Of course, Caesar was even more powerful after Pompey's defeat. He initiated a series of ambitious reforms and building programs, which included the foundation of colonies for his discharged veterans. This program alleviated the problem of inequitable land distribution. He revised the calendar, and to this day the "Julian" calendar is still in use among Orthodox Christians. He commissioned the construction of a number of monumental building projects. In 44, he miscalculated and proclaimed himself dictator for life—the last straw for conservatives in the Senate. The famous conspirators of the Ides of March (March 15, 43 BC) assassinated Caesar in the Senate House. His murderers had likewise miscalculated. Instead of being hailed as the saviors of the republic they thought they were, many in Rome wanted to avenge the great benefactor of the Roman masses.

Caesar's legacy fell to his best combat leader, Marc Antony, and Octavian, the grandson of his sister Livia, whom Caesar had adopted as his legal heir. These men first staged a great reign of terror, among whose victims was Cicero. They then assembled an army and in western Greece defeated the forces of Caesar's assassins at the Battle of Philippi (42). Antony and Octavian, ever suspicious of each other, proceeded to divide Rome's provinces between them. Octavian took control of Italy and Antony seized the riches of the East, which of course included Egypt, whose Queen Cleopatra seduced Antony into an alliance and a liaison. Relations between Antony and Octavian deteriorated, as both aspired to rule the whole Roman world. Eventually, they made war on each other. At the naval Battle of Actium (31 BC), Octavian's forces destroyed Antony's navy. Antony and Cleopatra retreated to Egypt, where they failed to raise another force against Octavian. They both committed suicide as Octavian's troops occupied Egypt.

Octavian returned to Rome in 29 BC. With the acquiescence of the Senate and the loyalty of about sixty-three legions, he began the task of reconstructing the Roman government, both in Italy and in the provinces. The Principate, as historians call that government, was a monarchy veiled in a sheer republican fabric. Essentially, the Principate invested all the republican magistracies in one figure—Octavian, whom the Senate granted the title/name of Augustus ("the great one") in 27 BC. Hardly any of the great old republican families survived in that assembly anymore, so few senators had a strong commitment to the ancestral constitution. Furthermore, Octavian was clearly the most powerful figure in the Roman world and only the suicidal would have stood in his way. The need for an end to civil strife meant that most senators were only too happy to play the public relations game through which Augustus reformed the government.

To be sure, the *concilium plebis* still met and held elections (but only, it seems, so long as Augustus lived, and not thereafter), but the contestants and the winners were men agreeable to Augustus. The Senate gave him the power of *censor* several times, so he remade the Senate according to his wishes, which meant the reduction of that body from one thousand to six hundred members. He served eight consecutive terms as consul. After 12 BC, Augustus was also *pontifex maximus*, the chief priest of the Roman state cult, one of the most treasured offices in the old republic. In 23 BC, he permanently assumed the powers of the tribunes, which gave him the power to convene the Senate, which he stripped of its political and deliberative powers, and made an arm of his administration. Most of the work of Augustus's regime was done by his household, which was, like the provincial adminis-tration of the late republic, dominated by equestrians. Over time, the impe-rial household grew, and eventually evolved into the imperial bureaucracy. At the same time, Augustus cultivated an image of simplicity and paternal solicitude. In public, he wore a simple senatorial toga made of homespun cloth. He preferred to be addressed by the title of *princeps*, which meant "first citizen." In 2 BC the Senate proclaimed Augustus *pater patriae*, "the father of his country." This particular honor was in no way unprecedented, for before he had departed to fight Antony, Octavian had demanded the *coniuratio Ital-iae* (32 BC), an oath which Octavian required of all Italians, and akin to the oaths sworn by clients toward their patrons. Ties between patrons and clients were second only to family bonds in importance for traditional Roman soci-ety. Patrons owed their clients preferment and aid of all sorts, and clients were required to support the social and political ambitions of their patrons. The patron/client relationship (as the word patron implies) was modeled on a Roman father's authority over his family.

Augustus was also known as *imperator*, the wielder of supreme military au-thority. In addition to his political reforms, he also restructured the Roman army and the provincial administration. He reduced the number of legions from sixty to twenty-eight, and resettled his discharged veterans on home-steads in territories to which they had been assigned as soldiers. He created a military force for Italy, which he called the Praetorian Guard. The provinces Augustus divided into two categories—pacified and insecure. He stationed a greater number of legions in the insecure provinces (such as Gaul, Spain, and Syria), but handed direct control of the others to the Senate. Of course, he retained final say on all decisions of the senators. Italy and Egypt were kept out of the provincial system. Because of its great wealth, a prefect, who answered directly to Augustus, governed Egypt. Italy's administration and government continued according to the settlements following the Social War of 90–88 BC.

The reforms of Augustus gave the Mediterranean world two centuries free of widespread war—the famous *Pax Romana*. Over those two centuries, the Principate also created something unique in the history of the Western world—a vast confederation of peoples, such that for most, by the turn of the third century, rule by Rome's emperor was unobjectionable, ordinary, and ha-bitual. At some point, Rome ceased to be a foreign, occupying power. The city became merely the seat of government. The point of the few rebellions that did take place was to replace the current emperor with a more agreeable figure, rather than to expel the Romans.[89] Thus, the *constitutio Antoniniana* (212) of the Emperor Caracalla, which made all free subjects of the Roman

Empire citizens of Rome, completed what the republican grants of *civitas sine suffragio* initiated.[90] Indeed, until the very end of the eastern Roman Empire (the Byzantine Empire), which came in 1453 when the Ottoman Turks seized Constantinople, residents of that city proudly called themselves not Greeks but *Rhomaioi*—Romans.

The Jurisprudence of the Classical Era

The classical era of Roman law (c. 200 BC–200 AD) coincided with the last days of the Republic and the heyday of the Principate. As in earlier centuries, the opinions of the learned jurists passed into the corpus of efficacious Roman law. In earliest republican days, these jurists were generally members of the college of pontiffs. Around 200 BC, the monopoly of the pontiffs on legal exposition seems to have yielded to a generally amateur field of keen expositors of the law:

> Before the time of Augustus the right of stating opinions at large was not granted by the emperors, but the practice was that opinions were given by people who had confidence in their own studies. Nor did they always issue opinions under seal, but most commonly wrote themselves to judges, or gave the testimony of a direct answer to those who consulted them.[91]

Characteristic of the Roman law is "the extreme prominence of jurists who, as such, have no connection with government."[92] Indeed, the great names in the republican Roman juristic tradition were not judges, nor did they collect fees for their opinions on the law. The Romans had no formal law schools; neophytes would simply apprentice themselves to a recognized luminary. Traditions grew up about these figures, and they were memorialized as a kind of priesthood.

In contrast, jurists of the Principate were usually professional legal advisors to the ruler. Of all the classic jurists, only the works of Gaius survived intact. His *Institutes*, which have been translated into English, were written (c. 168 AD) as an introductory text for law students.[93] The works of the other jurists are known from the Byzantine Emperor Justinian's *Corpus iuris civilis*. The edict of the Emperor Valentinian III (426), known as the Law of Citations, made authoritative the opinions of the jurists Ulpian, Paul, Papinian, Gaius, and Modestinus:

> We confirm all the writings of Papinian, Paul, Gaius, Ulpian, and Modestinus, so that the same authority attends Gaius as Paul, Ulpian, and the others. . . .

Where different views are produced the greater in number of authors prevails, if the number is equal, the authority of that party prevails in which Papinian, man of splendid intellect, shines forth. . . . Where their opinions cited in court are equal and their authority is thought to be equal, the decision of the judge decides whom he ought to follow.[94]

Of these figures, the careers of Ulpian and Papinian are the best known, and perhaps representative of their era. Unlike most other jurists, but akin to Cicero, the Syrian Ulpian also had interests in philosophy. His works date from 213–217 AD, and he served Emperor Alexander Severus (222–235) as praetorian prefect (none too well, apparently, as the emperor's guards murdered him in 223). Papinian seems also to have served the Emperor Septimius Severus (193–211) as praetorian prefect. Both men were Syrians, and may have taught at the law school in Beirut.

Most of the classical Roman law survives in two late antique codifications. The first was the *Codex Theodosianus* (*Theodosian Code*, so named for the Emperor Theodosius II, who commissioned the work), which was completed in 438. It is a compilation of imperial law from the reign of the first Christian Roman Emperor, Constantine I (312–337), to the reign of the eastern Roman Emperor Theodosius II (408–450). The *Codex Theodosianus*, then, consists of imperial rescripts and imperial edicts. Rescripts, which were the emperors' preferred form of legislation until 398, originated as letters of inquiry sent to the emperor by a provincial official. Once received, the emperor's legal staff read and considered the best answer. A formal letter of reply (*rescriptum*, *rescriptio*) was drafted, revised, and then returned to the provincial official who had made the enquiry. Copies of rescripts could often be found in the imperial archives, but some could only be found in the possession of private individuals, which accounts for their abandonment in 398.

The eastern Roman Emperor Justinian I (527–565) appointed Tribonian, his *quaestor sacri palatii* (chief legal advisor), to compile the second codification of Roman law. The *Corpus iuris civilis* ("The Civil Law") was published *seriatim* beginning in 533.[95] The *Corpus iuris civilis* consists of several parts.

Digest (*Digestum* in Latin, or *Pandecta* in Greek): Promulgated in 533, and divided into 50 books, each of which contains fragments from the classical jurists (citation Dig. 1.1.1.1). The Digest, which is the lengthiest part of the *Corpus iuris civilis*, also contains its oldest texts.

Institutes (*Institutiones*, in Latin): Promulgated in 533 and divided into four books. Tribonian's update of the second-century Institutes of Gaius served as an introductory work for law students (citation Inst. 1.1.1).

Code (*Codex*, in Latin): Promulgated in 534, divided into twelve books; consists mostly of late imperial law (citation Cod. 1.1.1.1).

Novels (*Novellae leges*, "new laws" in Latin): 134 laws promulgated between 535 and 548 by the Emperor Justinian (citation Nov. 1.1).

The *Digest* begins with an account of the nature of law, which the jurist Ulpian defined as "the art of goodness and fairness." He also justified the Roman law tradition which took the thoughts of the jurists as law: "Of that art we [jurists] are deservedly called the priests."[96] Like Cicero, he believed that the law issued from the nature of the cosmos and of humanity: "Law is sovereign over all divine and human affairs. It ought to be the controller, ruler and guide of good and bad men alike, and in this way to be a standard of justice and injustice and, for beings political, by nature a prescription of what ought to be done and a proscription of what ought not to be done," which, of course, might be taken as the basis of all law.[97] The jurists taught that there were "two branches of legal study: public and private law. Public law is that which respects the establishment of the Roman commonwealth, private that which respects individuals' interests, some matters being of public and others of private interest."[98] Public law might also be understood as constitutional law, of which the Romans throughout their history possessed little; indeed, most of what the Digest says about Roman government amounts to a history of the republic and early Principate. Like Babylonian and Athenian law, Roman law was predominantly civil law, what Ulpian here called private law.

Having made this essential distinction in the laws, the jurists focused their discussion on the civil law, which "derived from principles of *ius naturale, ius gentium,* or *ius civile*," that is, the natural law, the law of nations, and statute law. Of these, the natural law was the most sublime, the law which all things obeyed: "Natural law is that which nature has taught to all animals; for it is not a law specific to mankind but is common to all animals." The Roman jurists most often illustrated the natural law with the example of procreation and the raising of offspring: "Out of [natural law] comes the union of man and woman which we call marriage, and the procreation of children, and their rearing. So we can see that the other animals, wild beasts included, are rightly understood to be acquainted with this law."[99] Natural law, then, governed the universe—the heavenly bodies themselves obeyed the natural law, for the sun and the planets revolved around the earth in their appointed places in the cosmos. For human beings, the natural law brought human society into being, along with that society's basic unit, the family.

The law of nations referred to those laws which can be found in every human community: "The law of nations is that which all human peoples observe. That it is not coextensive with natural law can be grasped easily, since this latter is common to all animals whereas the law of nations is common only to human beings among themselves."[100] The examples of the law of nations were "religious duties . . . or the duty to be obedient to one's parents and fatherland."[101] The law of nations also enjoined self-defense and preservation against violence.[102]

The law of nations, however, sometimes contradicted the natural law, for all nations recognized and practiced slavery. Ulpian argued that by the natural law, all human beings were born free. The law of nations, however, permitted slavery, as preferable to mass slaughter during wartime. So, "we all being called by the one natural name 'men,' in the law of nations there came to be three classes: free men, and set against those slaves and the third class, freedmen, that is, those who had stopped being slaves."[103] And so, the law of nations governs all those enterprises, noble and degraded, pursued by all peoples: "Wars were introduced, nations differentiated, kingdoms founded, properties individuated, estate boundaries settled, buildings put up, and commerce established."[104] In particular, the law of nations mitigated the evils that human beings committed.

The civil law, particular to the Romans, consisted merely of the laws on the books—laws that the constitutionally competent authorities had promulgated into law. The civil law of the Romans, which by the time of the *Corpus iuris civilis* had a one-thousand-year history, took several forms: "Now the *ius civile* is that which comes in the form of statutes, plebiscites, *senatus consulta*, imperial decrees, or authoritative juristic statements."[105] Statutes, the broadest category of civil laws, were likewise defined broadly: "A statute is a communal directive, a resolution of wise men,"[106] and so the classical jurists preserved the tradition whereby legislation was the responsibility of aristocrats, senators, and the jurists themselves. Plebiscites were simply decisions of the old *concilium plebis*, important in republican days but long since fallen out of use. Resolutions of the Senate were *senatus consulta*, but since the senate had no direct, constitutionally mandated lawmaking powers, these were understood to be directions to the magistrates.[107]

Imperial legislation constituted a category of law-making altogether unique and supreme. The jurists calculated the weightiness of imperial decree by comparing it to statute law: "The emperor is not bound by statutes."[108] The emperor was the source of all legislation, indeed, by the mid-third century the only source of law in the Roman state apart from the jurists. At the same time, however, the jurists also preserved a dim memory of the popular sovereignty which lay behind the whole Augustan settlement of the Principate, wherein one magistrate was invested with the powers of the consuls, the priests, and the tribunes. Since Augustus received his powers from the Senate, a representative assembly of the old republic, the emperor's power to legislate theoretically derived from the people: "A decision given by the emperor has the force of a statute. This is because the populace commits to him and into him its *own entire authority and power*." The legislation of the emperors were known as constitutions.[109] Another important authority rested with the jurists. Since the legal history of the Romans was ancient, it was also disparate, and rules and rulings to iron out the inconsistencies and contradictions needed to be laid out. This responsibility had long rested with the learned jurists whose opinions, like the statutes, plebiscites, and imperial constitutions, passed into the body of the Roman civil law.

The classical jurists likewise enumerated the competencies of the law: "All our law concerns [either] persons or things or actions."[110] The Roman law of persons had mostly to do with the legal distinctions between persons, on the one hand, and family and marriage law, on the other. Like every other set of laws prior to the onset of the French Revolution in 1789, Roman law recognized legal distinctions between persons of servile and free status.[111] "Of slaves, to be sure, there is but a single condition, of free men, on the other hand, some are freeborn and some are freedmen,"[112] that is, "those who have been manumitted from lawful slavery."[113] The condition of slavery generally resulted from a selling of the self (owing to the need for money), capture in war, or birth to an enslaved woman.[114] The status of freedman meant that even should a slave be manumitted, a legal stigma carried over into freedom. In practice, freedmen became the clients of their former masters. Roman law also recognized another distinction between persons, namely, according to sex, wherein "the condition of the females is inferior to that of males."[115]

Thus, Roman family law rested upon distinctions between men and women, and between dependants generally, those who were *alieni iuris* (in the power of another), on the one hand and *sui iuris* (subject to no other), on the other.[116] The Twelve Tables themselves had listed minor children, the insane, slaves, and wives as *alieni iuris*, subject to the authority of the *paterfamilias*. By the third century, however, the powers of masters over their slaves had been restricted in law.[117] Early in Rome's history, a married women remained under the authority of her father; should she die, her dowry reverted back into the possession of the family into which she had been born, rather than becoming the possession of her husband. Unmarried adult women were also *alieni iuris* to a tutor the *paterfamilias* selected.

Like the Athenian, the Roman law of marriage allowed little room for the state. Rather, marriage was an agreement entered into by the husband and the wife. Classical Roman jurisprudence recognized two kinds of marriage. The most common form of marriage in the early republic was *cum manu* ("with the hand"), which was signified by the father handing his daughter over to her husband. *Potestas* ("authority") was thereby transferred from the father to the husband. Another marriage, *sine manu* ("without the hand"), became more common after 200 BC. Marriages *sine manu* had no accompanying ritual and the bride was taken to remain under her father's *potestas*. If she was *sui iuris*, she remained under the protection of her tutor.

Roman marriages usually took place in two stages. The fathers of the bride and groom first held a formal betrothal, "the announcement and mutual promise of marriage in the future,"[118] usually in the absence of the young man and woman. A ceremony might be held but some engagements took place less formally, often during dinner parties. A marriage valid in Roman law required that the bride be at least twelve years old, and that the husband and wife freely agree to the union: "Agreement and not sleeping together creates marriage."[119] Usually, the couple expressed their consent to the union in vows made in the bride's home in the presence of the families and an *auspex*, an expert in the divination characteristic of traditional Roman religion, for in the opinion of the jurists, a legally valid marriage was "the union of a man and a woman, partnership for life involving *divine as well as human law*."[120] After the vows had been exchanged, the couple and their guests processed to the groom's home, where the couple would begin their lives together.

Since valid marriage depended upon the free consent to the union, the jurists worked out legal impediments to marriage. They agreed that insanity nullified marriage, as well as legal status (because it created pressures owing to legal inequalities).[121] Personal disreputability might also invalidate a marriage, because "as far as marriages are concerned, it is always necessary to consider not just what is lawful but also what is decent."[122]

Although they were expected, as marriage required the maintenance of newcomers to the household, dowries were not essential to a valid marriage in Roman law. While the couple was married, the dowry belonged to the husband, who could exploit it according to his desires. In the early republic, the husband could retain the dowry in the case of divorce but by the late republic the wife's father could take legal action to recover the part of the dowry he had donated to the marriage, called the profectitious dowry.[123] In the case of the wife's death, the widower retained the dowry. In the case of the husband's death, his widow could recover the dowry from her husband's heirs. By the time of the Principate, the husband's power over his wife's dowry had become usufructuary; that is, he was able to enjoy the use and the profits of that property but he must also preserve the principal, and return it to his wife should the marriage be terminated. Divorce seems to have been rare before c. 230 BC; indeed, the implications of *cum manu* marriages would seem to make them legally impossible. After this date, however, and much to the chagrin of moralists thereafter, divorce was permitted both sexes for any reason. As far as the law was concerned, the hallmark of divorce was the intention of the couple to separate permanently: "A true divorce does not take place unless an intention to remain apart permanently is present."[124] A legally efficacious divorce merely demanded that some oral formula, such as "Keep your things to yourself" or "Look after your own things" be uttered "in the presence of seven Roman citizens of full age."[125] By the *lex Julia de adulteriis*, one of the moral reform measures enacted by Augustus, if the wife's infidelity prompted divorce, she would be banned from marrying her lover, suffer diminution of her property, lose her citizenship, and be subject to exile.[126]

Early Roman law recognized only a few criminal acts.[127] The sources permit a good picture of criminal law, also called public law, only from about 200 BC. Like the Athenian, Roman law defined crime as an act perpetrated against the Roman state and people. Most criminal proceedings seem to have been handled in the *comitiae*, which of course meant that in the republic crime and politics were often conflated, again, much as in Athenian law. The criminal proceedings with which the sources are preoccupied usually involve the crime of malfeasance in provincial administration, and, of course, treason, which the law took to be the greatest offense because of its direct threat to the Roman commonwealth: "The crime of treason is that which is committed against the Roman people or against their safety," which in the main meant that the crime of treason occurred if "anyone should bear arms against the state" or "does anything with malicious intent whereby the enemies of the Roman people may be helped with his counsel against the state."[128] Treason also included desertion from the army or melting the statues of the emperor.[129] Treason was believed so serious an offense that even those who normally were banned from bringing accusations (like women or slaves) could do so in a case involving treason.[130]

Over time, the number of crimes recognized in Roman law grew. By the time of Sulla, forgery, counterfeiting, murder, and assault had also been treated as crimes.[131] The Augustan moral legislation added adultery to the list.[132] Adultery became a crime because children inherited their parents' goods, and so the care of future generations of Romans was at stake. For the Romans, adultery did not mean extramarital relations in themselves, for the law of adultery reflected the sexual double-standard characteristic of pagan societies in the ancient world. Roman law, for instance, recognized the ability of an offended husband to murder his wife's lover in certain cases, but no wife could legally kill her husband's lover.[133] Only two legally free persons could commit the crime of adultery.[134] A husband's liaison with the slave of another man, for instance, did not legally constitute adultery. A liaison with a free woman, however, threatened the status of his wife within her own household and therefore threatened her children with loss of inheritance. The jurists agreed that the damage done to the social health of the commonwealth rendered such a sexual relationship adultery. In contrast, sexual relations between unmarried free persons were known as *stuprum*, a lesser offense. Sexual relations with a female or male slave carried no threat of reprisal, for concubinage was legal (although married men could not have concubines). Over the centuries, then, criminal law developed in an *ad hoc* manner, as laws and procedures were passed and developed in response to events. Acts that had been traditionally treated as delicts came to be treated as crimes, particularly during the late republican era and into the Principate. As Roman government grew and became bureaucratized, the ability of the state to investigate and prosecute crime improved. The government continually assumed more of the responsibility for punishing criminals.[135]

On the other hand, theft and assault long remained within the realm of the civil law. Roman law recognized two kinds of theft: manifest and nonmanifest.[136] A manifest thief had been caught in the act of theft.[137] The prosecution of theft the law left to the private persons, not government officials: "A person who has an interest in the thing not being stolen will have the action for theft."[138] Plaintiffs could establish ownership by describing the object stolen, in particular, idiosyncrasies about the item that only the owner would know.[139] By assault, the Romans understood not only physical attack but also forcible entry.[140] Victims of either could bring an action on the basis of having been insulted. Again, during the proceedings, the victim was required to account for his injuries.[141]

The Roman law of things (*res*) had mostly to do with property and inheritance. Roman jurisprudence drew its most careful distinctions with regard to property. The jurists first distinguished between things subject to divine and those subject to human law. Property subject to divine law included temples. Unlike Christian churches, for instance, only priests could enter temples. The altars, where worshippers made their sacrifices, were outside the temples. City walls (*res sacrae*, protected by the gods), as well as tombs (*res religiosae*) were also sacred, as they separated the living from the dead—the cemeteries of pagan Rome were all outside the city gates. Property subject to human law included *res communes*. Under *res communes* were common goods and natural resources such as the air, sources of running water, the sea, and riverbanks—owned by no one but whose use could be regulated in law. Other properties, such as bridges, roads, harbors, and ports were *res publicae*, owned by the Roman state and not subject to the civil law of property.[142]

The jurists distinguished between two types of private property: *res mancipi* and *res nec mancipi*. *Res mancipi* were goods important to agricultural communities: land, slaves, and beasts; *res nec mancipi* were all other forms of property.[143] Under the law, ownership of *res mancipi* could be transferred from one person to another by *mancipatio* or *in iure cessio*. *Mancipatio* was a formal ceremony which required the attendance of the transferrer, the transferee, five male adult Roman citizens, and the holder of a scale. The transferee took into his hand what was to be handed over, struck the scale with a copper or bronze ingot, and said "I declare this slave [for example] to be mine by the law of the citizens, and let him have been bought by me with this bronze and this bronze scale." The transferrer said nothing, a sign of his participation in the deal.[144] In contrast, *res mancipi* and *res nec mancipi* could be transferred by *in iure cessio*, a kind of fictive lawsuit before a magistrate where the transferee claimed to be the owner. The transferrer made no defense, so the magistrate declared the property transferred from the one party to the other.[145] Both *mancipatio* and *in iure cessio* could take place only between citizens of Rome.

Another kind of transfer was *usucapio*, which like *mancipatio* and *in iure cessio* was only available to Roman citizens. *Usucapio* was important because it transformed possession into ownership. *Usucapio* said that control of real estate for two years, or moveable property for one, conferred ownership, provided that that control was in good faith, that the land was not stolen, and that it could be owned privately. *Usucapio*, said the jurists, had been introduced to reduce litigation for people who acquired property but lacked full legal ownership to it. Such a condition created uncertainty and possible strife, which compromised the common good: "*Usucapio* was introduced for the common good, to wit, that the ownership of certain things should not be for a long period, possibly permanently, uncertain, granted that the period of time prescribed should suffice for owners to inquire after their property."[146] Such conditions must have been fairly common in a society without many written documents, and where the movements and relocations of peasant settlers would be nearly impossible to document. Furthermore, the whole commonwealth might benefit, since peasant settlers made uncultivated land fruitful.

Again, *res nec mancipi* consisted of everything not included in *res mancipi*. Such properties could be transferred through *traditio*, an actual, physical delivery, and a transaction available in Roman law to foreigners as well as citizens. The law also recognized two types of delivery: first, "by the long hand" (*longa manu*), when property was warehoused, and the seller gave the buyer the key; and second, "by the short hand" (*brevi manu*), where the goods had simply been handed over.[147] *Traditio* also demanded intention to transfer goods for "a lawful reason," generally understood to be signified by either sale, gift, or exchange.[148]

The Romans also drew distinctions between the ownership (*dominium*), the possession (*possessio*), and the use (*usus* or *usufructus*) of property. In the main, possession meant the control of a thing and the intention to keep it, and so differed from the legal claim to property, which was ownership. The distinction between ownership and possession may well have been for procedural purposes, in that possession was generally necessary to prove ownership, and indeed most possessors of property were in fact the owners. Ulpian sounds much like a law professor using a hypothetical to illustrate this principle: "Pomponius discusses the question whether, when stones had been sunk in the Tiber in a shipwreck and some time later salvaged, the ownership of them remained intact throughout the time that they were submerged. My view is that I remain owner of them but I do not possess them."[149] Should property become the subject of a legal dispute, having possession went a long way to proving ownership, for possession was protected by remedies called interdicts, which stipulated that when ownership was disputed the party who had possession was the defendant, and in these cases only the plaintiff need prove his case.[150] Again, possession was necessary for *usucapio*.

The rights to the use of property were very important, inasmuch as many people made livings from real property that they did not own, since the ownership of land rested disproportionately with great landowners. *Usufructus*, or usufruct, was the right to enjoy the use of property, along with its fruits, without impairing that property, for the span of the term agreed to, often an entire lifetime. So, for instance, a living could be made from wool or milk without ownership of sheep or cows, and housing could be likewise enjoyed. For his part, the usufructuary (the one with the right to use the property) had to maintain the numbers of the flocks or herds he exploited.[151] *Usus*, on the other hand, was the right to use property but not to enjoy its fruits; in the previous example, the usuary could not sell the wool or milk but had to consume them himself.[152] *Habitatio* was a kind of *usus* for housing, as it was the right to dwell in a particular building.

Of course, property was also transferred from the dead to the living through inheritance. As in any age, property owners died either intestate or testate. Roman law seems not to have penalized intestacy and the classic jurisprudence of inheritance depended heavily on what had first been set down in the Twelve Tables. The Roman law of testation granted complete freedom to testators—they could draw up a will entirely on their own terms, unlike the modern United States, where the law prescribes that a fair amount be given to the heirs.[153] Only a sane citizen past the age of puberty could make a will; after the reign of the Emperor Hadrian (117–138) adult women could also draft wills.[154] In the case of a Roman will, the heirs received only what the testator decided, no matter how small or great an amount, nor how inequitably the property be divided between them.[155] Heirs received not only the deceased's goods but also his debts, whether testate or intestate, and even if the debts exceeded the value of the inheritance: "An heir succeeds to the whole legal position of the deceased and not only to the ownership of the individual things, because the assets which take the form of debts also pass to the heir."[156]

The efficacy of the Twelve Tables for intestacy was probably longer-lived than any other part of that document. The order of succession for freemen enumerated in the Twelve Tables was (1) *sui heredes*, (2) the nearest agnate (that is, male relation), and (3) the *gens* (the deceased's clan). *Sui heredes* were everyone who became *sui iuris* upon the death of the deceased, in particular the children and widow (if the marriage was *cum manu*). Previously emancipated children and wives in free marriage (rare in the early republic) were not *sui heredes*. The opinion of the jurist Pauls illustrates well Roman thinking about property and family: "In the case of *sui heredes*, it is more clearly evident that the continuation of ownership leads to this, that no inheritance is regarded as having taken place, if they were already owners, being thought of as in some sense owners even in the lifetime of the father [should the sons already be adults]."[157] The family's goods, although under the control of the *paterfamilias*, nonetheless existed to serve the needs of the entire family and might even be understood as the common goods of the family. The nearest agnate generally meant a brother of the deceased.

Under the Principate, the legal position of widows improved relative to the agnates. The *senatus consultum Tertullianum* (130 AD) provided that mothers who had had at least three children (the *ius liberorum* of Augustan legislation) could inherit the children's property if they had died intestate. Previous legislation had denied it to them altogether in favor of the agnate. Under the later Empire, the Tertullian order was applied to mothers regardless of the *ius liberorum*. An even greater departure from earlier law was the *senatus consultum Orphitianum*, which gave children, whether legitimate or illegitimate, the first claim on the property of an intestate mother.[158] Last in the order of succession was the *gens*, or clan of the deceased, but the claim of the *gens* to the property of a deceased member seems to have dissolved early in the history of the Republic.

Historians and jurists have long admired the Roman law of contract. As with so many other aspects of their jurisprudence, the Roman jurists did not define contract but merely distinguished between the types of contract recognized in law. The jurists identified four types of contract: verbal, literal, real, and consensual. Verbal contracts required that a formula or pattern of words be spoken for them to be efficacious. Of these, the earliest was the *stipulatio*, wherein the promisee orally asked, "Do you promise?" and the promissor answered "I promise." This form of contract antedated even the Twelve Tables.[159] Literal contracts, of course, involved a written agreement; the law says little else about them.[160] Real contracts involved the delivery of an actual thing (*re*). There were four types of real contract: (1) *mutuum*, the oldest form, a consumption loan, for which the borrower was responsible for repayment for the full value of what had been loaned, (2) *commodatum*, a loan which required the return of the thing loaned, (3) *depositum*, where property was exchanged for safekeeping, and (4) *pignus*, a transfer of property as security by a borrower to a lender by way of mortgage.[161]

Consensual contracts came into being simply by the agreement of the parties involved and required no formalities. They first appear in the history of the middle republic and may have been a response to the needs of an expanding, imperial economy; if so, they probably also resulted from the legal work of the peregrine praetor. Each of the four consensual contracts were commercial in nature. The jurists identified four types of consensual contracts: sale, hire, mandate, and partnership. Sale (*emptio venditio*) was the most important, and required agreement, price, and a thing to be sold. No formalities were necessary: "Sale is a contract of the law of nations and so is concluded by simple agreement; it can thus be contracted by parties not present together, through messengers, or by correspondence."[162] An exchange of "earnest money (*arra*)" constituted proof of an agreement between the contracting parties, as did other items, most commonly a ring.[163] Anything, of course, could be sold so long as it was not excluded from trade (such as a freeman, for instance).[164] In most cases, a mutually agreeable price would be named in money.[165] The jurisprudence of the classical era had no theory of "just price" by which a sale might be nullified. The seller was responsible for maintaining the quality of his merchandise, and the buyer for handing over the price agreed (and any interest, should he be late in making payment).[166]

The second type of consensual contract was hire (*locatio conductio*), which of course closely resembled sale, and the two were often confused in law.[167] The law allowed that a *locator* (the one hired) could hire out a thing, his services, or a piece of work to a *conductor* (the one doing the hiring). In the first instance (*locatio conductio rei*), the *locator* provided the *conductor* with something to be used, such as land (rent) or farm tools, at a mutually agreed price. The thing to be used was generally imperishable. The *locator* was responsible for providing the thing to be used, and the *conductor* for returning the thing in good condition, as well as paying for the use of the thing. The hire for services (*locatio conductio operarum*) essentially constituted wage labor, and was usually entered into for labor often done by slaves. The hire for a piece of work (*locatio conductio operis*) was a hybrid of the first two contracts for hire, wherein the *locator* placed a thing with the *conductor* in order for the latter to do some work in relation to it; for example, one gives another some bronze with which to make a statute. In this case, the *locator*, not the *conductor*, paid.[168] Mandate (*mandatum*), the fourth type of consensual contract, dated from about the mid-second century BC. "There is no mandate unless it is gratuitous. The reason is that it derives its origins from duty and friendship, and the fact that payment for services rendered is incompatible with this duty: For if money is involved, the matter rather pertains to hire."[169] Mandate, then, stipulated that one friend had contracted to do another a favor, without remuneration. During the Principate, mandate acquired a wider commercial use, as a form of appointment of business managers and agents.

The final type of consensual contract was partnership, which had a long history in the Roman republic and empire. The Twelve Tables recognized *sui heredes* who did not divide inheritances as partners, although not as a consequence of contract. Simply put, in classical Roman jurisprudence partnership (*societas*) was a contract whereby more than one person voluntarily agreed to associate in a common endeavor for mutual benefit, which need not be, although often was, financial. All partners had to contribute to the common enterprise, and all received benefits therefrom but those contributions and benefits need not be equal. Losses were shared in the same way. The law recognized four types of partnership: for a single transaction, for a particular business, for all business transactions, for all assets.[170]

The law of procedure formed another great fraction of the whole of the Roman legal *corpus*. After the promulgation of the Twelve Tables, the next glimpse the sources afford into the history of republican legal procedure dates from the third century BC. During the Second Punic War, the Senate had, when necessary, established special commissions, called *quaestiones*, to investigate and prosecute the conduct of certain Italian allies. These evolved into the *quaestiones perpetuae*—permanent jury courts.[171] In the beginning, *praetors* supervised the work of the *quaestiones*; if the *praetor* was not available, other officials, known either as *iudices* (judges) or *quaesitores* (examiners) were appointed for the job. Juries usually consisted of senators; after the reforms of Tiberius Gracchus (tribune c. 130 BC), equestrians also served as jurors. Under the republic, any male citizen could ask government officials to investigate suspects. Accusers prosecuted cases. They took the oath of calumny and as such were subject to the same penalties the defendant would suffer if convicted. A formal accusation having been made, the defendant had to be in attendance at court; his absence was understood to be voluntary exile and a plea of guilty. Both defendants and plaintiffs were allowed at least ten days to prepare a case. After the trial began, the absence of the prosecutor dismissed the charges. The prosecutor began proceedings with a speech, after which the defendant's advocates (normally more than one) made a speech on his behalf. Each side then presented the proof for its case. The law recognized the validity of both documents and witnesses, of which the latter was weighed much more heavily. The character and reputation of the defendant, plaintiff, and witnesses likewise counted for much, and like the Athenians both parties often employed personal invective in the examination of witnesses.

Since Roman jurisprudence preferred testimonial to documentary evidence, a confession constituted irrefutable proof of guilt. Roman law, then, permitted the use of torture to obtain testimony: "It is customary for torture to be applied to unearth crimes."[172] However, the jurists also warned that "the confession of accused persons [under torture] should not be taken as equivalent to crimes established by investigation."[173] They agreed that torture was morally and procedurally troublesome:

> It is stated in constitutions that reliance should not always be placed on torture—but not never either; for it is a chancy and risky business and one which may be deceptive. For there are a number of people who, by their endurance or their toughness under torture, are so contemptuous of it that the truth can in no way be squeezed out of them. Others have so little endurance that they would rather tell any kind of lie than suffer torture.[174]

Their innate conservatism prompted them to find a place for torture in the legal order of their empire, and so they laid down rules for its application. According to the Emperor Hadrian, torture could only be used on slaves, and only in instances where the testimony of slaves was the only missing piece in an otherwise compelling case against the accused. Hence, a substantial body of evidence must already have been assembled before torturing a slave-witness. The law also prohibited torturing anyone under the age of fourteen, except in the instance of treason, since "it touches on the persons of the emperors."[175] Pregnant women were exempt from torture.[176] Torture should not result in death.[177] The investigator "should not ask specifically whether [someone] committed a homicide, but in general terms who did it; for the former seems rather the action of someone suggesting [an answer] than seeking [the truth]."[178] Evidence obtained by torture, then, was trustworthy only if it could be corroborated by other evidence.

After both sides had made their case, the jury deliberated on a verdict. Jurors voted on wax tablets, upon which they wrote either A[*bsolvo*], for not guilty, or C[*ondemno*] for guilty. A simple majority sufficed for conviction. Since most juries consisted of at least seventy jurors, unanimous decisions were impractical. The likeliest penalties for convicted criminals were either death, slavery (usually in the state-owned mines), or exile; long-term imprisonment was rare, as "prison ought to be employed for confining men, not for punishing them."[179]

The *quaestiones perpetuae* disappeared early in the history of the Principate. Criminal jurisdiction fell to the emperor and the prefect of Rome, whose authority extended to a radius of one hundred miles from the city. Another official of the capital, the Prefect of the Night Watch, had jurisdiction over petty crimes. The Senate itself also seems to have served as a court when the accused was a high-ranking noble. The Senate wielded a jurisdiction similar to the *quaestiones perpetuae*, which would not be surprising since those who served on them were usually senators.

The judicial powers of the emperor defy easy classification. Together with his chief advisors, among whom were leading jurists who composed responses to inquiries, the emperor handed down rulings on contested issues. He also sometimes heard appeals from lower officials. Governors, who after all wielded the emperor's authority in their jurisdictions, handled similar responsibilities. That imperial governors were known as *iudices* indicates the nature of many of their responsibilities. In Augustus's day law in the provinces differed appreciably from Roman law but over the next two centuries would come to resemble it ever more closely. A famous case-in-point involved Pliny the Younger, the governor of the Anatolian province of Bithynia. Christians were denounced to Pliny for refusing to make the customary sacrifices to the statue of the emperor (in this case Trajan), and so seemed to be guilty of contumacy, the crime of stubbornly refusing to carry out the command of the magistrate. Without legal experts of his own, Pliny wrote to the emperor asking for advice and direction:

It is my custom to refer all my difficulties to you, Sir, for no one is better able to resolve my doubts and to inform my ignorance. I have never been at an examination of Christians. Consequently, I do not know the nature or the extent of the punishments usually meted out to them, nor the grounds for starting an investigation and how far it should be pressed. Nor am I at all sure whether any distinction should be made between them on the grounds of age, or if young people and adults should be treated alike; whether a pardon ought to be granted to anyone retracting his beliefs, or if he has once professed Christianity, he shall gain nothing by renouncing it; and whether it is the mere name of Christian which is punishable, even if innocent of the crime, or rather the crimes associated with the name.[180]

Trajan assured Pliny that he had followed the correct procedures but encouraged him only to examine Christians who had been denounced to him. Pliny should not investigate and apprehend the Christians of his own volition:

> You have followed the right course of procedure, my dear Pliny, in your examination of the cases of persons charged with being Christians, for it is impossible to lay down a general rule to a fixed formula. These people must not be hunted out; if they are brought before you and the charge against them is proved, they must be punished, but in the case of anyone who denies that he is a Christian, and makes it clear that he is not by offering prayers to our gods, he is to be pardoned as a result of his repentance however suspect his past conduct may be.[181]

An essentially judicial procedure would then serve as the occasion for imperial legislation, as the rescript returned to Pliny from the emperor would then become.

Finally, the jurists insisted that equity and liberality inform all judicial proceedings. Since plaintiffs risked the same penalties as the defendants whom they had accused, the burden of proof rested on the shoulders of the defendant: "Someone who has been charged must clear himself and cannot bring an accusation until he has been discharged."[182] The Romans preferred the testimony of eyewitnesses to documentary evidence, perhaps a concession to the possibility of forgery and widespread illiteracy. Witnesses themselves were to be examined and questioned for their reliability.[183] That reliability was to be evaluated on the basis of legal status, personal reputation, wealth, and relation to the accused. The extremely poor, for instance, could not accuse in court.[184] The jurists taught that "evidence can be admitted if it is free from suspicion,"[185] which must have been mostly honored in the breach, since the sources from all eras of Roman history resound with complaints about corruption and dishonesty.[186]

Fairness dictated that "nothing must be permitted a plaintiff which is not permitted to a defendant."[187] The jurists argued that the spirit of the law be considered as well as its letter.[188] Generosity was to inform all legal proceedings so, for instance, "in a case where the wish of the manumitter is uncertain, preference is to be given to liberty," which "is more desirable than anything."[189] Penalties should be as lenient as justice permitted.[190] "In doubtful cases, the more generous view is always to be preferred."[191] The jurists held "preferable that the crime of a guilty man go unpunished than an innocent man be condemned."[192]

Their law, then, could be as enigmatic as the Romans themselves. They could be both cruel and magnanimous, and their judicial procedures terrifying and dignified.

Late Roman Law and the Christian Church

At the death of the last of the great classical jurists, the Roman world was well advanced into an era of great military and constitutional alteration. While peace blessed the first two centuries of the Roman imperium, the third was often troubled and violent. Between 238 and 284 rival generals fought each other for the throne, and in the meantime presented foreign invaders and raiders with the opportunity to plunder the provinces. New, great confederations of German nations and an expansionist and aggressive Persian Sassanid Empire exploited Rome's vulnerabilities to the fullest. Whereas the Augustan reformulation of the Roman state and military had in the first two centuries generally been a source of strength, the emergencies of the third exposed the weaknesses of the Principate.

Augustus could have established no formal protocol for the transference of power. The Senators, who endorsed his reforms, might well have decided that a formally enacted dynastic protocol had gone too far in the direction of monarchy. Besides, for most of the first two centuries AD, power did pass from one generation to another without incident. Too often, however, the third-century possession of the throne was decided in the supreme court of war, and the legions of victorious generals determined the succession. Of course, while the Romans fought among themselves, they could not fight external enemies, and Germanic tribes such as the Goths and the Franks raided and invaded across the Rhine and Danube rivers. Rome's traditional eastern rival, the Persian Sassanid Empire, attacked across the Euphrates. In 260, the Sassanids inflicted the most humiliating defeat on the Romans (since the disaster at the Teutoberg Forest in 9 AD) when they smashed a Roman army and captured the Emperor Valerian.

Despite such unhappy events, much strength remained to the Roman Empire. Not all was a disaster. Throughout the third century, several able leaders, such as Philip the Arab (244–249), Gallienus (253–268), Claudius II (268–270), Aurelian (270–275), and Probus (276–282) emerged to stop the hemorrhaging (which meant that only sixteen of forty-six years between 238 and 284 were abjectly awful). Probably few other governments could have held together during these years, as the sheer number of enemies made defense difficult; indeed, the Persians and the Germans sometimes coordinated their attacks, and still the Romans defeated them, often decisively.

With the advent of the Emperor Diocletian, who won the throne in 284, the immediate emergency had passed and another reinvention of the Roman state was at hand. Diocletian was a Dalmatian rustic who rose to the rank of general; his reforms bore all the subtlety of a peasant. Convinced, rightly, that the Empire now confronted too many enemies for one man to defeat or contain, he expanded the military and the government dramatically. Ironically, his model for reform was Rome's traditional enemy, Persia.

Diocletian first attempted to formalize the protocol for the succession, and thereby reduce the occasions for civil war. He introduced an imperial college, in which the eastern and western halves of the empire would be shared between two co-rulers, whom he gave the title of *Augustus*. Each *Augustus* would have a junior colleague with the title of *Caesar*. Upon either the death or resignation of his *Augustus*, the *Caesar* would succeed. The new ruler would then appoint his own successor. Historians have sometimes called this regime the *Tetrarchy* (*tetra*, "four," and *arche*, "authority," in Greek). He also introduced a Persian-style protocol at the Roman imperial court. Instead of the traditional toga, Diocletian wore a robe entirely dyed in purple and a golden tiara.

> He was, in fact, the first who really desired a supply of silk, purple, and gems for his sandals, together with a gold-brocaded robe. Although these things went beyond good taste and betrayed a vain and haughty disposition, they were nevertheless trivial in comparison with the rest [of his achievements].[193]

Whereas Augustus had sat on a simple Roman bench, Diocletian sat on an elevated throne. Incense perfumed the imperial court and a red curtain hid the emperor from view. Court functionaries controlled entrance into the imperial presence and those who approached the throne were required to make a full prostration (*proskynesis*), face to the floor, before the emperor. Since the emperor was now addressed as lord, historians have sometimes called the regime founded by Diocletian the Dominate, as opposed to the Principate.

Diocletian reformed the provincial administration. He increased the number of the provinces and thereby decreased their size. He also diminished the responsibilities of provincial officials. He enacted a precedent of the Emperor Gallienus, who had separated the military and civilian jurisdictions of provincial magistrates, in the hope that that uncoupling would discourage rebellion. Diocletian incorporated Italy, which under the Principate was administratively autonomous, into the provincial organization, which reflected the blending together of Rome with her conquests that had begun during the republic. The provinces Diocletian organized into four dioceses (of Gaul, Italy, Illyria, and the East), whose highest civilian official bore the title of *praetorian prefect*. Over the past century, *praetorian prefects*, who under the Principate commanded the Praetorian Guard, had been responsible for much mischief. Diocletian transformed that office from a military into a civilian jurisdiction. He might have liked to dispense with it altogether but the great families of the empire coveted the position. Of course, all these bureaucrats (and the soldiers whose needs they served) had to be paid, and Diocletian inflicted an often-crushing burden of taxation on the subjects of the Roman Empire. Diocletian created a whole host of bureaucrats, such as the *magister officiorum* ("master of offices," head of the imperial civilian bureaucracy), the *quaestor sacri palatii* (chief imperial legal advisor), and the *comes sacrarum largitionum* (chief finance minister). Some scholars speculate that a fourth of the empire's citizens might have been working for the government by the end of his reign.

Diocletian's reform of the military reflected his determination to reduce the incidence of rebellion but he was also convinced that he needed more soldiers to defend the Empire. He (probably) doubled the size of the army, and required that the sons of soldiers follow in their fathers' professions.[194] Under the Principate, legions had been assigned to generals, and the loyalties thus created had contributed to rebellions. Diocletian replaced personal with regional commands, under leaders called dukes (*dux*, singular in Latin). In his system, commanders were assigned to regions, so that when a legion was reassigned, the commander lost control of those soldiers.

Finally, Diocletian also promulgated a number of economic and social reforms intended to restore a more harmonious society. He bound unfree peasant laborers (*coloni*) to the estates on which they worked.[195] In an unsuccessful attempt to quiet social unrest owing to high bread prices, he enacted a series of wage and price controls. The preceding half-century of tumult had badly damaged the monetary system, as rival generals minted more coins, with which they bought the loyalty of soldiers. Most of the new coins contained less precious metal than earlier mintings. Diocletian ended the debasement of the coinage.

While much of Diocletian's program succeeded rather well, the imperial college failed to eliminate the ambitions of the generals. Almost immediately after his retirement in 303, his junior colleagues began another round of civil wars for the thrones of both east and west. The Romans had ancient political habits, formed by the Principate's lack of a formal protocol for the succession, which could not be undone in one generation. After a decade of conflict, the Emperor Constantine I emerged as the most powerful man in the Roman world. He ruled the western half of the empire from 312, and the whole empire from 324 until his death in 337.

Constantine further reformed the Roman state. A tactical and strategic genius, he restructured the Roman army. He created two classes of troops, the *limitaneus* and the *comitatus*. Commanded by dukes, *limitanei* were unpaid frontier conscripts, mostly responsible for reconnaissance and for the garrison of fortifications. The *comitatus* was a highly paid, well-trained, mobile infantryman, stationed in the rear of the frontier. They formed the strategic reserve of the new Roman military. Their job was to move to meet any breach of the frontier. They relied at least as much on maneuver and containment of the enemy as on defeating them in a costly battle in the open field. The equipment of the Roman soldier also changed a bit—shields became smaller, and armor became lighter. Roman armies also deployed more archers and cavalry than in the days of the Principate. Eastern armies in particular had more mounted archers and heavy cavalry (*clibanarius* or *kataphraktos*), much like their Persian and Gothic enemies.

Of course, as the first Roman emperor to convert to Christianity, Constantine's religious policies changed world history. A religious and sensitive man, he became convinced that the God of the Christians had delivered imperial rule into his hands and he was determined to keep the favor of that deity. One year after conquering the western half of the empire, with his eastern colleague Licinius, he proclaimed the Edict of Milan (313), which legalized Christianity throughout the Roman world.[196] Constantine made other proclamations in support of the Christian church. He exempted Christian clergy from compulsory public services and the taxes on the unmarried first proclaimed by Augustus:

> Those persons who were formerly considered celibates by the ancient law shall be freed from the threatening terrors of the law, and they shall live as though numbered among married men and supported by the bonds of matrimony, and all men shall have an equal status in that they shall be able to accept anything to which they are entitled.[197]

In his imperial capacity as *pontifex maximus*, he made grants of money to churches, extended rights of sanctuary to Christian churches, and built and endowed churches himself, such as the first St. Peter's in Rome and the first Church of the Holy Sepulchre in Jerusalem.[198]

Constantine also granted the Christian church important legal duties. Roman law had long recognized the ability of agreed-upon, impartial private third-parties to adjudicate disputes. Bishops had long judged disputes between

Christians. Constantine expanded the judicial responsibilities of Christian bishops:

> Pursuant to his own authority, a judge must observe that if an action should be brought before an episcopal court, he shall maintain silence, and if any person should desire him to transfer his case to the jurisdiction of the Christian law and to observe that kind of court, he shall be heard.[199]

Constantine also proclaimed that manumissions performed in the presence of a bishop were legally valid.[200] Thus were the bishops made a kind of officer of the Roman state, and the institution of church courts were thus initiated.

Constantine also intervened in two serious theological disputes, convinced, like other Christians, that correct belief was as indispensable as correct worship for the salvation of the soul. In 314, he called the Council of Arles, the task of which was to consider the teachings of Donatism. Donatism was a North African church movement and a reaction to third-century persecutions. Some African bishops, in an effort to mitigate the severity of the torturers and executioners, cooperated with the government by handing over the sacred books for destruction. Many other Christians, of course, renounced the faith under the compulsion of torture and death. After the storm had passed, however, many of these so-called *lapsi* wished to return to the church. North African Christians often quarreled over the reception of the *lapsi*. Some also denied the efficacy of sacraments administered by bishops who had handed over the sacred books. Generally, *lapsi* were readmitted to communion after the completion of a lenient penance but some North Africans demanded that they be rebaptized, which in turn suggested that the mark of sacramental baptism could be eradicated. The conflict between these two factions, which involved essential Christian teachings on redemption and salvation, grew very heated. Those who favored rebaptism (called Donatists, after Donatus, one of their leaders) and denied the validity of the sacraments conferred by bishops who cooperated with the government pleaded with Constantine to intervene. They also asked that the council take place outside of Africa, as that province had become too torn by religious strife. The Donatists, for whom Constantine had little sympathy, must have been disappointed when the Council of Arles ruled against rebaptism, a ruling that later passed into the law of the Roman Empire.[201]

In 325, Constantine called another, more famous council, in response to a controversy that had originated in the great Egyptian city of Alexandria. A priest of that city by the name of Arius taught the inequality of God, the Creator and Father, and of Jesus Christ. In Arius's view, Jesus must be lesser than the Father, since Jesus had been flesh and blood and appeared in time, according to Arius's mantra, "There was a time when he was not." Arius cited Scripture on behalf of his teaching as well. The bishop of Alexandria, Alexander, aided by his brilliant protégé Athanasius, countered that Jesus was in fact the equal of the Father. Whereas Donatism got only a small hearing outside of North Africa, Arianism won adherents all over the eastern half of the Empire. Constantine decided to take action for the peace of the church and called the Council of Nicaea (in northwest Anatolia), the first council recognized as "ecumenical," because bishops from all over the empire attended. Presided over by Constantine himself, Nicaea taught that Jesus and the Father were equal and the same in substance (*homoousios*, in Greek, *consubstantialis*, in Latin). The council fathers condemned Arianism as heresy. While Constantine may have had little appreciation for the nuances of theology, he understood full-well how division damaged the Christian church. He denied heretics the benefits available from the Roman state: "The privileges that have been granted in consideration of religion must benefit only the adherents of the Catholic faith."[202] Constantine thus transferred to the Christian church the Roman state's traditional relationship with paganism, that is, its benefactor and protector.

Constantine's reign, therefore, sowed the seeds of the later, distinctively Western debates concerning the respective powers and spheres of the church and the state. While that debate intensified and matured in later centuries, the dualism at its heart first emerged in the Christian Roman Empire. Bishops first challenged the ruler's power over the church during the fourth and fifth centuries. For instance, the Emperor Theodosius I (379–395) had ordered the Greek city of Thessalonica destroyed for its support of a rebellion. Ambrose, the bishop of Milan, forbade the emperor from entering church and demanded that he do penance for so great a massacre of mostly innocent folk. Theodosius complied and was reconciled to the church. So convinced was he that the welfare of the empire depended upon the Christian church, the Emperor Theodosius declared Christianity the state religion in 395.

In the late fifth century, Pope Gelasius I (492–496) wrote a letter to Emperor Anastasius in Constantinople that served later jurists as the earliest delineation of the imperial and sacerdotal powers:

> Two there are, august emperor, by which this world is chiefly ruled, the sacred authority [*auctoritas*] of the priesthood and the royal power [*potestas*]. Of these the responsibility of the priesthood is more weighty in so far as they will answer for the kings of men themselves at the divine judgement. You know, most

clement son, that, although you take precedence over all mankind in dignity, nevertheless you piously bow the neck to those who have charge of divine affairs and seek from them the means of your salvation, and hence you realize that, in the order of religion, in matters concerning the reception and right administration of the heavenly sacraments, you ought to submit yourself rather than rule, and that in these matters you should depend on their judgement rather than to seek to bend them to your will. For if the bishops themselves, recognizing that the imperial office was conferred on you by divine disposition, obey your laws so far as the sphere of public order is concerned lest they seem to obstruct your decrees in mundane matters, with what zeal, I ask you, ought you to obey those who have been charged with administering the sacred mysteries? Moreover, just as no light risk attends pontiffs who keep silent in matters concerning the service of God, so too no little danger threatens those who show scorn—which God forbid—when they ought to obey. And if the hearts of the faithful should be submitted to all priests in general who rightly administer divine things, how much more should assent be given to the bishop of that see which the Most High wished to be preeminent over all priests, and which the devotion of the whole church has honored ever since. As Your Piety is certainly well aware, no one can ever raise himself by purely human means to the privilege and place of him whom the voice of Christ has set before all, whom the church has always venerated and held in devotion as its primate. The things which are established by divine judgement can be assailed by human presumption; they cannot be overthrown by anyone's power.[203]

Gelasius's letter to the emperor was written after the deposition of the last western Roman emperor in 476, so he could afford a display of audacity. Still, he here stated the fundamental division of the secular and religious power, a division fully accepted in a later novel promulgated by the Emperor Justinian (527–565):

The greatest gifts given by God to men from his heavenly clemency are priesthood and empire [sacerdotium et imperium]. The former serves divine things, the latter rules human affairs and has care of them. Both proceed from one and the same source and provide for human life. Therefore, nothing shall so preoccupy emperors as the moral wellbeing of priests, since priests pray constantly to God for the emperors themselves. For, if the priesthood is everywhere blameless and filled with faith in God and the imperial authority orders rightly and efficiently the commonwealth committed to it, a good harmonious relationship will exist, providing whatever is useful for the human race. We, therefore, exercise the greatest care concerning the true doctrines of God and the moral wellbeing of priests through which, if they preserve it, the greatest gifts of God shall be bestowed on us and we shall both hold firmly what we have and acquire what we have not yet received. Now all things are conducted well and properly if a foundation is established which is fitting and pleasing to God. This, we believe, will come about if care is taken for the observance of the sacred rules which the venerable and justly praised apostles handed down as witnesses and ministers of the word of God, and the holy fathers preserved and expounded.[204]

Justinian here was merely taking up the responsibility left him by his predecessors. From Constantine until the Investiture Controversy of the eleventh century, the more powerful partners in the "harmonious relationship" were either the emperors or, in the west, their successors the Germanic kings.

Scholars continue to debate the impact of Christianization on Roman family law. By and large, the Christian Roman Emperors enacted legislation to restrict the ability of spouses to divorce. They also altered intestacy legislation, which traditionally benefited fathers and husbands, to benefit children. Since about 200 BC, Roman law had essentially recognized what today would be called "no-fault divorce." Unlike their pagan or Jewish contemporaries, Christians rejected divorce in all but a few cases, based on Mt 5.31–32, Mt 19.9, Mk 10.2–12, Lk 16.18, and 1 Cor 7.10–11. In 331, Constantine sent this rescript to the *praetorian prefect* Ablabius:

> It is pleasing that a woman not be permitted to send a notice of divorce to her husband because of her own depraved desires, for some carefully contrived cause, such as his being a drunkard or gambler or womanizer. However, neither should husbands be permitted to divorce their own wives for just any reason whatsoever. But in the sending of a notice of divorce by a woman these crimes only are to be looked into: if she has proven that her husband is a murderer or a preparer of poisons or a disturber of tombs, so that only then, after being praised, she shall receive back her entire dowry. For if she has sent a notice of divorce to her husband for any reason other than these crimes, she should leave the dowry, down to a hairpin, in her husband's home, and in return for such great confidence in herself, should be deported to an island.
>
> Also in the case of men, if they send a notice of divorce, it is fitting that these three crimes be inquired into: if they wanted to repudiate an adulteress or a preparer of poisons or a go-between. For if he has ejected a woman who is free of these crimes, he ought to restore the entire dowry and not marry another woman. But if he does, the former wife will be given the opportunity to invade his home and to transfer to herself all the dowry of the second wife, in return for the injury brought against her.[205]

Some scholars have questioned the influence of Christianity on such legislation because it was harsher on women than men, while other Christian influences were more egalitarian. In light of the conservatism of Roman law, however, that any change was attempted argues for a Christian influence. Constantine's successors, the emperors Theodosius and Honorius (western emperor from 395 to 423) likewise required that a *repudium* (bill of divorce) must have good reason for the dissolution of the marriage. If the wife had proved no causes for the divorce, she should lose her dowry, be subject to exile, and be unable to remarry. If, on the other hand, she had proven satisfactorily "serious causes" against her husband, she would repossess her dowry and any betrothal gifts. She would also be eligible to remarry five years after the divorce.[206]

Late imperial legislation sometimes explicitly expressed concern for the welfare of children. A novel of the Emperor Majorian (western emperor from 457–461), for instance, expressed anxiety for the material welfare of the empire's children. That concern, in turn, required that a legally valid marriage involve a dowry:

> What is advantageous for children is of concern to us, and we wish that they be begotten more numerously for the increase of the Roman name and do not allow benefits for those who have been begotten to be lost. Therefore, as a necessary consequence, we have considered that precautions must be taken so that an equal condition on both sides constrain the male and female who are to be joined by the nuptial bond . . . girls and the parents of girls, or whatever persons are about to marry, shall know that both parties who have been joined without a dowry are to be branded with the stains of infamy, with the result that it shall not be judged a marriage nor shall legitimate children be born from them.[207]

The emperor here effectively broke with centuries of Roman jurisprudence— still upheld in the eastern half of the empire, which merely required consent to the union. Majorian therein also condemned parents who forced their daughters to become nuns.[208] The same sentiment is unmistakable in a novel of Theodosius II, the purpose of which was to make divorce more difficult to obtain, "for the favor that should be shown to children demands that the dissolution of marriage ought to be rather difficult."[209] At the same time, however, Theodosius's novel characterized as "harsh" this departure from the "ancient laws," and so revoked it. Still, only thirteen years later, Valentinian III (425–455) once again enacted divorce legislation He repealed dissolution of marriage "solely on the basis of an opposing desire."[210] Theodosius seems to have thought better as well, and in a later novel enumerated criteria and penalty for just and unjust divorce. He permitted *repudium* to spouses of criminous mates; such women could remarry within a year (so that the paternity of any children born in the meantime should be certain); no interval was prescribed for husbands. If a divorce was unjustified, both husbands and wives "shall be struck with the avenging penalty of this most providential law." The novel also provided that

> If a *repudium* has been sent when there is a son or sons, a daughter or daughters extant, we decree that everything acquired from the marriage is to be preserved for [them] after the death of the person receiving it; that is, if the father rashly sent a *repudium*, the pre-nuptial gift is to be preserved by the mother, (or) if the mother (sent a *repudium*), the dowry itself is to be given up to the same son/s or daughter/s when the father dies.[211]

That legislation like this so obviously contradicts republican and early imperial law seems to refute arguments for the legislative fecklessness of late imperial Christianity.

The Christian emperors of late Rome also altered the law of intestacy to benefit child heirs. The Principate had already moved in this direction, since the *senatus consultum Tertullianum* and the *senatus consultum Orphitianum* had both improved inheritance prospects of mothers and children in the case of an intestate child in the first instance, and of an intestate mother in the second. In two *novellae* promulgated in 543 and 548, the Emperor Justinian introduced a new scheme of intestate succession. The order was (1) descendants, meaning primarily all natural and adopted children, (2) ascendants and full brothers and sisters, (3) half-brothers and sisters, (4) nearest collaterals, and (5) surviving spouse. That Justinian relegated spouses much lower in the order than had previous imperial legislation might at first glance seem an injustice; however Justinian's dowry legislation stipulated that the first charge on the estate of the deceased was to restore the full value of the dowry to the widow—others stood to inherit whatever was left.

By the late fifth century in the west, the Roman legacy was in great danger, as enemies eventually overwhelmed the imperial armies and government. The state vanished in 476, but the Roman legal legacy long survived the empire. The law of the Romans, like Latin, their language, had become part of a larger cultural inheritance. Their law and their language would flourish once again, in medieval and modern Christian Europe.

Notes

1. Livy, *Ab urbe condita*, 3.35 [Aubrey de Sélincourt, trans., *The Early History of Rome* (New York, NY: Penguin Books, 1960), p. 221].

2. Cicero, *De legibus*, 2.59 [Niall Rudd, trans., *Cicero: The Republic and the Laws* (Oxford, UK: Oxford University Press, 1998), p. 146].

3. *Twelve Tables*, 11.1 [*Loeb* 329:505].

4. *Twelve Tables*, 7.7 [*Loeb* 329:471].

5. *Twelve Tables*, 8.2 [*Loeb* 329:477].

6. *Twelve Tables*, 8.10 [*Loeb* 329:481].

7. *Twelve Tables*, 8.12–13 [*Loeb* 329:483].

8. *Twelve Tables*, 8.23 [*Loeb* 329:491].

9. *Twelve Tables*, 9.5 [*Loeb* 329:497].

10. *Twelve Tables*, 8.1a [*Loeb* 329:475].

11. *Twelve Tables*, 5.7c [*Loeb* 329:453].

12. *Twelve Tables*, 5.1 [*Loeb* 329:445].

13. The standard treatment of Roman marriage law is: Susan Treggiari, *Roman Marriage* (Oxford, UK: Clarendon Press, 1991).

14. Livy, 3.55 [Sélincourt, p. 243].

15. Alan Watson, *The Digest of Justinian*, 4 vols. (Philadelphia, PA: University of Pennsylvania Press, 1985), Dig. 1.2.2.8.

16. Livy, 4.1–6 [Sélincourt, pp. 269–276].

17. Livy, 6.35 [Betty Radice, trans., *Rome and Italy* (New York, NY: Penguin Books, 1982), p. 83]. Plebeians had been elected to the consulship in the past but by mid-fourth century had been customarily excluded. Since custom had legal efficacy, a law was needed to overcome it.

18. Livy, 8.28 [Radice, p. 196].

19. Livy, 10.6 [Radice, pp. 295–296].

20. Dig. 1.2.2.25 [Watson, 1:6].

21. Tacitus, *Annals*, 11.22 [*Loeb* 312:285] says that the people took over the bestowal of the *quaestorship* "sixty-three years after the expulsion of the Tarquins," so in 447 BC.

22. Livy, 4.8 [Sélincourt, p. 279].

23. After other *praetorships* were created, this official was known as the *urban praetor*.

24. Dig. 1.2.2.21 [Watson, 1:6], and Cicero, *De legibus*, 3.7 [Rudd, p. 152].

25. Dig. 1.2.2.18–19 [Watson, 1:5].

26. Cicero, *Letters to Quintus*, 1.1.10 [*Loeb* 4562:397].

27. The government of the late republic had no bureaucracy comparable to the Internal Revenue Service of the United States government and so relied on private contractors to collect revenues. Tax contracts, stipulating the assessment for a jurisdiction, were auctioned off and sold to the highest bidder. The contractors had every incentive to extract as much money from the provincials as possible, as they were only bound to deliver to the government as much as their contract stipulated. The rest of the money covered the costs of collecting the taxes. Whatever was left over after that constituted their profits.

28. Cicero, *Letters to Quintus*, 1.1.8–35 [*Loeb* 462:395–427].

29. Cicero, *De legibus*, 1.5 [Niall Rudd, trans., *Cicero: The Republic and The Laws* (Oxford, UK: Oxford University Press, 1998) p. 98].

30. Cicero, *De republica*, 2.2 [Rudd, p. 35].
31. Cicero, *De republica*, 2.5, 2.7, 2.16 [Rudd, pp. 36–37, 39–40].
32. Cicero, *De republica*, 2.27–29 [Rudd, pp. 43–44].
33. Cicero, *De republica*, 2.39 [Rudd, p. 47].
34. Cicero, *De republica*, 2.58 [Rudd, p. 54].
35. Cicero, *De republica*, 2.53–56 [Rudd, pp. 52–53].
36. Cicero, *De legibus*, 2.23 [Rudd, p. 131].
37. Cicero, *De republica*, 1.65–68, 2.3 [Rudd, pp. 30–32, 35–36].
38. Cicero, *De republica*, 1.45 and 2.15 [Rudd, pp. 21, 39].
39. Cicero, *De republica*, 2.57–58 [Rudd, pp. 53–54].
40. Cicero, *De republica*, 3.44 [Rudd, pp. 72–73].
41. Cicero, *De republica*, 1.39 [Rudd, p. 19].
42. Cicero, *De legibus*, 2.11 [Rudd, p. 125].
43. Cicero, *De legibus*, 1.32 [Rudd, p. 108]. Cf. Plato, *Laws*, 880d–880e [Hamilton, p. 1439]: "Laws . . . are made in part for the virtuous—to teach them what rule they should follow in their intercourse with one another, if they are to live in peace and good will."
44. Cicero, *De legibus*, 1.44 [Rudd, p. 112].
45. Cicero, *De legibus*, 1.17 [Rudd, pp. 102–103].
46. Cicero, *De legibus*, 1.14 [Rudd, pp. 101–102].
47. Cicero, *De legibus*, 1.28 [Rudd, pp. 106–107].
48. Cicero, *De legibus*, 1.30 [Rudd, p. 107].
49. Cicero, *De legibus*, 1.33 [Rudd, p. 108].
50. Cicero, *De republica*, 3.33 [Rudd, pp. 68–69]. Cf. *De legibus*, 1.18 [Rudd, p. 103].
51. Cicero, *De legibus*, 1.42 [Rudd, pp. 111–112].
52. Cicero, *De legibus*, 2.8 [Rudd, p. 124].
53. Cicero, *De legibus*, 2.20 [Rudd, p. 129], and Livy, 1.59 [Sélincourt, pp. 99–100].
54. Cicero, *De republica*, 3.24 [Rudd, p. 64].
55. Cicero, *De legibus*, 2.13 [Rudd, p. 126].
56. Cicero, *De legibus*, 1.42 [Rudd, pp. 111–112].
57. Cicero, *De legibus*, 1.43 [Rudd, p. 112].
58. Cicero, *De legibus*, 1.47 [Rudd, pp. 113–114].
59. Cicero, *De republica*, 1.34 [Rudd, p. 17].
60. Cicero, *De republica*, 1.51 [Rudd, pp. 23–24].
61. Cicero, *De legibus*, 3.32 [Rudd, p. 162].
62. Cicero, *De republica*, 1.47 [Rudd, pp. 21–22].
63. Cicero, *De republica*, 1.49 [Rudd, pp. 22–23].
64. Cicero, *De republica*, 1.35 [Rudd, p. 17].
65. Cicero, *De republica*, 1.36 [Rudd, pp. 17–18].
66. Cicero, *De legibus*, 2.4–5 [Rudd, p. 122].
67. Cicero, *De republica*, 1.19 [Rudd, p. 11].
68. Cicero, *De republica*, 1.28–29 [Rudd, p. 14–15].

69. Cicero, *De legibus*, 1.56 [Rudd, p. 117].
70. Cicero, *De legibus*, 1.58 [Rudd, p. 118].
71. George F. Will, *Statecraft as Soulcraft: What Government Does* (New York, NY: Simon & Schuster, 1983).
72. Cicero, *De republica*, 5.5 [Rudd, pp. 82–83].
73. Cicero, *De republica*, 1.2 [Rudd, p. 4].
74. Cicero, *De legibus*, 1.48 [Rudd, p. 114].
75. Cicero, *De legibus*, 1.29 [Rudd, p. 107].
76. Cicero, *De legibus*, 1.34 [Rudd, p. 108–109].
77. Cicero, *De legibus*, 1.23 [Rudd, p. 105].
78. Cicero, *De legibus*, 3.3 [Rudd, p. 150].
79. Cicero, *De legibus*, 1.48 [Rudd, p. 114].
80. Cicero, *De legibus*, 3.2 [Rudd, p. 150].
81. Cicero, *De legibus*, 3.12 [Rudd, pp. 154–155].
82. Cicero, *De legibus*, 3.6 [Rudd, pp. 151–152].
83. Cicero, *De republica*, 5.7 [Rudd, p. 83].
84. Cicero, *De legibus*, 2.30 [Rudd, p. 134].
85. Cicero, *De legibus*, 1.60 [Rudd, pp. 118–119].
86. Cicero, *De republica*, 1.41 [Rudd, p. 19].
87. Cicero, *De republica*, 5.11 [Rudd, p. 83].
88. Cicero, *De legibus*, 3.42 [Rudd, p. 166].
89. Except, of course, in the great Jewish rebellion of 66–73.
90. Dig. 1.5.17 [Watson, 1:16].
91. Dig. 1.2.2.49 [Watson, 1:10].
92. Alan Watson, *The Spirit of Roman Law* (Athens, GA: University of Georgia Press, 1995), p. 57.
93. Gaius, *The Institutes of Gaius*, trans. W. M. Gordon and O. F. Robinson (Ithaca, NY: Cornell University Press, 1988).
94. Cod. Theo. 1.4.3 [Pharr, p. 15].
95. The definitive edition is Theodor Mommsen, *et al.*, eds., *Corpus iuris civilis*, 3 vols. (Berlin: Weidmann, 1899). The Digest has been translated into English by Alan Watson, *The Digest of Justinian*, 4 vols. (Philadelphia, PA: University of Pennsylvania Press, 1985). The Institutes have been translated into English by Peter Birks and Grant McLeod, *Justinian's Institutes* (Ithaca, NY: Cornell University Press, 1987). A somewhat archaic translation of the whole *Corpus iuris civilis* is S. P. Scott, ed., *The Civil Law*, 17 vols. (New York, NY: AMS Press, 1973).
96. Dig. 1.1.1.1 [Watson, 1:1].
97. Dig. 1.3.2 [Watson, 1:11].
98. Dig. 1.1.1.2 [Watson, 1:1].
99. Dig. 1.1.1.3 [Watson, 1:1].
100. Dig. 1.1.1.4 [Watson, 1:1].
101. Dig. 1.1.1.2 [Watson, 1:1].
102. Dig. 1.1.3 [Watson, 1:1].

103. Dig. 1.1.4 [Watson, 1:2].
104. Dig. 1.1.5 [Watson, 1:2].
105. Dig. 1.1.7 [Watson, 1:2].
106. Dig. 1.3.1 [Watson, 1:11].
107. See Watson, *Spirit of Roman Law*, Ch. 6.
108. Dig. 1.3.31 [Watson, 1:13].
109. Dig. 1.4.1 [Watson, 1:14].
110. Dig. 1.5.1 [Watson, 1:15]. Cf. Dig. 48.19.18 [Watson, 4:850]: "No one is punished for thinking."
111. Dig. 1.5.3 [Watson, 1:15].
112. Dig. 1.5.5 [Watson, 1:15].
113. Dig. 1.5.6 [Watson, 1:15].
114. Dig. 1.5.4.2 [Watson, 1:15] and Dig. 1.5.5.1 [Watson, 1:15].
115. Dig. 1.5.9 [Watson, 1:16].
116. Dig. 1.6.1 [Watson, 1:17].
117. Dig. 1.6.2 [Watson, 1:18].
118. Dig. 23.1.1 [Watson, 2:656].
119. Dig. 23.2.4 [Watson, 2:657], Dig. 23.2.2 [Watson, 2:657], and Dig. 50.17.30 [Watson, 4:958].
120. Dig. 23.2.1 [Watson, 2:657].
121. Such is the sense of Dig. 23.1.8 [Watson, 2:656], "insanity is an impediment to betrothal," and Dig. 23.2.44.1 [Watson, 2:663], which prohibited marriages between senators and freedwomen, on the one hand, and senators and actresses, on the other, for example.
122. Dig. 23.2.42 [Watson, 2:662].
123. Dig. 23.3.6 [Watson, 2:669].
124. Dig. 24.2.3 [Watson, 2:715].
125. Dig. 24.2.2.1 [Watson, 2:714] and Dig. 24.2.9 [Watson, 2:716].
126. Andrew Borkowski, *Textbook on Roman Law*, 2nd ed. (Oxford, UK: Oxford University Press, 1997), p. 128.
127. See the discussion of the Twelve Tables above.
128. Dig. 48.4.1 [Watson, 4:802].
129. Dig. 48.4.2 [Watson, 4:802] and Dig. 48.4.6 [Watson, 4:803].
130. Dig. 48.4.7.1 [Watson, 4:803] and Dig. 48.4.8 [Watson, 4:804].
131. Murder was understood not only to be the actual commission of the taking of a life but also the making of poison or the setting of fire with intent to kill. Abortion was also considered murder, punishable by exile (Dig. 48.8.8 [Watson, 4:820]).
132. Dig. 48.1.1 [Watson, 4:795]: "Not all trials in which an offense is concerned are public criminal trials, but only those which arise from the statutes on criminal proceedings, such as the lex Julia on treason, the lex Julia on adultery, the lex Cornelia on murderers and poisoners, the lex Pompeia on parricide, the lex Julia on embezzlement, the lex Cornelia on wills, the leges Juliae on vis privata, and vis publica, the lex Julia on electoral corruption, the lex Julia on extortion, and the lex Julia on the corn dole."

133. Dig. 48.5.25 [Watson, 4:811].

134. Dig. 48.5.6 [Watson, 4:805].

135. O. F. Robinson, *The Criminal Law of Ancient Rome* (Baltimore, MD: The Johns Hopkins University Press, 1995), pp. 3–5.

136. Dig. 47.2.2 [Watson, 4:737].

137. Dig. 47.2.3 [Watson, 4:737].

138. Dig. 47.2.10 [Watson, 4:738].

139. Dig. 47.2.19 [Watson, 4:741].

140. Dig. 47.10.5 [Watson, 4:772].

141. Dig. 47.10.7 [Watson, 4:773].

142. Inst. 2.1 [Birks, pp. 55–61].

143. Gaius, Inst. 2.14 [Gordon, pp. 130–131].

144. Gaius, Inst. 1.119 [Gordon, pp. 79–80].

145. Gaius, Inst. 2.24 [Gordon, pp. 134–135].

146. Dig. 41.3.1 [Watson, 4:517], and Inst. 2.6 [Birks, pp. 63–65].

147. Dig. 41.2.1.21 [Watson, 4:503] and Dig. 41.1.9.5 [Watson, 4:490].

148. Dig. 41.1.31 [Watson, 4:495].

149. Dig. 41.2.13 [Watson, 4:507–508].

150. Dig. 43.17.2 [Watson, 4:589] and Dig. 41.2.35 [Watson, 4:513].

151. Dig. 7.1.68.2 [Watson, 1:230], and Inst. 2.4 [Birks, p. 61].

152. Dig. 7.8.2 [Watson, 1:243], and Inst. 2.5 [Birks, p. 63].

153. Dig. 28.1.1 [Watson, 2:815]: "A will is a lawful expression of our wishes concerning what someone *wishes to be done* after his death."

154. Dig. 28.1.2 [Watson, 2:815] and Dig. 28.1.5 [Watson 2:815]. See Watson, *Spirit of Roman Law*, p. 21.

155. Watson, *Spirit of Roman Law*, p. 174.

156. Dig. 29.2.37 [Watson, 2:880].

157. Dig. 28.2.11 [Watson, 2:820].

158. Inst. 3.3 [Birks, p. 97] and Inst. 3.4 [Birks, p. 97].

159. Dig. 45.1.5.1 [Watson, 4:651], and Inst 3.15.1 [Birks, p. 107].

160. Inst. 3.21 [Birks, p. 113].

161. For *mutuum*, Dig. 12.1.2.1–2 [Watson, 1:357], for *commodatum*, Dig. 13.6.15–16 [Watson, 1:404], for *depositum*, Dig. 16.3.1 [Watson, 2:469], and for *pignus*, Inst. 3.14.4 [Birks, p. 107].

162. Dig. 18.1.1.2 [Watson, 2:513].

163. Dig. 18.1.35 [Watson, 2:518].

164. Dig. 18.1.34.1 [Watson, 2:517].

165. Dig. 18.1.1.1 [Watson, 2:513].

166. Dig. 19.1.1.1 [Watson, 2:544] and Dig. 19.1.13.19–20 [Watson, 2:549].

167. Dig. 19.2.2.1 [Watson, 2:559].

168. Borkowski, *Textbook on Roman Law*, p. 285.

169. Dig. 17.1.1.4 [Watson, 2:479].

170. One of the more infamous partnerships in particular business were partnerships of tax farmers (*publicani*) that the republican government contracted with for the collection of revenues from Roman provinces.

171. For the *quaestiones perpetuae*, I am indebted to O. F. Robinson, *The Criminal Law of Ancient Rome* (Baltimore, MD: Johns Hopkins University Press, 1995), pp. 3–6.

172. Dig. 48.18.1 [Watson, 4:840].

173. Dig. 48.18.1.17 [Watson, 4:841].

174. Dig. 48.18.1.23 [Watson, 4:841].

175. Dig. 48.18.10 [Watson, 4:843].

176. Dig. 48.19.3 [Watson, 4:845].

177. Dig. 48.18.7 [Watson, 4:843].

178. Dig. 48.18.1.21 [Watson, 4:841].

179. Dig. 48.19.8.9 [Watson, 4:847].

180. Pliny the Younger, *Letters*, 10.96 [*Loeb* 59:285–287].

181. Pliny the Younger, *Letters*, 10.97 [*Loeb* 59:291–293].

182. Dig. 48.1.5 [Watson, 4:795].

183. Dig. 22.5.1 [Watson, 2:650].

184. Dig. 48.2.10 [Watson, 4:798].

185. Dig. 22.5.3 [Watson, 2:650].

186. Like, for instance, Augustine, *Letter* 153.23–24 [E. M. Atkins and R. J. Dodaro, eds., *Augustine: Political Writings* (Cambridge, UK: Cambridge University Press, 2001), pp. 85–86].

187. Dig. 50.17.41 [Watson, 4:959].

188. Dig. 50.16.6.1 [Watson, 4:934].

189. Dig. 50.17.179 [Watson, 4:968] and Dig. 50.17.122 [Watson, 4:964].

190. Dig. 48.19.42 [Watson, 4:854].

191. Dig. 50.17.56 [Watson, 4:960] and Dig. 50.17.155.2 [Watson, 4:966].

192. Dig. 48.19.5 [Watson, 4:846].

193. Aurelius Victor, *Lives of the Emperors*, c. 39 [H. W. Bird, trans., *Liber de caesaribus of Sextus Aurelius Victor* (Liverpool, UK: Liverpool University Press, 1994), p. 41].

194. Cod. Theo. 12.1.18 [Pharr, pp. 344–345]: "It is our will, indeed, that the sons of military men, according to the former regulation, either shall pursue the aforesaid service of their fathers, or, if they refuse to perform military service and have reached the age of thirty-five years, they shall be assigned to the municipal councils."

195. Cod. Theo. 5.17.1 [Pharr, p. 115]: "Coloni who meditate flight must be bound with chains and reduced to a servile condition, so that by virtue of their condemnation to slavery, they shall be compelled to fulfill the duties that befit freemen."

196. Eusebius of Nicomedia, *The History of the Church*, 10.5.1–10.5.12 [G. A. Williamson, trans. (New York, NY: Penguin Books, 1988), pp. 322–324].

197. Cod. Theo. 8.16.1 [Pharr, p. 217]; also *History*, 10.7.2 [Williamson, p. 327].

198. Eusebius, *History* 10.6.1 [Williamson, pp. 326–327], and *Life of Constantine*, 3.29–3.40 [Averil Cameron and Stuart G. Hall, trans. (Oxford: Oxford University Press, 1999), pp. 133–137].

199. Cod. Theo. 1.27.1 [Pharr, p. 31], and Cod. 1.4.8 [Krueger and Mommsen, 2:40].

200. Cod. Theo. 4.7.1 [Pharr, pp. 87–88].

201. Cod. Theo. 16.6.1 [Pharr, p. 463], and Cod. 1.6.2 [Krueger and Mommsen, 2:60]. Constantine's own legislation, cited in Cod. Theo. 16.6.2 [Pharr, pp. 463–464], is not extant.

202. Cod. Theo. 16.5. [Pharr, p. 450].

203. D. 96 c. 10, [*Crisis of Church and State*, pp. 12–13].

204. Nov. 6, pr. [*Crisis of Church and State*, p. 15].

205. Cod. Theo. 3.16.1 [Judith Evan Grubbs, *Women and Law in the Roman Empire* (London, UK: Routledge, 2002), p. 203].

206. Cod. Theo. 3.16.2 [Grubbs, *Women and Law*, p. 204].

207. Novel 6.9 (Majorian, 458), [Grubbs, *Women and Law*, p. 119]. Valentinian III (western emperor from 425–455) promulgated a similar law in 452 (Cod. Theo. 4.6.7 [Pharr, p. 87]).

208. Novel 6.10 (Majorian, 458), [Grubbs, *Women and Law*, p. 119].

209. Novel 12 of Theodosius II (439) [Grubbs, *Women and Law*, p. 205].

210. Novel 35.11 of Valentinian III (452) [Grubbs, *Women and Law*, p. 206].

211. Cod. 5.17.8 [Grubbs, *Women and Law*, pp. 206–208].

PART III

The Laws of the Middle Ages

For many years the Middle Ages were also known as the Dark Ages—a long era of ignorance, superstition, and barbarism that followed upon the great, enlightened civilizations of Greece and Rome. Fortunately, the reputation of the Middle Ages has been rehabilitated over the years, as scholars have drawn attention to the great cultural achievements of the era. Law may well be ranked among the chief of those achievements, for the Middle Ages constitute a golden era in the study of law and jurisprudence. That period of a thousand years was extraordinarily rich in its legal legacy, for during the Middle Ages Germanic law appeared on the Western cultural scene, the canon law of the Catholic Church matured, Roman law reestablished itself as the great secular legal system of the European continent, and the tradition of the English common law was born.

Germanic and Customary Law

During the unusually frigid winter of 405–406, a number of Germanic tribes crossed the frozen Rhine into Roman imperial territory. Over the next half-century, the Vandals, Visigoths, Burgundians, and Franks fought each other and the western empire's dwindling military. In the meantime, they occupied new homelands within the empire's frontiers. The Vandals first settled in Spain. They then crossed the straits of Gibraltar and established a kingdom in north Africa (c. 435). Rome was thus cut off from what was probably the most populous and wealthiest province of the western empire. The Vandal kingdom lasted until 535. In that year, East Roman/Byzantine armies under the command of the great general Belisarius reconquered the province for the Emperor Justinian. Africa remained a Byzantine province until 699, when it passed permanently into the hands of Muslim conquerors, and out of the Christian concert of kingdoms. In Spain, the Visigoths founded a kingdom which was the forerunner of the later principalities of Leon, Castile, Aragon, Navarre, and Catalonia. Important church councils were held in Spain in the seventh century, and the Visigothic kingdom produced one of early medieval Europe's best scholars, Isidore of Seville (c. 560–636), whose *Etymologies* influenced so many subsequent works of learning. In the great provinces of Gaul, the Burgundians settled in the Rhone valley. The kingdom of the Franks (in northern Gaul) was the lone, permanent survivor of the German successor states. By the end of the sixth century, the Frankish kingdom also encompassed trans-Rhenish territories that had never recognized the authority of the Roman emperors.

Although the Germans had long been in contact with Romans, they had no written law until they occupied Roman territory. The Goths had had Bibles in their native language since the fourth century, but no law codes. German law, then, was *customary*; that is, the law and unwritten custom were virtually synonymous. According to the *Bavarian Laws* (c. 750):

> An ancient custom, in fact, is to be considered as a law. *Lex* is a written constitution; *mos* is custom derived from antiquity, although an unwritten law. For *lex* is named from *legere*, since it is written. *Mos*, however, means an ancient custom, which is derived only from usage; however, custom is a type of law, defined through usage, from which law is derived. Law should be universal, which alone is established with reason, which serves order, and which produces well-being. Custom is named [i.e., unwritten], but it is in common use.[1]

Inheritance law, family law, and torts were addressed in accord with the unwritten customs handed down from generation to generation of the people. Law was an integral part of culture, rather than an edict of government. Since literacy was long confined to professed religious over the course of the Middle Ages, *most medieval people lived by customary law*. Such laws of course had certain similarities from village to village, and region to region, but there was often an element of the idiosyncratic as well. Consequently, when villagers had disputes, they sought redress in the manor court, not before a magistrate of the ruler, unlike the case under the late Roman imperial regime. Over the early medieval centuries, customary law established itself in northern Gaul, although Roman law continued to serve as the legal foundation of southern Gaul and northern Italy.

When the Germans came to rule great numbers of Romans, they clearly felt the necessity to have their laws written down, partly in imitation of the emperors, whose heirs they claimed to be. Indeed, before its final demise in 476, the western government often bestowed Roman honors on German leaders and kings. For a number of generations after the establishment of the German kingdoms, Romans continued to be ruled by Roman law but the Germans by their native law. During the Roman Empire, Roman law had become territorial law, that is, applicable to all residents/citizens of the Roman Empire. In the post-Roman west, however, the law had become personal; that is, the Romans lived according to their law and the Germans theirs. Thus, the Burgundian King Gundobad (474–516), the Frankish King Clovis (c. 481–511), and the Visigoth Receswinth (649–672) all had their laws set down in writing, to stand alongside the law of the Romans.

The *leges barbarorum* ("laws of the barbarians"), then, represent some intermingling of German and Roman elements.[2] Like early Roman law, however, the laws of the barbarian codes contain very little in the way of public or constitutional law (indeed, the Germans had virtually no state at all, but rather war-chiefs and their followers), and are overwhelmingly private law; that is to say, most crimes were taken to be offenses committed by one person against another, or one family against another, and so should be settled between the perpetrator and the victim. German law, like Roman republican law, assumed that family members would seek out vengeance-justice for aggrieved relatives.[3] The Germans had no long-term imprisonments, state executions, or state investigation and prosecution of crime, although the war-chiefs had a great interest in the limitation of private violence, lest their followings disintegrate into chaos. Again, the Burgundian code reminded relatives of murder victims that "no one can be pursued except the killer."[4] Thus, the great majority of German laws cite the compensation (*wergeld*) owed one party by another, for theft of or damage to property. The law codes also listed *wergeld* for offenses such as assault and murder, and in such cases the compensation was very high, so as to encourage plaintiffs to take the money and thereby avoid further violence and bloodshed, for acceptance of the *wergeld* was taken to mean rejection of blood feud, and thereby conclude the case. The *wergeld* increased or decreased according to the seriousness of the offense, the legal status of the offender, and the legal status of the victim:

We decree that this rule be added to the law by a reasonable provision, that if violence shall have been done by anyone to any person, so that he is injured by blows of lashes or by wounds, and if he pursues his persecutor and overcome by grief and indignation kills him, proof of the deed shall be afforded by the act itself or by suitable witnesses who can be believed. Then the guilty party shall be compelled to pay to the relatives of the person killed half his *wergeld* according to the status of the person: that is, if he shall have killed a highly-ranking noble, we decree that the payment be set at one hundred fifty *solidi*, i.e., half his *wergeld*; if a person of middle estate, one hundred *solidi*; if a humble person, seventy-five *solidi*.[5]

If a slave had been harmed, his owner collected the compensation, and where a slave had been the offender, the owner might be liable to pay compensation, although the usual penalty for criminous slaves was either flogging, mutilation, or death. Masters who employed slaves as assassins were subject to death.[6] Like Roman law, German law codes permitted the torture of slaves to obtain evidence of guilt.

In German law codes, legal procedure depended much upon compurgation (*compurgatio*, a swearing of oaths) and ordeal, wherein the war-chief's responsibility was to ensure that proof of an offense could be produced and that the proper procedures were observed.[7] The aggrieved parties brought their own compurgators, or fellow oathtakers, before the chief or his agents. They swore oaths attesting to guilt or innocence, as in the Burgundian code: "If a slave has committed the theft while under the dominion of his master, and if he flees after committing the theft, let his master prove by oaths that he should not be held liable to punishment either for the theft or for the flight of the slave."[8] Both the plaintiffs and the defendants were permitted to present compurgators, as in the laws of the Lombards: "In a case between freemen involving twenty or more *solidi* where an oath is to be given, the parties shall swear on the sacred gospels with twelve oathhelpers or oathtakers selected in such a way that six of them are named by that one who brings the case, he against whom the case is brought is the seventh, and the accused shall choose five additional freemen to make twelve."[9] The compurgators needed to be freemen of good reputation. If the accused failed to assemble enough compurgators by the holding of court, then the law demanded that he undergo ordeal to be declared innocent. The most common ordeal was probably that of boiling water. The accused plunged his hand into a pot of boiling water, and if the burns healed well enough in the estimation of the chief's officers, the defendant was declared innocent. If the hand had not healed well enough, he was pronounced guilty and ordered to pay the appropriate *wergeld* to the plaintiff.[10] The Germans permitted ordeal by combat in certain circumstances to elite warriors:

> If the party to whom oath has been offered does not wish to receive the oath, but shall say that the truthfulness of his adversary can be demonstrated only by

resort to arms, and the second party (the one accused) shall not yield (the case charged), let the right of combat not be refused; with the further provision that one of the same witnesses who came to give oath shall fight, God being the judge.[11]

Whether by compurgation or ordeal, the burden of proof rested upon the accused.

German family law had its own idiosyncrasies. German law generally assumed a reverse dowry, rather than a dowry, because the marriage market favored women.[12] The pagan Germans were polygynous, and so the number of women on the marriage market tended to concentrate in the households of the wealthy, thus skewing the available number of mates. While couples could marry without the permission of either father, such marriages carried very high fines for both nobles and peasants.[13] Women could not divorce their husbands, although men could divorce their wives with the payment of twelve *solidi*, unless the wife admitted to adultery, witchcraft, or grave despoliation, in which case he owed her nothing.[14] Inheritance law, of course, was closely related to family law. While wives and daughters might inherit the family patrimony, only sons could inherit Frankish Salic land (held as a consequence of service to the ruler): "But concerning Salic land no portion of the inheritance shall pass to a woman, but the male sex acquires it, that is, the sons succeed to the inheritance."[15]

By the turn of the fifth century, the kings had replaced war-chiefs for most of the responsibilities for the protection of the "nation" from enemies without and for the provision of justice within. Of course, the king could not possibly hear every grievance in the kingdom nor preside at every compurgation or ordeal. By the sixth century, officers of the king had taken on the responsibilities of the local administration of justice. Councils of seven freemen, known as *rachimburgi*, served as local legal experts. They were empowered to "speak the law" on the king's behalf, that is to say, to determine the proper action in any case. Officials possessed of the old imperial title of count (*comes*) served as the king's governor, chief military commander, and supreme judicial authority within his jurisdiction.

Customary Germanic law flourished until the twelfth century, when the kings of France and the German emperors increasingly relied on feudal and the newly rediscovered Roman law to further their political ambitions. Roman imperial law in particular endowed the ruler with far-reaching powers ("what pleases the prince has the force of law"). German imperial apologists could take Roman law at its face value; French royal defenders simply stated that the king of France was like unto an emperor in France. Customary law thus began a long period of decline that terminated in early nineteenth-century France with the promulgation of the *Code Napoleon* (based on south French Roman law), valid for the whole of France, in 1806.

The Carolingians

By the mid-eighth century, the kingdom of the Franks had established itself as a permanent political and national fixture in western and central Europe. By the reign of Charlemagne (768–814) the Franks had succeeded in bringing almost all of Latin Christendom under their rule. With his coronation as emperor on Christmas day, 800, by Pope Leo III (795–816) the Roman Empire itself was reborn in the west. Unlike the later Roman Empire, however, the government of Charlemagne's realm depended in no way on a vast imperial civil service, but rather on Germanic ideas about loyalty and personal service to the chief/king. The great king and his successors relied heavily on the services of elite families and their loyalists in the provinces. Charlemagne appointed "his men," with the title of count, to wield the royal authority within territorial jurisdictions known as counties. Late Romans used the word *comes* to describe commanders of the elite, mobile field army, as well as heads of some civilian departments of government. They called territorial commanders *duces*. After the collapse of the empire in the west, the Germans appropriated these titles unto somewhat different purposes. German dukes were territorial princes and largely independent of the kings. The title of count fell mostly out of use until the establishment of Charlemagne's regime. Like their Roman ancestors, Frankish counts were understood to be close associates—companions—of their ruler.

The frontiers of the Frankish counties closely followed those of the old Roman unit of subprovincial administration, the *pagus*. Roman provincial administration was centered on cities, and the surrounding countryside that those cities dominated. Counts were established in much the same way, with the same territorial responsibilities. The responsibilities of the counts, whose resources included vast secular and ecclesiastical lands, were to wield the royal authority on behalf of the king, and to defend the county against foreign invaders. The tie between the counts and the king was another instance of the ancient bond of patron and client, which was ritualized in the rite of homage, which in turn consisted of two elements. The *immixtio manuum* involved the inferior partner, who came to be called a vassal, kneeling bareheaded and unarmed before the standing, superior partner, his lord. The vassal extended his hands, folded as in prayer, towards the lord, who took them into his own. The second element was a solemn pledge of fealty, wherein the vassal promised not to harm his lord, although Charlemagne demanded more from counts than had traditionally been the case among the Germans. The Emperor declared that fealty was

> not as many have thought up til now, involving simple fidelity to the lord emperor as far as his life is concerned—that is, the obligation of refraining from any action against him which will put [his] life in danger—and the obligation of not introducing into his kingdom any enemy out of hostility towards him, and of declining to be a party to the disloyalty towards him of others or keeping silent regarding such.[16]

After the pledge of fealty, the lord helped his new vassal to his feet, and they kissed on the lips. A symbolic exchange might also follow, for instance, a clump of soil to represent the vassal's landed jurisdiction, received from his lord. Of course, once in their jurisdictions, the counts needed the services of men upon whom they could depend for military and government service. In time, vassals were required to provide military support and counsel to their lords. Lords, on the other hand, owed their vassals enough resources to do their jobs properly.[17] These resources, called "benefices" (*beneficia* in Latin) or "fiefs" (in Old French, or "fees" in Old English), might consist of churches and monasteries, manors, or offices at court; indeed, the early Carolingians provided for their followings with land confiscated from the Christian church. During Charlemagne's lifetime, counts served at the pleasure of the ruler. Upon the count's death or deposition, the county reverted back to the king, who would find a successor to that position. Often, the son of the deceased predecessor would be named to the post. Families often handed down traditions of royal service, so sons could be relied upon to be as loyal as their fathers.

Only two generations removed from Charlemagne, however, two crises beset the Frankish monarchy. The ancient Frankish custom of partible inheritance, where all the sons received a portion of their father's patrimony, ran up against the wish of Charlemagne's son, Louis the Pious (814–840), to bequeath the entire empire to his eldest son Lothair. Louis hoped that in this way he might avoid the civil wars that had erupted again and again between rival branches of the royal family. His other sons, Louis and Charles, however, insisted on their traditional rights. Instead of avoiding armed struggle, Louis the Pious had instigated yet another civil war, which resulted in the division of the empire in 843 into western, eastern, and Rhenish components. The eastern realm, which in time became the kingdom of Germany, fell to Louis the German (843–876), while Lothair (840–855) inherited the imperial title, along with the Rhenish territories of the Franks, and the Italian and Burgundian kingdoms. West Frankland, which eventually became the kingdom of France, passed to the youngest of the sons of Louis the Pious, Charles the Bald (843–877).

During these wars, however, another great wave of invasions—perhaps the most devastating yet—had begun to descend upon the Frankish realm. From the east, the Magyars, a steppe people closely related to the Huns and Avars of earlier centuries, devastated Germany. Muslim pirates attacked Italy and the valley of the Rhone river. They burned the Vatican in 843 and established bases as far north as Switzerland. In west Frankland, the lightning-quick raids of the Vikings, who with their longships were able to take advantage of west Frankland's wide and navigable rivers, ravaged much of the territory between the Loire and the Seine. The position of the west Frankish king in particular was poorly suited to deal with the Viking threat. For one, his capital city was Rheims, in the eastern part of the realm, while most raiders attacked from the west. The traditional Frankish national levy of heavy infantry took a long time to muster, and could only remain in the field for about six weeks. Frankish commanders either hoped they could deliver the enemy one decisive blow, like Charles Martel against the Muslims at Poitiers in 732, or take strategically significant cities through siege. The Vikings generally avoided field battles and wherever possible concentrated on easy targets, such as monasteries or unfortified settlements. Thus, the Carolingian military initially had great difficulty defending the realm against their depredations. Royal authority atrophied in the confusion. Beginning in the 880s, another round of succession crises further compounded the troubles of the Carolingian dynasts. They either lacked direct heirs or left their thrones to young boys.

The Frankish nobility of the Loire-Seine valleys filled the royal military and administrative vacuum in their region. Counts petitioned the Carolingian monarchs to make their fiefs heritable. To refuse was unthinkable, for it would leave endangered regions defenseless, as embittered comital families could well rebel or ignore their responsibilities. Local nobles of all ranks, upon whom the burden of defense now fell, quickly learned that fortifications not only repelled Viking depredations effectively but also solidified their own personal control of the immediate territory. Although the construction of fortifications was illegal without royal permission, castles quickly began to dot the countryside of Latin Christendom. From the safety of their garrisoned fortifications, castellans could defy comital power as merrily as greater lords could defy comital or royal power. In addition to heritable fortifications and lands, nobles also treasured the power of the *ban*, that is, the right to erect a gallows and to exercise high (that is capital) justice, which had traditionally belonged to the ruler, for the crimes of murder, treason, rape, heresy, sodomy, and counterfeiting. Secondary offenses, like maiming and insult, were punished with imprisonment. Low justice, which included crimes like public disturbance and assault, were punished with fines. Essentially, whether counts or castellans, nobles wanted to wield royal powers, merely within a territory rather than the entire realm. Just as kings had men in their service, so also did the counts and the barons. The greatest and most powerful lords wanted to rule their territories without deference to either royal or comital authority.

These same legal, military, and political impulses worked at society's humblest levels as well. In such a brutal age, peasants suffered the depredations of invaders and raiders, and the intimidation of the nobles, whose fortified houses and armed followers served as instruments of exploitation. Increasing numbers of peasants became serfs, a legal status between freedom and slavery. The movement from freedom into servitude seems to have been very subtle, but generally included an increase in the obligations of peasants towards the lords, as in a capitulary of Charles the Bald:

> Certain tenants of the royal and ecclesiastical demesnes owe cartage and manual services according to ancient usage; so much is noted in the *polyptyques* and they do not deny it. But they refuse to carry marl and other things which do not please them because in the old days, perhaps, marl was not carried (in many places indeed its transport began in the time of our grandfather and our father).[18]

Charles's capitulary invoked the customary law from both sides. These peasants conceded that they owed their lord (in this case the king himself) certain services, but they refused to cart marl because their ancestors had no such obligation. Charles admitted as much, but countered that cartage had first been demanded during the reign of Charlemagne, and so might be understood as customary anyway. This capitulary hints at negotiation, rather than terrorization, between the peasants and their monarch. At the very least, the capitulary shows that customary law was fungible, sometimes worked to the advantage of the peasants, and at others to the advantage of the lord.

In some cases, peasants became serfs in rituals similar to those by which a man became the vassal of his lord. The monastery of Marmoutier thus recorded the enserfment of a peasant named William, sometime during the middle of the eleventh century:

> Be it known to all who come after us, that a certain man in our service called William, the brother of Reginald, born of free parents, being moved by the love of God and to the end that God—with whom is no acceptance of persons but

regard only for the merits of each—might look favorably on him, gave himself up as a serf to St. Martin of Marmoutier; and he gave not only himself but all his descendants, so that they should for ever serve the abbot and monks of this place in a servile condition. And in order that this gift might be made more certain and apparent, he put the bell-rope round his neck and placed four pennies from his own head on the altar of St. Martin in recognition of serfdom, and so offered himself to almighty God.[19]

The serf William, however, unlike a vassal, received no kiss from his lord, a reminder of a kind of equality between the two partners. The bell-rope and the head-price of four pennies that William placed on the altar, furthermore, are clear signs of his subordination to the monks of Marmoutier. William's descendants would also suffer the stigma of his servitude.

Still, the collapse of royal power in west Francia and the enserfment of many peasants are only part of the post-Carolingian story. By 950, the devastations of the Viking, Magyar, and Muslim raiders had largely ceased. The numerous fortifications built over the last century effectively frustrated foes that relied on swift military operations. The German king/emperor Otto I (936–973) smashed the Magyar threat at the great Battle of the Lechfeld in 955. Southern French nobles drove out the Muslim raiders. In the west Frankish kingdom, the Carolingians coopted the Vikings into their weak regime. In 911, Charles (III) the Simple granted the lands surrounding the bay of the Seine to a Viking chieftain named Rollo, along with the title of duke. Over the next several centuries, the Normans demonstrated their genius for administration, and the duchy of Normandy became one of the best-governed regions in western Europe. Other great lords, such as Fulk Nerra, the count of Anjou (972–1040), and his enemy Odo, the count of Blois (983–1037), among others, provided order and predictability as they consolidated their governments. These possessors of both castles and fortified cities assumed the right to hold their own courts, which gave a greater depth to the administration of justice than in any other period of history until then. Again, insofar as lords behaved like territorial princes, they exercised jurisdiction over rural peasants; after 1000 AD, municipal councils served the same purposes for the increasing number of towndwellers. Kings often gave towns charters of liberties, which released the townsmen from their duties to the local lord. Municipal councils then assumed the juridical powers that the lords had formerly wielded over the townsmen.

Out of these competing jurisdictions—royal, comital, and municipal—came "the notion that argument about rights and justice constituted the standard way of setting the boundaries of rule and of confronting and correcting misrule."[20] Much of the litigation recorded in medieval documents involved disputes over infringement of rights or dereliction of responsibilities. In medieval justice, rights rarely referred to abstract concepts, but rather the enjoyment of specific lands or privileges. Litigation had still, as in former times, to be initiated by plaintiffs, and heard before the lord with jurisdiction over the case. Trials began when both plaintiff and defendant could appear before the judge. Defendants could claim, on their behalf, that the present court had no jurisdiction over the case, or that the case had already been ruled upon, or that the judge had a conflict of interest. None of these, of course, established his innocence, and were called "dilatory" defenses because they merely served to delay the proceedings.[21] Consequently, many trials dragged on interminably, for defendants could reasonably hope that delay might abort the proceedings. As in Roman law, defendants carried a high burden of proof, for accusations were not idly made, as a plaintiff stood to suffer the same penalties as the defendant, if he could not prove his case.[22] By the thirteenth century, plaintiffs more commonly presented documentary evidence to prove their cases. But in all trials, the testimony of witnesses remained paramount. As in modern litigation strategies, the parties to a suit undermined the testimony of witnesses, for instance, by pointing out that a witness was a relative of either the plaintiff or the defendant, and the evidence obtained from that witness should be omitted from the case. The testimony of witnesses had to be independently corroborated (thus cross-examination of witnesses was not permitted, so as not to suggest certain testimony through questioning). Special officers of the court conducted the questioning but the questions themselves were submitted to these officers by the parties to the suit.[23] Corroborated testimony was taken to be *ipso facto* true.[24] After both parties had concluded their arguments, the case was decided by either a judge or a jury. The decision was read to the parties to the suit, and if no appeal was made, the judgment was final and executed immediately.[25]

Of course, the law of persons was a central preoccupation of medieval law. Principally, that law enumerated the privileges that nobles enjoyed but were denied to other freemen, not to mention the servile, like serfs and slaves. Nobles suffered lesser penalties when they committed the same crimes as commoners; for instance, a commoner suffered loss of limb for unprovoked assault upon his lord but a noble suffered loss of fief.[26] Denied to commoners, the law permitted private warfare to nobles, as a means of self-defense, even if they should take up arms against the king himself:

> If a baron has a liegeman and he says to him: "Come away with me, for I want to make war on my lord the king who has refused me a hearing in his court,"

the man should answer his lord this way: "Sir, I will be glad to go to find out from the king if it is the way you tell me." Then he should go to the king and say to him: "Sir, my lord has told me that you refused him a hearing in your court; for this reason I have come to you to find out the truth; for my lord has summoned me to go to war against you." And if the king says: "I will never give your lord a hearing in my court," the man should immediately return to his lord; and the lord should reimburse his expenses. And if he would not go away with him [to war], he would lose his fief as a penalty. And if the king had answered; "I will willingly give your lord a hearing in my court," the man should come back to his lord and say: "Sir, the king told me that he will willingly give you a hearing in his court;" and if the lord says: "I will never enter his court, but come away with me as I summoned you," then the man could say: "I will not go." He would not lose any part of his fief as a penalty.[27]

Nobles prized other privileges, such as the right to fish and hunt game.[28] These legal distinctions between persons characterized European law until the French Revolution.

By the time of Charlemagne's reign, the authority and ideology of the Frankish monarch had grown insofar as the conception of the ruler as the font of justice had become more common. Much of this conceptual alteration was the work of Christian clerics who portrayed the Frankish kings in images drawn from King David in the Bible, or from the example of the Emperor Constantine. For their part, many of these barbarian kings aspired to fulfill the rhetoric. The very compilation of law codes, such as the Salic under Clovis, suggests that even by turn of the sixth century Frankish monarchical ideology was headed in this direction. Even so, according to the chronicle of Fredegar, the presence of Dagobert I (629–638) created reactions that Clovis's probably would not have:

> The profound alarm that [Dagobert's] coming caused among the Burgundian bishops, magnates and others of consequence was a source of general wonder; but his justice brought great joy to the poor. On arrival at the city of Langres he gave judgement for all, rich and poor alike, with such equity as must have appeared most pleasing to God. Neither bribe nor respect of persons had any effect on him: justice, dear to the Almighty, ruled alone. Then he went to Dijon and spent some days at Saint-Jean-de-Losne, and did what he could to bring justice to his people throughout his realm. Such was his great good will and eagerness that he neither ate nor slept, lest anyone should leave his presence without having obtained justice.[29]

Thus, Merovingian kings had grown from little more than war-chiefs to kings, with the accompanying expectations of ultimate authority and supreme stewardship of peace, order, and justice.

The Twelfth-Century "Legal Revolution"

Extraordinary achievements in all the systems of law—feudal, canon, and Roman—took place in the High Middle Ages (1000–1300). Historians sometimes speak of a virtual twelfth-century "legal revolution," which had four basic features. First, Roman law was rediscovered and adapted to medieval purposes. Second, a specifically legal education, rooted in the conviction that the exercise of power should be rational and legitimate, came into being in the universities.[30] Third, that legal education created a cadre of legal professionals. Finally, new bodies of applied law were established all over Europe. The legal revolution was responsible for three changes in the legal regime. Old systems of law yielded to new systems, human juridical competence replaced reliance on divine intervention (as in the case of trials by ordeal), and clergy and laity accepted the changes.

First, the study of Roman law once again flourished in twelfth-century Latin Christendom. Advocates of imperial and royal authority sought out proof texts to support the claims of kings and emperors. The written, systematic bodies of Roman and canon law demanded well-trained, professional legal scholars. Thus, formal legal education became a prominent feature of the medieval university, in particular the University of Bologna, the most famous law school in medieval Europe. Because university students studied both bodies of law, historians speak about Romano-canonical procedure, as scholars employed insights and texts from both traditions. Roman law also came to be the conceptual framework used to sort out confusions from feudal and customary law.[31] These parallel traditions of legal reasoning medieval scholars described as the "common law" (ius commune), not to be confused with English common law.[32]

Like their theological and medical counterparts in the new medieval universities, law students studied the authoritative texts, the standard commentaries, known as the "ordinary glosses" (glossae ordinariae), and summae written on those texts by medieval scholars. The study of Roman law focused on the texts in the Corpus iuris civilis, which had been lost in western Europe until the discovery of the Codex Florentinus (now in the Laurentian Library in Florence), which preserved a copy of Justinian's code, in a south Italian library around 1050. Historians generally credit the half-legendary figure Irnerius (c. 1055–c. 1130) with the renewal of scholarly interest in Roman law. Irnerius, along with an equally mysterious scholar named Pepo, began to read Roman law in Bologna around 1100. These two figures were the first in the series of jurists who have come to be called the Glossators, from their method of reading and commenting on—known in the Middle Ages as "glossing"—the text. Irnerius had four especially gifted pupils: Bulgarus (d. 1166),

Hugo, Jacobus, and Martinus. Bulgarus was especially influential because he served as advisor to Frederick I. Other important figures in this tradition include Azo (c. 1150–1230), whose *summa* on Justinian's Code became so influential that jurists sometimes quipped that "whoever does not have Azo should not go to court."[33] Azo's student Accursius (c. 1182–1263) compiled the *glossa ordinaria* on the *Corpus iuris civilis.* Accursius's career marked the end of the classical Glossators. Roman jurists called post-glossators succeeded them. Their thought features a greater interest in applying civil law to daily legal difficulties. Of these jurists, the two most famous were Bartolus of Sassoferato (c. 1313–1357), who laid the foundations of post-glossator thought, and Baldus de Ubaldo (1327–1400).

The *Decretum* and the Decretals served as the textual authorities in canon law. Law students in the universities studied both canon and Roman law and received degrees "in both laws" (*utriusque iuris*). Neophytes listened and took notes as their professors read the authoritative texts. Professors also interrupted their readings to make comments. Advanced students debated legal issues and were expected to present the authorities that supported their side of the argument. Of course, law school graduates formed a cadre of legal professionals whose learning might find them employment in government, the church, or as legal counsel to litigants. Above all, the legal revolution made the laws more systematic.

Finally, rulers erected new systems of law during the legal revolution of the twelfth century. The prestige of Roman law meant that ordeal and compurgation yielded to new juridical procedures that weighed the testimony of witnesses or obtained the confession of the accused. Gradually, the Roman replaced customary procedures—earlier in France, much later and more slowly in Germany. For instance, both Roman and feudal law influenced the policies of Emperor Frederick I. From Bulgarus he learned the exalted legislative powers granted to the emperor in Roman imperial law, which Frederick often invoked in his disputes with the popes. Frederick also employed feudal law to reconstitute German imperial authority. Early in his reign, he attempted to bind the great princes of the empire, who had vastly increased their power as a consequence of the Investiture Controversy, to himself as feudal tenants-in-chief, that is, that the princes must acknowledge their holdings as fiefs of the crown. Frederick compensated the princes by granting them authority over the nobilities within their fiefs. He granted to his powerful cousin, Henry the Lion, royal powers within his duchy of Saxony, in exchange for Henry's support. Frederick's uncle, Henry Jasomirgott, was Henry the Lion's enemy. To placate his uncle, Frederick in 1156 created the entirely new duchy of Austria. In 1176, Henry the Lion failed to support Frederick's military campaign in Italy. The cities of the Lombard League defeated Frederick at the great Battle of Legnano. Frederick was convinced that he would have been victorious had Henry the Lion fought alongside him. He summoned Henry to Worms in January 1179 to answer for himself. Henry failed to appear, violating an essential feudal obligation. In 1180, with the support of many German nobles, he stripped Henry the Lion of titles and lands, save for those he held independently of the crown. He was exiled to the court of his father-in-law, Henry II of England, for three years.

Over time, however, the feudalization of the German territorial princes proved counterproductive to imperial government. As they consolidated control over their nobilities, the power of the princes rivaled the emperor's. The princes also found allies among the popes, who opposed imperial power as a potential threat to their rule over the church. By the end of the Middle Ages, the emperors resembled the authority that Frederick had bestowed on his tenants-in-chief—efficacious only within the territory under the direct control of the ruler.

The Law of the Fief

The legal revolution involved other systems of law as well. By the late eleventh century, a movement towards the legal systematization of personal relationships and landed possessions began to produce the feudal law. For many years, historians had located the origins of these laws in the early Middle Ages, but over the last generation scholars have pointed out that references to laws involving fiefs, along with the subordinate relations between king and nobles they imply, date from rather later periods. Before 1025, the great dynasts approached the royal family as near-equals. Renewed study of Carolingian texts, along with increased concern for peace and order, contributed to the implementation of feudal institutions and laws. In sum, feudal law meant that benefices were ultimately held through the king, and that the king was the ultimate arbiter of the law. In France, feudal laws and institutions aided the recovery of royal power. Instead of war, the great feudatories often argued their disputes in the king's court, even if the ruler was deciding a case between nobles more powerful than he (like Fulk Nerra and Odo of Blois, for instance). The mere fact of serving as judge in such cases implied royal supremacy. The church's advocacy of the Truce or Peace of God likewise worked in favor of the king. Limitations on feudal warfare inhibited the noble acquisition of territory and granted the king a monopoly on licit violence. *The Truce of God criminalized private violence, and implied that only public violence might be licit.* To be sure, the Capetian kings of France were exceedingly weak until the twelfth century. Although suzerains of all France, they controlled less territory in the kingdom than, for instance, did such barons as Fulk Nerra, whose control over Anjou was firmer than the king's over the Ile-de-France. The king was just as subject to the laws governing fiefs as every other French aristocrat, but those laws demanded that lords and vassals deal justly with each other, with a sense of fair play. Another advantage enjoyed by the king was that he figured as a major player throughout the kingdom, but the counts and dukes only in their regions. Even as early as 1122, the great feudatories of France rallied so enthusiastically around King Louis VI (1108-1137) that the more powerful German Emperor Henry V (1106-1125) abandoned his plans to invade France. Two generations later, when King Philip II (1180–1223) Augustus took the cross, he levied a tax on the whole of the French church to help pay the costs of the campaign. No other prince could do so; therefore, no other prince could exploit the resources of the entire kingdom. In the name of feudal sovereignty, Philip waged a number of wars against his troublesome vassal, the duke of Normandy, who was also King John of England. Philip was one of the best field commanders of his day, and in a series of clever campaigns which culminated in his great victory over both John and his ally Emperor Otto IV at the Battle of Bouvines (1214), he conquered most of the Plantagenet empire in France, which only a generation before had stretched from the Mediterranean to the Firth of Forth. Philip benefited as well from the extinction of a number of comital families; the feudal law said that those fiefs reverted back to the crown. While Philip lacked the resources to maintain direct control of those fiefs, he could grant them to loyalists. Thus, the land controlled by the king of France, whether directly or indirectly, increased dramatically during Philip's reign.

Of course, the recovery of French royal fortunes presented the king with new administrative challenges. When the king was only in control of the Ile-de-France, he could travel about and see to its government firsthand, but as the ruler of a region which stretched from the Mediterranean to the English channel, he needed reliable ministers. Philip created a number of government positions to serve the king outside the original royal demesne. *Prévôts* were responsible for collecting the king's revenue and managing the royal estates. They also detained suspects in criminal cases. *Baillis* were usually knights who served as royal judges. *Serjeants*, in turn, served the *baillis* and carried out their rulings. The expansion of royal power created another jurisdictional nightmare, however, as provincials claimed that royal law conflicted with customary law. Furthermore, documentary proof began to assume a greater importance in litigation.

At the same time, the king's court, called a *Parlement*, (from a "meeting of the king and his councillors," a parley, from French *parlée*) came into being. As their names suggest, both the English Parliament and the French *Parlement* originated as a king's court (remember that court had a broader meaning in the Middle Ages). Until the seventeenth century, the speaker of the English Parliament served as advisor to the king. However, the English Parliament became involved in more political issues than would the French *Parlement* because of the earlier development of the English courts. The *Parlement* was responsible for more judicial responsibilities than its English counterpart, and so never obtained the position in the government that the Parliament did in England. The feudal law influenced the constitution of the *Parlement*, for the barons demanded that they should be judged by their peers, rather than royal ministers. Thus, royal knights and diocesan clergy who had been brought up on the customary law of the Ile-de-France served on the *Parlement*'s panel of judges.

Parlements did not serve as vehicles for the dissemination of a French common law like the court of common pleas did for England. First of all, the feudal baronage of France remained much more powerful than did that of England. The power of the nobility meant that regional particularisms of all sorts remained a prominent feature of French law, government, and administration. Such particularisms were no more obvious than in the use of Roman law in the south of France, rather than the customary and feudal law of northern France.

Nor did the French Estates-General, which first met in 1302, develop into a regular deliberative body. Customary and feudal law said that rulers could not arbitrarily despoil their subjects of property, so if they wanted to expand their revenues, they would have to make a case for it, and obtain the consent of their subjects. In any event, kings collected taxes infrequently, for customary law also said that everyone should live by his own resources. The peasant survived on his hovel, but aristocrats flourished by their estates. However, the arms race of the High Middle Ages meant that even kings were short of money when they waged war, so they needed permission to levy tax (an idea also found in Magna Carta). In particular, King Philip IV (1285–1314), who called the first Estates-General, was fighting the English and the Flemish. Philip quarreled with Pope Boniface VIII (1298–1303) over the taxation of the French clergy. He called the first meeting of the Estates-General to rally the support of France against the pope. From its beginning, then, the kings called *Estates-General* when they wanted to enact legislation that nullified custom. Philip also found that new taxes were easier to collect when the taxpayers had approved them (even if grudgingly). In the *Estates-General*, the king was forced to make an argument for new initiatives. Noble status largely meant freedom from new taxes in particular and the church could be taxed (theoretically, at least) only with the permission of the pope. That left the commons to bear the brunt of the new revenues and to restrain the demands of the crown. Customary law thus ordered French society into its three traditional estates. The Third Estate—the commons—was subject to different tax laws and penal laws than were the first and second (clergy and nobility). Of course, taking formal vows officially enrolled one into the first estate. Enrollment in the second estate required an act of the king. Commoners who aspired to a noble's privileges had to purchase a *lettre d'anoblissement*. Ennoblement, in turn, required military service and a "noble income"—never defined and rarely acted upon. Nobles, in turn, fell into two categories. The old nobility (nobles of the sword) occupied provincial governorships and town captaincies. The new nobility (nobles of the robe) served as royal financial officers and judges. In 1484, Charles VIII (1483–1498) ordered his bailiffs and seneschals to assemble the clergy, nobles, and commons in their *baillages* to elect one deputy from each estate, "who should carry to the Estates-General the corporate *doléances* [grievances] of their *pays*."[34] Each of the estates had one collective vote. The Estates met only when summoned and the rebellion of the Jacquerie in 1353 suggested to the kings that commoners could not be trusted as partners in government. The kings of France also distrusted the nobility, especially after noble alliances with England during the Hundred Years' War and the Wars of Religion from 1562–1589. For their part, the nobles were antagonistic to alterations of custom and new taxes and so royal calls for an Estates-General alarmed them. As a result, no Estates-General met from 1614 until 1789. Instead, French royal apologists employed the arguments of the Roman jurists, and argued that reason and the common good served as restraints upon royal power. Thus did the elements of both feudal and Roman jurisprudence affect the development of administration and constitutional law in the kingdom of France.

The Law of the Medieval Catholic Church

From the eleventh century on, the Catholic Church was in the vanguard of the legal history of medieval Europe. Like its Jewish antecedent, the Christian religion was legalistic from the beginning and the first compilations of canon (church) law followed soon after Constantine's edict of toleration in 313. In the eleventh century, the law of the church came to be the chief vehicle whereby a great reform of Western Christian life and worship was enacted.

The series of invasions that beset Western Christian civilization between 850 and 950 likewise affected the church, whose defense became the responsibility of local nobles. Their protection often came at a price in lands and income; indeed, the early Carolingians themselves had seized church property. Monasteries, in particular, accepted advocates (*avoués*, in French), lords who pledged to protect the monks from personal harm, and their property from destruction or theft. The advocates would often help themselves to a portion of the monastery's income. Contrary to the Benedictine Rule (perhaps the most widespread organizational guidelines for European monasteries), some lords assumed the position of abbot. Thus did lay lords come to dominate many monasteries, which were integral parts of Frankish society.

In addition to religious houses, numerous diocesan churches were also under the thumb of lay lords. Old German custom required that local nobles provide sacred space, on their own lands, for worship. When the Germans became Christians, they no longer built temples but churches. As in pagan days, however, the relationship between that church and its founding family continued, generally through rights of presentment, also known as the *advowson*. Advowson was the right of the founder and his descendants to choose the priest who would serve as rector of the church, although of course only the bishop could ordain that candidate. The same principles extended to the rank of bishop. Like Constantine, the Christian German kings much preferred that bishops support their aims. More than either Constantine or Charlemagne, the German kings of the tenth and eleventh centuries cultivated an ideology of imperial theocracy, whose best example was Emperor Henry III (1039–1056). Like most medieval rulers, Henry traveled about his realm to show his power and live off of his landed possessions. As he traveled about, peasants brought the sick, in hopes that the touch of Henry's gown would work a cure. Henry was also committed to the renewal of the church. He deposed several popes and once put a cousin, Leo IX (1049–1054), upon the chair of St. Peter. For the rest of his pontificate, Leo worked with his imperial kinsman to reform the Western church.

Indeed, by the mid-eleventh century support for church reform had gained great momentum. Many of the early reformers were monks, who had come to believe that lay domination had infested the church with three great abuses. The first of these was clerical marriage, which damaged the church's pastoral effectiveness in several ways. First, by law sons inherited the benefices of their fathers but did so whether or not they possessed any real zeal for service to the church. Inheritance of church offices also threatened to alienate church lands. If the same family collected the income from the same lands over several generations, the difference between owners and users could easily get confused. Another reason for the insistence on celibacy was that, since antiquity, sexual relations were believed to render a man unfit to celebrate the sacraments. The church fathers preferred, but did not insist upon, a celibate priesthood.

The reformers also attacked simony, which was the buying and selling of church offices. Simony was clearly condemned in Acts 8.9–25. However, agreement on what constituted simony in the medieval church was often difficult. Germanic custom required that the granting of benefices be reciprocated by gift-giving. Thus, bishops and abbots in the German Empire often gave the emperor a handsome return for having appointed them to their offices. The reformers argued that rulers distributed episcopacies and abbacies in expectation of these return gifts, rather than for the saintliness and pastoral effectiveness of the beneficiaries.

Finally, lay investiture also attracted the opprobrium of the reformers. Simply put, lay investiture was royal appointment of bishops, who were described as having been "invested with ring and staff"—the symbols of their pastoral office. Reformers believed that lay investiture made the church an instrument of imperial or royal policy, when she should be the instrument of human salvation through her administration of the sacraments. Rulers elected bishops with political, rather than holy, aims in mind. The church, however, received great incomes from her vast landed possessions, along with the soldiers who could be paid from those possessions. Bishops often sent the kings warriors supported by church estates. Kings understood that their authority depended upon the loyalty of their bishops and abbots.

The reformers thus aimed to restore the liberty of the church (*libertas ecclesiae*) from lay control. While reformers employed many strategies, the law was paramount. Medieval canon law, which the Catholic Church followed until 1917, survives in two great compilations. The Italian monk Gratian compiled the first, called the *Decretum*, sometime around 1140. Gratian's work, in turn, depended on earlier texts, in particular, that of Burchard, bishop of Worms (c. 965–1025), and Ivo, bishop of Chartres (c. 1040–1115). Gratian's *Decretum* is divided into four sections:

Distinctions (*distinctiones*), of which there are 101, concerning the sources of the law, ordination, the life of the clerical order, and church organization (citation D.1c.1).

Causes (*causae*), of which there are 36, each divided into questions (*quaestiones*), usually about hypothetical legal issues (citation C.1 q.1 c.1).

Treatise on penance (*De penitentia*, citation De pen. d.1 c.1).

De consecratione, five distinctions on the sacraments and worship (citation De cons. D.1.c.1).

Distributed throughout the *Decretum* are the decrees of church councils, biblical texts, excerpts from the church Fathers, early papal decrees and letters, as well as excerpts from Roman law. Essentially, Gratian tracked down the legal materials relevant to the important canonistic issues of the era. The full title explains his purposes: *Concordantia discordantium canonum*—the concordance of discordant canons. The *Decretum*, then, stands as a great display of systematic canon law.

The second volume of medieval canon law is contained in the Decretals, which consists of the following compilations:

Decretals of Pope Gregory IX (1227–1241), known also in Latin as the *Liber extra* ("extra book" to the Decretum) containing conciliar and papal decrees dating from about 1179 until the promulgation of this collection in 1234; subdivided into five books (citation X 1.1.1).

Liber sextus, the "sixth book" of Pope Boniface VIII (1294–1303), adds conciliar and papal decrees issued up to the promulgation of this compilation in 1298 (citation VI1.1.1).

Clementinae or "Clementines," named for Pope Clement V (1305–1314), which adds more such material up to 1317 (citation Clem. 1.1.1).

Extravagantes or "more such bits of legislation," promulgated by Pope John XXII (1316–1334) in 1327 (citation Extrav. 1.1.1).

Extravagantes communes, published in 1500, which contains other, early fourteenth-century papal decrees (citation Extrav. comm. 1.1.1).

Standard commentaries (known as the "ordinary gloss"—*glossa ordinaria*, in Latin), generally accompanied the texts themselves in manuscripts of the *Decretum*, the *Liber extra*, and the *Liber sextus*. A canonist (jurist of the canon law) known as Joannes Teutonicus (John the German, c. 1170–1245) wrote the commentary on the *Decretum* in the early 1200s. The Italian jurist Bernard of Parma (d. 1266) composed the gloss on the *Liber extra* in the 1260s. Joannes Andraea (Giovanni d'Andrea, c. 1270–1348) wrote the gloss on the *Liber sextus* in the early 1300s. By the end of the Middle Ages, a veritable legion of other formidable figures contributed their own commentaries on the canon law, which was thus "formed from authoritative text and academic commentary."[35]

Recurrent Issues in Canon Law

Numerous authorities over the centuries of Christian history considered the election of worthy bishops and priests. These authorities began with the Scriptures themselves: "A presbyter must be irreproachable, married once, the father of children who are believers and are known not to be wild and insubordinate"

(Ti 1.6), on the theory that a man who failed to raise his children in the virtues and the Christian faith could not be trusted to shepherd the Lord's flock at all well. Above all, he should be a man of virtue, prayer, and good works: "[He] should . . . be hospitable and a lover of goodness; steady, just, holy, and self-controlled" (Ti 1.8). For the high medieval reformers, however, he must also be free of domination by others. They took as precedent a ruling of Pope St. Leo I (440–461): "None of the bishops shall presume to ordain the slave of another to the priesthood."[36] Leo's text suggested later impediments to ordination. A ninth-century Spanish council included serfs and *coloni* as likewise unworthy of priesthood because of their unfree legal status.[37] Because illegitimate children lacked the protection of the laws, they too could not be ordained.[38] Other impediments included great birth defects and epilepsy, as they were believed to hinder the pastoral effectiveness of those afflicted by them.[39] There was no "right" to ordination.

In addition to personal fitness, the church reformers insisted that the pastoral effectiveness of the church depended upon her freedom, which meant that elections of bishops and popes take place without undue lay influence, and that priests and other clerics must freely choose to serve God and His church. Thus, the canon law must establish procedures for the free, canonical election of bishops. A decree of Pope Calixtus II (1119–1124) laid down that "no one is a bishop without canonical election."[40] As with most of their other initiatives, the reformers took as their model the earliest church (*ecclesia primitiva*)—the church of the apostles. The reformers argued that canon law must reestablish what the early church had observed in electing successors to the apostles. The purpose of reform, then, was to restore and recover what had been lost over the centuries. The reformers used scholarship to make their arguments. They consulted ancient and early medieval authorities in support of their vision for the government of the church.

A text attributed to Pope Leo I enumerated three requirements for canonical election of bishops: "In no way should a candidate for bishop be accepted, who has not been elected by the clergy, acclaimed by the people, and consecrated by the bishops, along with the metropolitan, of the province."[41] The canonical, valid election of a bishop, then, demanded the approval of clergy and laity, but in unequal proportion, for the people were often mistaken, as in a rescript attributed to Pope Celestine I (422–432): "If [the people] do not know [something], we ought to teach, not follow, the people, lest they prescribe that which should or should not be, nor ought we to approve consent in this way."[42] Furthermore, bishops should be selected "from the deacons and the priests," that is, the clergy, rather than the laity.[43] Pope Lucius III (1144–1145) confirmed these canons: "No one [shall be a bishop] in a church, where two or three brothers shall be assembled, unless he is chosen by the canons of the church."[44] Still, the reformers could not entirely eliminate lay influence over episcopal appointments. Rulers traditionally played an important role in church appointments, and the theory of popular sovereignty implicit even in the Roman imperial tradition meant that rulers received their power from the people, and so the wishes of the ruler had to be taken into consideration. Thus, the church law grudgingly conceded that princes had the right of selection in cases where bishops had been deposed because of heresy, which had happened numerous times in the late Roman Empire.[45]

The pope, of course, was an exception for he was not only a bishop but the universal pontiff. At the Council of Rome in 1059, during the minority of Emperor Henry IV, Pope Nicholas II (1059–1061) famously proclaimed: "Since the Apostolic See is superior to all the churches in the world it can have no metropolitan set over it, and so the cardinal bishops who raise the chosen pontiff to the summit of apostolic dignity undoubtedly act in place of a metropolitan."[46] This decree was unprecedented, in that no role for the Christian Emperor was recognized at all, and so it represented a break from a tradition that dated to Constantine himself. In 1179, Lateran III formally laid out the protocols for the election of popes.[47] That council declared that a two-thirds majority of the Roman cardinals validly elected a pope.

The papal primacy over the whole Christian church was taken to rest on the authority of Scripture: "I say to you, you are Peter, and upon this rock I will build my church, and the gates of Hell shall not prevail against it" [Mt 16.18]. Another Gospel text was invoked as well: "I have prayed for you, Peter, that your faith may not fail" [Lk 23.32]. As in the ancient tradition of Judaeo-Christianity, the law served as commentary and elucidation of what the sacred texts upheld, as in another decree of Nicholas II: "The Roman church establishes the dignities of all other churches of every rank, the eminence of each patriarch, the primacy of metropolitans, the sees of bishops. But she herself was founded and built on the rock of the dawning faith by Him who conferred simultaneously on the blessed key-bearer of eternal life the rights of a heavenly and an earthly empire."[48] Since Christ Himself had established the Petrine primacy, no one could question it: "No mortal shall presume to rebuke [the pope's] faults, for he who is to judge all is to be judged by no one, unless he is found straying from the faith."[49] While the pope's authority rests on no hint of popular sovereignty, his authority lasted only as long as he taught orthodox Christian doctrine.

Very important developments in sacramental theology accompanied the church reform movements of the High Middle Ages. During this period, definitive teachings on the sacraments were worked out. The sacrament of baptism, of course, had vast legal as well as theological consequences, since that sacrament made the baptized a member of a huge, transnational corporate body. In keeping with the era's insistence on the Christian life as a life of liberty, church law conceded that forced baptisms did not lead to salvation, and that Jews, for instance, ought not to be forced into baptism.[50] What, then, of the baptism of infants? For years, scholars had believed that until the fourth century, most baptisms had been conferred on adults. Recent scholarship, however, suggests that infant baptisms were the norm much earlier than that, as Christian parents sought the sacrament for their newborns. Since infant baptism constituted the practice of the inerrant universal church, how did reformers confront this seeming contradiction, a difficulty that heretics had raised as well? In response, church law recalled the singularity of baptism's role in human redemption.[51] Since God desired the salvation of each and every human being, and since baptism cancelled original sin, intent, while necessary for adults, could be waived for infants.[52] Baptism conferred an indelible mark on the baptized that even apostasy could not erase.[53] The valid baptism of infants, then, did demand right intention, but on the minister's part, not the child's. The administrator of the sacrament did not even have to get the child's name correct, but only his or her sex. In any event, the *rigor iuris* should be relaxed to the benefit of the one baptized.[54] This principle came in very handy, as the canonists had to account for differing traditions with regard to the administration of the sacrament. Some churches baptized by aspersion (a sprinkling of holy water); others by immersion (the plunging of the whole body into a pool of water)—they accepted the validity of both. Although in general the canonists dismissed the baptism of a dead body, some canonists allowed for special circumstances.[55]

Marriage and Monastic Vows

Liberty was also the basic concept in the canonists' teachings about matrimony and the monasteries. In the Middle Ages, almost every adult was either married or a member of a religious order; in either case, vows—a promise made to both God and neighbor—admitted the new spouses, monks, and nuns to a holy way of life. The making of vows had also wide-ranging legal ramifications. Both Scripture and tradition taught that matrimony was holy, for Jesus worked his first miracle at the wedding celebration in Cana [Jn 2.1–11], and St. Paul offered a series of rules for married Christians to observe [1 Cor 7.1–6 and Eph 5.21–33]. Among the church fathers, St. John Chrysostom (c. 347–407) and St. Augustine (354–430) taught that matrimony conferred numerous spiritual blessings. The early church, however, had no marriage ritual. Roman law said little about private matters, and since marriage was a private matter, no public ritual was necessary to contract a marriage. During the early medieval centuries, however, Christians began to solemnize their nuptial unions with sacred rites. In a letter written in 866, Pope Nicholas I (858–867) described the Latin rite of marriage:

> Our people, both men and women, when they make the marriage contracts do not wear on their heads bands of gold, of silver, or of any metal. After the betrothals, which are a promise of future marriage, with the consent of those who have made them and of those under whose authority they stand, certain agreements are struck. After the groom has betrothed the bride through a ring of fidelity which he puts as a pledge on her finger, and after the groom has given to her the dowry upon which both have agreed together with the written instrument from both sides, then, immediately or after a suitable interval, lest it be presumed that such an act was done before the legal age, both are brought to the marriage vows. And first the vows are taken in the church of the Lord with offerings, which they ought to offer to God through the hands of the priest. Thus finally they are given the blessing and the celestial veil.[56]

The exchange of vows closed a long ritual of preparation for marriage. The preparatory period was designed to ensure that both partners were not acting impetuously, but were mature enough to pledge fidelity to God and each other.

Twelfth-century theologians and canonists systematized sacramental theology. They officially accepted matrimony as one of the seven sacraments, and addressed the question of what constituted valid marriage. While some thinkers, like Gratian, believed that consummation validated a marriage, the consensus opinion essentially adopted the view expressed in Roman law: "Marriages should be free," and so, "no one is to be compelled to marry."[57] The canon law merely required that the bride and groom utter a formula of common consent to the nuptial union, such as "I accept you unto myself."[58] The insistence that the commitment to marriage be made freely surfaced in numerous marriage cases, such as the following:

> Coming to us, G., the bringer of the present case, revealed to us by his account, that in his house he received a certain woman, from whom he had offspring, and to whom in the presence of many he gave his faith, that he would take her as his wife. But meanwhile, he spent the night at the house of his neighbor, whose daughter slept with him that night. The father of the girl, coming across them together in one bed, forced the man to betroth himself to her through the words of present consent. Having been recently brought before us, he has consulted us on which of them he ought rather to stay with.

Because truly by no means has it become known to us whether after the manifest pledge of faith he knew the first person, therefore we hand him over to
you, to the extent that you inquire diligently into the truth of the matter,
and, if you shall have found out that he knew the first person after the manifest pledge of faith, make him remain with her; but if you find that, being in
a position to settle into the role of constant husband (*and not being forced by
fear*), he contracted himself to her, make him cling to the second woman as
his wife.[59]

Medieval Christian teachings on matrimony revolutionized families. The insistence on the consent of the partners alone placed limitations on the ability of parents (especially fathers), lords, and even the church herself, to interfere with the marriages of willing adult men and women. Although
marriages continued to be arranged and negotiated, a refusal on the part of
either the prospective bride or groom would invalidate the union. In particular, "the Church's doctrine was a damaging blow to paternal authority
within the medieval household, and by itself assured that the medieval family could never develop into a true patriarchy. The Church had been traditionally wary of the claims of the family over its offspring, which might well
conflict with the claims of God. Its teaching on marriage gave practical, powerful expression to this ancient suspicion."[60] Indeed, according to Christian
teaching, husband and wife were equals, since the same sexual ethics were
enjoined on both sexes. That equality extended to numerous other endeavors as well. For instance, canon law commanded that married crusaders must
receive the permission of their wives before they could "accept the cross."
Spouses could also recall their partners from the religious life, which was permitted only if *both* desired to enter religion, like Abelard and Heloise.[61] In
keeping with the Gospel injunction against divorce, legal separations were
available only in the cases of cruelty, heresy, or adultery. Divorce or annul-
ment could be obtained on the grounds of consanguinity or affinity, but
rarely were these invoked to invalidate a marriage.[62]

Initiation as a monk or nun also required the making of vows. The monastic vows of conversion, stability, and obedience had been set down in the Rule
of St. Benedict.[63] The law of the church accepted no compulsion into the
monastic life: "Let no one be tonsured, unless of legitimate age and acting of
his own free will."[64] The canons thus reflected the monastic reform movements
of the day, in particular the Cistercians, who refused to accept oblates, who
were very young boys given to monasteries to be brought up, most of whom
would remain in the monastery after they had reached the age of majority. Just
as divorce was forbidden to spouses, canon law prohibited a monk from leaving his monastery, unless he wished to join a stricter monastic observance.[65]

Pope Innocent III and the Principle of Subsidiarity

As heads of the church, the popes assumed leadership of the high medieval reform movement. Their advocacy of reform made them the enemies of the German emperors, whose rule in the tenth and eleventh centuries depended upon imperial allies among the German episcopate. The government of no other kingdom in Latin Christendom was as inextricably interwoven with the church as that of the German Empire, for reasons that date back into the early Middle Ages. The reign of Charlemagne, of course, had resurrected the imperial dignity in the West after a hiatus of three hundred years. After Charlemagne died, the imperial title fell to one or another of his descendants for several generations, only to disappear again in 924. The king of Germany, Otto I of Saxony, was named emperor again in 962. In the cases of both Charlemagne and Otto, the consecration and anointing of the pope conferred the imperial authority. Since investitures became the chief contested issue between the popes and the emperors, the long conflict between them has been named the Investiture Controversy. The tensions between papacy and empire continued long after the Investiture Controversy had been settled.

The question then ensued about the relationship between the empire and the papacy. Did the pope's consecration mean that the emperor was subordinate to the pope? Or was the pope merely confirming what the candidate already possessed? How did the authorities of pope and emperor interrelate? For that matter, what of the competing claims of the papacy and other secular authorities in Christian Europe?

The answers to all these questions got more complicated owing to the victory of the popes in the Investiture Controversy. Until about 1100, the relationship between bishops and rulers followed the traditions set in place back during the reign of Constantine. Bishops were a sort of imperial magistrate, and thus they owed loyalty to a king or emperor more powerful than themselves. The ruler expected no opposition to his policies from the bishops, who by and large resisted only a ruler's theological positions, if those were heretical. Everyone knew that making a public enemy of the ruler was asking for a lot of trouble, so generally bishops came from high-ranking noble families allied (or at least indifferent) to the ruler.

The Investiture Controversy changed all this. Antagonism replaced the cooperation characteristic of relations between church and state in late antiquity and the early Middle Ages. The emergence of the church's power in the Middle Ages quite naturally introduced entirely new questions into the workings of governments and the law, as both the civil authority and the religious authority claimed powers over the lives of men and women, and the possession of property. Could their jurisdictions be sorted out? In a series of decretals, Pope Innocent III (1198–1216) explained the relative jurisdictions of the pope and the princes.

Innocent may well have been the youngest man ever elected pope. Lothario dei Segni was only thirty-seven years old when he was chosen to succeed to the chair of St. Peter. He was probably the most powerful pope in history, as he managed to bend each of Western Christendom's monarchs to his will. Innocent became embroiled in several controversies during his pontificate. One involved the succession to the German Empire. In 1197, Emperor Henry VI of Hohenstaufen died without a son to succeed him. His brother, Philip, inherited the Hohenstaufen claim to rule. As far as Innocent was concerned, Philip promised disaster for the church, for he already possessed Sicily and southern Italy. Should he become emperor, the Hohenstaufens would surround the papacy. Innocent therefore supported the claim of Otto of Brunswick, a Welf, the longtime rivals of the emperors. Henry's young son, named Frederick, Innocent took as his ward—Innocent's strategy being that Otto would rule until his death, which would give the popes time to sunder the dynastic alliance between the empire and southern Italy. Frederick would then rule after Otto's demise.

One question was, of course, whether the pope had any right to thus interfere in the imperial succession. Innocent proclaimed his reasoning for his actions in the decretal *Venerabilem*:

> We do indeed acknowledge, as we should, that the princes, to whom this belongs by right and ancient custom, have the right and power to elect a king who is afterwards to be promoted emperor; and especially so since this right and power came to them from the apostolic see which transferred the Roman empire from the Greeks to the Germans in the person of the great Charles. But the princes should acknowledge, and indeed they do acknowledge, that right and authority to examine the person elected as king, who is to be promoted to the imperial dignity, belong to us who anoint, consecrate and crown him; for it is regularly and generally observed that the examination of a person pertains to the one to whom the laying-on of hands belongs. If the princes elected as king a sacrilegious man or an excommunicate, a tyrant, a fool or a heretic, and that not just by a divided vote but unanimously, ought we to anoint, consecrate and crown such a man? Of course not.[66]

The pope had no role in the election of the German king. That authority rested with Germany's princes. But since the pope anointed the emperor, he possessed the power to approve whomever they elected. The pope could not in good conscience anoint a madman or a heretic. Neither could he anoint a "sacrilegious man," a rather more plastic label that might serve the pope's purposes very well. In any event, Philip's assassination in 1208 terminated the dispute to the imperial succession.

Innocent also intervened in a war between King Philip II Augustus of France and King John of England (1199–1216), who were contesting possession of the duchy of Normandy. Philip claimed that John had been an unfaithful vassal, and so was trying to take possession of Normandy by conquest. Innocent attempted to broker an agreement between John and Philip. At Philip's instigation, the bishops of France protested that the pope had no right to intervene in a dispute over a fief. Innocent replied with the decretal *Novit*:

> Let no one suppose that we wish to diminish or disturb the jurisdiction or power of the king when he ought not to impede or restrict our jurisdiction and power. Since we are insufficient to exercise all our own jurisdiction why should we want to usurp another's? But the Lord says in the Gospel, *if thy brother shall offend against thee, go, and rebuke him between thee and him alone* (Mt 18.15). . . . We do not intend to judge concerning a fief, judgment on which belongs to [the king] . . . but to decide concerning a sin, of which the judgment undoubtedly belongs to us, and we can and should exercise it against anyone.[67]

Innocent here first stated that the possessors of authority ought to respect their jurisdictions, and he had no intention of interfering with feudal law or a feudal court (which had already ruled against John). As a priest, however, the pope was obliged to offer paternal correction to sinners (another very plastic formulation). In this case, he was carrying out his pastoral mission, for the fate of souls was at stake. In the end, the supreme court of war decided the possession of Normandy. Philip defeated John.

In the decretal *Per venerabilem*, Pope Innocent clarified the pope's authority relative to that of princes other than kings and emperors. In 1202, Count William of Montpellier petitioned the pope to legitimize his bastard children. No one questioned whether the pope could legitimize children for the purposes of ordaining them priests, but William asked Innocent to legitimize them in the secular sphere as well, so that they could inherit his titles and estates, a power exercised until then only by kings. Furthermore, Innocent had already legitimized two sons of King Philip II. The pope's reply must have disappointed William:

> That the Apostolic See has full power in the matter seems clear from the fact that, having examined various cases, it has given dispensations to some illegitimate sons . . . legitimizing them for spiritual functions so that they could be promoted to be bishops. From this it is held to be more likely and reputed to

be more credible that it is able to legitimize children for secular functions, especially if they acknowledge no superior among men who has the power of legitimizing except the Roman pontiffs. . . . Now the king of France acknowledges no superior in temporal affairs and so, without injuring the right of anyone else, he could submit himself to our jurisdiction and did so. It seemed to some indeed that he could perhaps have granted the dispensation himself, not as a father to his sons but as a prince to his subjects. But you know that you are subject to others and so you cannot submit yourself to us in this matter without injuring them unless they give consent.[68]

Innocent refused on the grounds that to grant William's request would damage King Philip's authority within the kingdom of France on a matter of secular law. Innocent then would be challenging the king's authority over his subjects. Still, Innocent could have legitimized William's children had the king agreed, so the pope maintained that he had the authority, but in this case he had not the will. In the decree *Licet,* Innocent admitted other cases wherein the church could have no jurisdiction.

If it happens that laymen of Vercelli have obtained letters from the Apostolic See on matters which pertain to secular jurisdiction, we command that you adjudge them by our authority to be void and of no effect, provided that the consuls and commune will do full justice to the plaintiffs in a secular trial.[69]

Even with letters from the pope, laymen must submit to the justice of secular courts in secular matters.

These decrees of Innocent III remained important for Catholic thinking about government and society. They anticipated what later generations came to call the principle of subsidiarity, which Pius XI (1922–1939) defined thus in his encyclical *Quadragesimo anno:* "A community of a higher order should not interfere in the internal life of a community of a lower order, depriving the latter of its functions, but rather should support it in case of need and help to co-ordinate its activity with the activities of the rest of society, always with a view to the common good."[70] Thus, higher jurisdictions could take action in lower, if the lower failed in an issue of justice. If the lower could manage on its own, the higher should refrain from action. Once again, the medieval canonists provided for the common good through their advocation of liberty.

The "Wretched Poor"
At the onset of the thirteenth century, then, several formidable systems of law and parallel jurisdictions had established themselves in Latin Christendom. The jurists—both civil and canonistic—sorted out what actions and

procedures pertained to the various courts. Marriage, of course, resided safely and unquestionably under the jurisdiction of the church. In contrast, secular courts wielded jurisdiction over such malefactions as arson and murder. In the Byzantine Empire, where the ruler presided over both the church and the state, civil and canon law were almost synonymous. The Emperor Justinian had declared blasphemy a secular crime, since blasphemy was the cause of earthquake, famine, and plague.[71] In Latin Christendom, however, the Investiture Controversy demanded that sharper distinctions between the secular and canon laws be made. At the same time, the various laws and jurisdictions had their hands in the same legal pie. Many cases and persons might be in the legal "gray area," with nightmarish jurisdictional confusions. Heresy cases, for instance, were tried in ecclesiastical courts, but in capital cases the secular authorities carried out sentences, because canon law forbade churchmen from taking lives. Criminous clerks occasioned many a dispute between rulers and the church—should clerks accused of crime be tried in secular or canonical courts? Lay criminals had no such options, and so cases of criminous clerks raised the specter of injustice. Through ecclesiastical courts, criminous clerks would almost certainly receive a lighter sentence than a secular court would hand down. Furthermore, such trials pitted the authority of the church against secular jurisdictions.

In *Licet*, Innocent III claimed for the church courts an appellate secular jurisdiction:

> If those who have taken their cases before the consuls feel themselves oppressed in any way, they are permitted to appeal to you [the bishop of Vercelli] for a hearing, as has been the custom, or to me if they prefer. This is especially so when the empire is vacant so that those who are oppressed in the courts of their superiors cannot appeal to a secular judge. If there is reasonable cause of suspicion against the consuls they shall be accused before mutually selected arbitrators and the grounds of suspicion investigated. If they prove just, recourse is to be had to you or to me for justice.[72]

The church, of course, traditionally served as the protector of the vulnerable—especially orphaned children and widows. In *Licet*, Innocent taught that the church's solicitude for what later canonists called "the wretched poor" (*miserabiles personae*) created an appellate jurisdiction for church courts.[73] In promulgating *Licet*, of course, Innocent honored ancient legal traditions and the authoritative texts of Judaeo-Christianity. Long before the compilation of the Scriptures, Hammurabi's law singled out widows and orphans as in need of the special protection of the law. The Old Testament portrayed Yahweh as the impartial Judge of the Universe, but also the special protector of defenseless women and children: "For the Lord, your God, is the God of gods, the Lord of lords, the great God, mighty and awesome, who has no favorites, accepts no bribes; who executes justice for the orphan and the widow" (Dt 10.17–18). The earliest church fathers understood the scriptural injunction perfectly well. Shortly before his martyrdom (c. 115), St. Ignatius of Antioch urged St. Polycarp to "take care that widows are not neglected; next to the Lord, be yourself their guardian."[74] Early medieval canon law was especially concerned about the vulnerability of widows and children in a time of war; they were declared to be under the protection of the church during open hostilities, as any harm done to them would merit excommunication.[75] Thus, early canon law commanded bishops to protect them, and implored secular authorities to join the bishops in this charitable endeavor.[76] Church authorities believed so strongly in the church's solicitude for widows and orphans that the law allowed clerics to serve as legal guardians for orphans, an important exception to the general tendency of the canon law to separate church personnel from the laity, in particular from the responsibility of raising children, a responsibility the reformers deemed essential to the laity, but a hindrance to the clergy.[77]

Of course, such laws complicated judicial procedures. A claim to the status of *miserabiles personae* might circumvent the law, rather than advance the cause of justice, as in a case involving Pope Gregory IX. A decretal of that pope considered a widow who, claiming that she was poor, sought papal help in recovering goods she had lost. The papal letters were revoked when she was discovered to have been a wealthy noble.[78] Medieval jurists, both civil and canon, were fully aware of possible abuses. The civil jurists, however, helped only a little. In his famous commentary on the Codex, the Roman jurist Azo (c. 1150–1250) defined *miserabiles personae* as "all those whom nature moves us to pity."[79] The advantages of flexibility that such a vague formulation provided were nullified by the procedural difficulties raised therein. Even if the understanding of *miserabiles personae* was limited to children whose parents had perished, noble children, who had many powerful relatives to defend their interests, would still be included. Even the orphans of kings, however, might need protection against rapacious uncles. The law required a formulation that would meet the requirements of charity, justice, and practicality. The canonists ultimately agreed that fatherless children should be considered *miserabiles personae*, but that only the poor or aggrieved could appeal decisions of secular courts to the church courts. Pope Innocent IV (1243–1254) added other deserving persons to the list of *miserabiles personae*: lepers, merchants, and pilgrims.[80]

The canonists also decided that being a *miserabile persona* was a necessary, but not sufficient, condition for making such appeals. The wealthy must also prove that they had suffered *ex defectu justiciae*, "from a defect of justice," by which they meant that the secular court of first instance committed a procedural violation. The glossator of the *Liber sextus*, the lay canonist Joannes Andraea, taught that a defect of justice resulted when (1) no secular judge had heard the case, (2) the competence or impartiality of the judge was suspect, and (3) the judge had refused to do justice.[81]

The influence of the canons on the law's subsequent treatment of the legally disadvantaged cannot be exaggerated. The conviction that appellate courts and jurisdictions protect the powerless and politically marginalized has ever since figured prominently in Western jurisprudence, and no more so than in American civil rights cases such as the landmark Supreme Court decision in *Brown vs. Board of Education* in 1954. At the same time, the principles of subsidiarity figured into the deliberations of the medieval canonists. If a secular court had in fact administered justice, church courts had no reason to nullify its decision.

Medieval Poor Law

In addition to their concerns for the poor in the courts, the canonists thought and wrote often about alleviating their suffering owing to lack of food, clothing, and shelter. Once again, the canonists depended upon the Scriptures and the Fathers, who implored worshippers of the Christian Trinity to aid the poor.[82] Among the church Fathers, John Chrysostom, Ambrose of Milan (c. 339–397), and Augustine were influential. Chrysostom, an Antiochene who became bishop of Constantinople around the year 400, taught that Christians were bound to aid anyone who came to them for money and food. Ambrose, who had a long career in civil service before he became a churchman, argued for discernment, because giving alms to conmen deprived the truly poor of help they really needed: "Since there are plenty of people who solicit help by behaving deceitfully and feigning hardship, mercy ought to flow more generously where the legitimacy of the cause is obvious."[83] He also taught that every bishop should set aside a fourth part (not necessarily one-fourth) of his income for poor relief.[84] A number of early church councils and popes echoed Ambrose's recommendations: "Bishops, insofar as they are able, ought to provide food and clothing to the poor and infirm who, *because of disability*, are unable to work with their hands."[85] Anyone who could work, then, had little claim to the relief others might offer. In one of his letters, Pope Gregory I (590–604) scolded Althelm, bishop of Naples, for attending too much to his boats, "so much so that neither his church nor the monasteries, nor his laymen and suffering poor feel the support of his love to-wards them . . . he should be intent on defending the poor with discretion."[86] Ambrose's pupil in things religious, Augustine, likewise argued for discern-ment between the deserving and undeserving poor: "The church ought not to provide for a man who is able to work . . . for strong men, sure of their food without work, often do neglect justice."[87] The scope of Augustine's influence established Ambrose's as the standard view.

Indeed, the medieval canonists employed an impressive sophistication to the subject of poor relief. They further articulated the differences between voluntary and involuntary poverty, for monks and nuns over the centuries had willingly become poor to imitate Christ: "They venerate poverty, not the penury of the idle and negligent, but a poverty directed by the necessity of the will and sustained by the thoroughness of faith, and approved by divine love."[88] The new mendicant (begging) orders of the early thirteenth century increased the ranks of the voluntary poor. While their critics argued that the friars' adoption of voluntary poverty deprived the truly poor of aid, the Fran-ciscans could quote from their great founder himself: "I have worked with my hands and I choose to work, and I firmly wish that all my brothers should work at some honorable trade. And if they do not know, let them learn."[89] Consistently, then, church law condemned idle poverty, praised voluntary poverty, and sought to relieve involuntary poverty.

The canonists keenly analyzed the moral ramifications of poverty. Squalid, involuntary poverty they deemed dehumanizing and an impediment to the cultivation of virtue. Poverty created inordinate temptations for theft and perjury, as Thomas More later affirmed in *Utopia*: "Where will you find more squabbling than among beggars?"[90] But, whereas Roman law prohibited the poor from making an accusation in court,[91] the canonist Joannes Teutonicus argued that only a person's integrity excluded anyone from the courts.[92] Poverty created its own moral handicaps but the poor might learn virtue nonetheless—a point noted by several, probably overly romantic, medieval poets, who wrote that while many of the materially comfortable failed in their duties and obligations, poor villagers rarely did. In his gloss on the *Liber sextus*, Joannes Andraea likewise rejected the exclusion of the poor from court: "Poverty is not a kind of crime."[93]

The poor were also deprived of learning and of justice. The law of the church ordered the bishops to maintain teachers for poor scholars:

> Since the church of God is bound to provide like a mother for those in want, with regard to both the things which concern the support of the body and those which lead to the progress of the soul, therefore, in order that the op-

portunity of learning to read and progress in study is not withdrawn from poor children who cannot be helped by the support of their parents, in every cathedral church a master is to be assigned some proper benefice so that he may teach the clerics of the church and the poor scholars.[94]

This decree, promulgated by Lateran III in 1179, was in keeping with the spirit of Carolingian decrees that required that cathedral churches and monasteries maintain schools. Universities, most famously that of Paris, later developed out of these cathedral schools. Lateran IV repeated this decree.[95] Church law, then, conceded that poverty impeded access to learning. The church also understood that poverty constituted a source of injustice. Pope Honorius III (1216–1227) commanded that courts should provide lawyers to those too poor to afford legal counsel themselves.[96]

Of course, any consideration of poverty required a theory of property. The canonists agreed that by natural law all property was held in common, although civil law permitted private property. The jurists' reconciliation of the natural and civil law included no condemnation of private property but rather an insistence that charity is an obligation of the natural law. As the authority of Ambrose made clear, men are the stewards, not owners, of God's abundance and generosity:

> But you say, 'Where is injustice if I diligently look after my own property without interfering with other people's?' O impudent words! You own property, you say. What? From what stores did you bring it into this world? When you came into the light, when you came forth from your mother's womb, with what resources, with what reserves did you come endowed? No one may call his own what is common, of which, if man takes more than he needs it is obtained by violence. . . . Who is more unjust, more avaricious, more greedy than a man who takes the food of the multitude not for his own use but for his abundance and luxuries? The bread that you hold back belongs to the needy, the clothes that you shut away belong to the naked, the money that you bury in the ground is the price of redeeming and freeing the wretched.[97]

Although Ambrose denounced the acquisition of surpluses as a violence, the canonists accepted that inequalities of wealth were inescapable, but almsgiving alleviated the suffering of the poor. Both justice and charity, they argued, demanded that Christians give alms to the poor. As the late thirteenth-century canonist Guido de Baysio (c. 1250–1313) remarked in his commentary on the *Decretum* (called the *Rosarium*): "Say briefly it is a precept to give alms from our superfluities and also to give to a man in extreme necessity. . . . To give alms in other circumstances is a matter of counsel."[98]

Since justice rendered to all their deserts, any lack of basic necessities was unjust and so "the poor had a right to be supported from the superfluous wealth of the community."[99] Thomas Aquinas, for instance, argued that theft in the case of need was neither a crime nor a sin, for by natural law human need made all goods possessed in common, for the sake of human dignity:

> Each one is entrusted with the stewardship of his own things, so that out of them he may come to the aid of those who are in need. Nevertheless, if the need be so manifest and urgent that it is evident that the present need must be remedied by whatever means be at hand (for instance when a person is in some imminent danger, and there is no other possible remedy), then it is lawful for a man to succor his own need by means of another's property, by taking it either openly or secretly; nor is this, properly speaking, theft or robbery.[100]

At the same time, the canonists accepted the idea that a certain rank in society was accompanied by a certain standard of living, and in no way did they argue, for instance, that the donor's standard of living must be compromised by almsgiving: "Discretion is to be observed . . . so that not everything is poured out at once, except when a man wishes to strip himself of all worldly responsibilities, nakedly to serve God," that is, become a professed religious.[101] Otherwise, as Ambrose and Augustine both agreed, immediate family had the first claim on anyone's generosity.[102]

The canonists were also interested in the effects of almsgiving on both the donor and the beneficiary, who were bound to each other in a moral economy. The canonists flatly rejected Robin Hood—a benefactor does nothing meritorious if he gives ill-gotten gains as alms. The thief's first obligation is to make restitution towards whomever he has stolen.[103] Almsgiving only benefited donors with the right intentions. The thief could not please God by donating stolen money to the poor; nor was lavish almsgiving a license to wickedness. If the purpose of almsgiving was to rid oneself of revolting beggars, no merit was thereby obtained; rather, a sin had been committed.[104]

Church law urged that donors prioritize their almsgiving. St. Augustine wrote that although most actors and prostitutes were able-bodied their frequent solicitation of alms should be refused.[105] They had no regular source of income but that was owing to their decision to follow vile, itinerant professions, rather than till fields, manufacture goods, or pasture flocks. In canons excerpted from Ambrose's De officiis, church law taught that faithful Catholics must be helped, as well as the sick and aged, and those in need through no fault of their own. Parents must be supported.[106] The canonists agreed with Ambrose and Augustine that charity begins at home, and then spreads out in concentric circles. The first responsibility was spouse and children, then parents, extended family, neighbors, and everyone else.

Otherwise, the identification of the deserving poor was vital, for "every student of poor relief administration knows that there are some cases where prompt and generous assistance does more harm than good."[107] Joannes Teutonicus, for instance, pointed out that Roman law condemned to slavery an able-bodied man who accepted public relief.[108] The canonist Rufinus's (d. 1192) thoughts are worthy of consideration:

> By all this it is shown that we ought not to show ourselves generous indiscriminately to all who come. But it should be known that in providing hospitality these four things are to be considered: The quality of the one seeking alms, the resources of the giver, the cause of the request, and the amount requested. The quality of the one asking—whether he is honest or dishonest; the resources of the one giving—whether they can suffice for all or only for some; the cause of the request—whether a man asks only for food for the love of God or says he is sent as a preacher and therefore claims a due stipend from you; the amount requested—whether it is excessive or reasonable. If the one who asks is dishonest, and especially if he is able to seek his food by his own labor and neglects to do so, so that he chooses to beg or steal, without doubt nothing is to be given to him, but he is to be corrected . . . unless perchance he is close to perishing from want, for then, if we have anything we ought to give indifferently to all such. . . . But if the one who asks is honest, you ought to give to all of this sort if the resources available suffice. . . . But if you cannot give to all asking of you then you should give first to those close to you; in this case the authorities on discrimination in giving are to be applied.[109]

Gamblers and the profligate should not be allowed to starve to death but they had only a few claims to the commonwealth's charitable giving. The canonists argued that the commonwealth was under no obligation to "enable" the squandering of necessities in wicked wastefulness. The canonists did, however, prescribe fraternal correction—what might today be called "tough love." Gamblers should never starve to death but sometimes they should go hungry.

For the canonists, then, poverty was more than a dearth of necessities and possessions. Rather, poverty amounted to a moral condition caused by scarcity. True, involuntary poverty resulted from a host of misfortunes—illness, death, handicap, crop failure, or invasion—but not from idleness or obsessions. The canonists equated the alleviation of poverty with the full restitution of human dignity—the cultivation of the virtues and endowment with the Earth's goods.

The Theory of the Corporation

Medieval canonists were, of course, preoccupied with issues concerning the government of the church.[110] They not only interpreted the sources and meaning of papal authority but of all the church's government. Indeed, they had also to think about the meaning of the word *ecclesia* (church) itself. In its original Greek, *ekklesia* referred to the Athenian assembly, where citizens debated and voted on legislation, and where some criminal cases were heard and decided, the most famous of these being the capital trial of Socrates in the *Apology* of Plato. For the canonists, however, *ecclesia* had two possible meanings, first the whole body of the faithful, second the institutional structures of the church. As lawyers and jurists, they were more concerned with the latter.

Then as today, the diocese formed the basic unit of church government. The bishop, the successor to the apostle who, by the tradition of that diocese, had introduced Christianity there, served as chief magistrate. Even from the earliest days of the church, however, the bishops had helpers in presiding over the church. Hellenized Jewish-Christians complained to the Twelve that their widows were being ignored during the distribution of the church's goods, and so the Apostles named administrators, while they attended to preaching, healing, and worship (Acts 6.1–6). For a long time, only bishops preached and celebrated the liturgy. When churches grew too large for one man to preside at all the liturgies, bishops ordained associates to confer the sacraments—priests. The first diocesan priests served as companions and servants of the bishops.

From the beginning, then, the church distinguished between her sacramental and secular responsibilities. The church's sacramental ministrations were invested primarily in the bishop, secondarily in his priests. Other church officers, who sometimes were called deacons (from the Greek for service, *diakonía*), administered the church's poor relief efforts and were responsible for maintaining church-owned lands and buildings. As the number of priests increased to meet the needs of the growing flock of the church, priests took on more such responsibilities, as for instance the maintenance of the sanctuary of the parish church. Lay officers were charged with other expenditures. Known in England as churchwardens, these officers spent the money needed to maintain the nave of the church building, as well as the money needed to buy candles, liturgical vestments, and books.

Thus did medieval clergy and laity administer the church. Of course, the bishop and his clergy formed the weightier part of this partnership. In time, a further distinction developed between the diocesan clergy, on the one hand, and the "bishop's clergy," otherwise known as the chapter, on the other. The bishop and chapter paralleled the pope and the cardinals. Like the cardinals of the Roman church, the chapter first comes into clear view in the eleventh century. That era's reformers wanted the diocesan clergy to live more like monks, with assembly for common prayer at certain times of the day. According to the Rule of St. Benedict, the monks elected their abbot. After the Investiture Controversy, canonical election of bishops took place in the chapter. Newly elected bishops were then presented to the laity for acclamation. Members of the chapter, most often drawn from prominent families, were priests called canons. Each canon generally possessed an endowment of his own; these endowments originated as pious donations granted to their predecessors in exchange for masses celebrated for the dead of a donors' family. The bishop had merely a theoretical authority over these lands and revenues, and had vaster endowments under his direct control. Again, church law said that bishops and priests served as the stewards, rather than owners, of the church's property.[111] Each diocese, then, formed the sum of the following parts: the diocese as a whole, the bishop, the chapter, the diocesan clergy, the laity. Because of these administrative structures, to say nothing of St. Paul's teaching about the mystical body of Christ (Rm 12.3–8; 1 Cor 12.12–31), as well as the unification of the community in the liturgical celebration, the canonists imaged the church as a body with many members—a corporation, a legal unity made up of a number of parts.

The juristic theory of the corporation was the contribution of two of the finest jurists ever to serve the church. Pope Innocent IV wrote a brilliant and influential commentary on the Decretals during his pontificate. Hostiensis (Henry of Segusa, 1190/1200–1271) did likewise in his *Summa aurea* (completed around 1251). These canonists taught that in the ordinary course of affairs the bishop governed the church of his diocese. However, when a particularly important issue was at stake, one that might affect the welfare of the whole diocese, they expected the bishop to take counsel with the chapter. The *Ordinary gloss* on the Decretals had already identified three sets of issues: those pertinent to the bishop, those pertinent to the chapter, and those pertinent to both. Hostiensis, however, argued that bishop and chapter possessed unequal authority. While the chapter enjoyed the balance of power on issues chiefly pertinent to it, the bishop's authority carried more weight on issues pertinent to both. Many issues fell only unclearly into one category or another. Furthermore, even on issues wherein both sides agreed that the bishop had the balance of authority, canonists argued that there were limits on how the bishop might pursue his policies. Chapters had *dominium*, a kind of veto, on alienations of church property. The canonists also taught that in the case of a vacancy, chapters wielded episcopal authority. Since authority was divided, all sorts of arguments between bishops and chapters might blow up, and often did. Long court cases between bishops and chapters fill the histories of the medieval church.

Of course, the canonists extended this analysis to the church as a universal body. The government of the universal church resembled the government of diocesan churches. The canonists recognized that the pope had the "fullness of power" (*plenitudo potestatis*) over the church but they also taught that the pope could not impair the good of the church. Despite the great power of the pope, the church is nonetheless a corporation, because the cardinals are invested with authority, as they elect the head of the church. Furthermore, as Hostiensis argued, the church must never be headless, and so in the case of vacancy the College of Cardinals becomes the highest authority in the church.

The Great Western Schism of 1378–1417 formed a critical test-case of canonistic corporate theory. From 1305 until 1378 the popes had resided in Avignon, a city on the Rhone River in imperial territory. All of the popes during this period were French. After seventy-three years and numerous exhortations to return to Rome from such spiritual luminaries as Catherine of Siena, and Bridget of Sweden, along with the humanist scholar Petrarch, Gregory XI (1370–1378) moved back to Rome in 1377. He died the following year and the conclave that followed elected Bartolomeo Prignano, the archbishop of Bari, as pope; he took the name of Urban VI (1378–1389). He soon thereafter announced a program of curial reform—a worthwhile aim—but threatened and terrorized the cardinals as well. A number of the cardinals fled Rome for Anagni, where they declared that Urban's election had taken place under duress and was therefore invalid. During the conclave the Romans had rioted. Fearing that another French pope might return to Avignon, they clamored for an Italian. The cardinals thus demanded that Urban resign. He refused. The cardinals in exile elected a Frenchman named Robert of Geneva pope. He took the name Clement VII (1378–1394) and resided in Avignon in the south of France, where a palace-castle had served as the papal residence from 1305–1378. Urban, of course, continued to reside in Rome. Two rival popes had thus been established. Papal schisms had happened in the past but not since Lateran III (1179), which established the protocol for a two-thirds majority vote of the cardinals. Furthermore, while past schisms were relatively short-lived, this one dragged on interminably, owing in part to the stubbornness of both sides. In addition, the Hundred Years' War (1337–1453) between England and France encouraged intransigence, since England and her allies recognized the Roman line of popes while France and her allies recognized the Avignonese.

By the 1390s, Latin Christendom looked to the theologians and canonists of the University of Paris to end the schism, because after twenty years, neither force nor diplomacy had proved equal to the job. Important members of the university's faculty invoked both the conciliar tradition of the early church and corporation theory to restore unity to the church. Both popes had clearly failed in their responsibility to unify and shepherd the church; indeed, both could have been argued to forfeit their authority owing to their persistence in schism, which in turn amounted to heresy. Both lines had equally culpable colleges of cardinals. However, the body of the faithful still constituted the infallible, universal church. The government of the church, having been perverted by the popes and their lackeys, defaulted to the whole of the church, as invested in a duly convened council, which was called for the imperial city of Constance by the German Emperor Sigismund (1410–1437) in 1414.

> That this synod, legitimately assembled in the Holy Spirit, constituting a general council, representing the catholic church militant, has power immediately from Christ, and that everyone of whatever state or dignity, even papal, is bound to obey it in those matters which pertain to the faith and the eradication of the said schism.[112]

The Council of Constance managed to depose all rivals and elect in their place a universally accepted pope, Martin V (1417–1431), thus ending the last Catholic papal schism.

Corporation theory, then, was symptomatic of medieval intellectual endeavors generally. Themselves part of the church, the canonists devised distinctions and categories they used to understand and think about the law and government of the church. Their ideas reflect their "doings" as members of the universal church. Furthermore, like the priestly law-givers of Leviticus, the canonists' work depended ultimately on the Scriptures, in particular, St. Paul's imagery of the mystical body.

The Courts and Procedure of the Medieval Church

In the wake of the Investiture Controversy, the amount of business conducted by church courts increased dramatically. St. Bernard of Clairvaux lamented to Pope Eugene III, the first Cistercian pope and his protégé, that litigation even threatened the pope's physical health:

> I ask you, what is the point of wrangling and listening to litigants from morning to night? And would that the evil of the day were sufficient for it, but the nights are not even free! Your poor body scarcely gets the time which nature

requires for rest before it must rise for further disputing. One day passes on litigation to the next, one night reveals malice to the next; so much so that you
have no time to breathe, no time to rest and no time for leisure.[113]

The prelates of the church—bishops and abbots—were forced to yield many
of their jurisdictional responsibilities to full-time professionals, called officials-
principal. In time, officials-principal came to head sophisticated episcopal departments with servants of their own—registrars who managed the work
schedule, clerks who drew up documents, and bailiffs who served summonses
to court. Episcopal courts handled marriage cases, moral misdemeanors, tithes,
heresy, benefices, and infractions of the church's laws for Sundays and holi-
days. Parallel developments took place in Rome, where the Rota—named for
the round room it originally met in—had emerged by the end of the twelfth
century as the pope's court of appeal. So many cases were now appealed to the
pope that cardinals were entrusted with much of the Rota's business. Since
only the wealthiest clients could litigate a case all the way to Rome, the popes
also named local church officials to serve as their judicial representatives
throughout Latin Christendom, which in turn aided the popes' aim of establishing their jurisdiction throughout the universal church. Litigants also benefited from the establishment of these officials, called judges-delegate, for they
could consult the highest courts at less cost. These courts and officials also
created their own cadre of servants, in particular the increasingly numerous
notaries—officials who wrote court documents.

Ecclesiastical courts followed the procedures of the civil courts. Plaintiffs
initiated proceedings when they submitted to an official-principal written
petitions for redress of grievance. If the plaintiff convinced the official-principal
that the case had merit and that his court had jurisdiction over it, the official-principal cited the defendant to appear before the court within ten days,
and either to render satisfaction to the plaintiff or make an argument against
the plaintiff's petition. If the defendant failed to appear in court, or to refute
the plaintiff's petition, the official-principal generally ruled in the plaintiff's
favor—so there was no presumption of innocence. However, once plaintiff
and defendant both appeared before the court, the trial began, usually with
lawyers arguing the respective positions. The church courts placed a very
high burden of proof on plaintiffs, requiring "evidence that was clearer than
midday light," usually meaning a confession, "the queen of proofs," or two
credible witnesses.[114] Because of the fear of forgery, the testimony of sworn
witnesses carried greater weight than documentary proof. As Innocent IV
wrote, to trust the skin of a dead animal more than the voice of a living man
was contrary to nature.[115] Since then, as now, criminals preferred secrecy or

darkness, witnesses were difficult to find; so the plaintiff's case rested upon confession of the accused. In contrast, defense lawyers cast doubts on the plaintiff's argument, evidence, or overall case. Unlike modern counsel, medieval defense lawyers offered no alternative theories of crime's commission. The judge, rather than the lawyers, interrogated witnesses privately, using lists of questions lawyers submitted. The testimony of witnesses was written down. After the witnesses had been interviewed, the lawyers for both parties "cross-examined" their testimony, and pointed out to the judge what was most advantageous for their clients. After these oral arguments had been heard, the judge set a date for his ruling, if he made one. Many cases failed to run the full course, for one reason or another, and were never ruled upon.

Since the testimony of witnesses was so difficult to obtain, some canonists argued for lower standards of proof. These canonists devised another procedure called *per notorium*, which stipulated that if the fact of a crime and the criminal were well-known, the normal procedure (*ordo iudicarius*) could be ignored. If the judge could find two witnesses who believed that someone was guilty of a crime, he could then impose sentence. A trial *per notorium* was particularly useful for prosecuting clerks who kept concubines. Such trials streamlined procedure but also threatened to diminish the rights of the accused.

Innocent III also introduced reforms that set aside the accusatorial procedure. A procedure *per inquisitionem* permitted judges to investigate suspected offenders, on the basis of a widespread belief of their having committed an offense.[116] "The whole conduct of a proceeding *per inquisitionem*—determining when and if to initiate the procedure, deciding what charges to prefer and against whom, producing witnesses, taking their testimony, responding to the claims and arguments of the defendant, arriving at a decision, and pronouncing sentence—rested in the hands of the judge, who thus combined the functions of investigator and prosecutor with his judicial role."[117] Innocent's reform constituted a move towards something like the modern attorney general—state prosecution of crime. A procedure *per inquisitionem* still had to satisfy the evidentiary requirements of the *ordo iudicarius*.

Whatever the judicial procedure, the canonists appropriated the spirit of Roman jurisprudence and insisted that reason must justify the law and its interpretation. For Gratian, law sprang from two sources: the *ius naturale* and custom. Human laws, said Gratian, must be reasonable and must conform to the practices of a polity. The decretist Huguccio would later add that unreasonable law was no law at all, for the author of justice is God, who is Reason Itself.[118] The decretist Hostiensis drew a distinction between justice and equity. He argued that justice secured retribution for wrongs, while equity was justice moderated by compassion for the offender.[119] The job of judges, then, was to apply the law equitably from case to case. He also taught that divine law (in the Scriptures) was an extension of the natural law.[120] Gratian also subjected custom and tradition to the test of reason and justice: "The authority of longstanding custom and practice is not insignificant; but its power is certainly not of such moment as to prevail over either reason or ordinance," and "whatever has been done without consideration for justice, against her discipline, may in no way be considered valid."[121]

The canonists also formulated the limits within which the law operates. The general rule was that interpretation of law should be guided by the law's *causa*, the legislator's reason for making the law. When the *causa* was clear, little work needed to be done, but when it was unclear, other canons and jurists' opinions should be brought to bear on it.[122] Another relevant principle here was that where the law was unclear, it should be applied as narrowly as possible.[123] When the reason for making the law no longer existed, that law's efficacy lapsed.[124] Like the Roman jurists before them, they argued that the law governed only future actions.[125] Law could not revoke prior transactions.[126]

Finally, the canonists also introduced the importance of intention as a legal concept. This development followed logically from the canonists' advocacy of the church reform movement's insistence on liberty of conscience and rightness of intention. For the classical Roman jurists, motivation had no legal efficacy: "Persons who administer abortion potions or love philtres—even if they do not do so with evil intent, nevertheless, it is an evil practice—are, if humble, deported to the mines; if of superior rank, deprived of part of their property and relegated to an island."[127] In contrast, the canonists argued that candidates for the clergy should freely choose to serve God and neighbor as a priest of His church. A young man and young woman should freely choose to love and serve each other as husband and wife. The legal validity of matrimony and orders depended on the action and the motivation. The canonists, then, devised a legal theory of culpability that took into account the intentions of the accused. Earlier systems of law had focused on the harm the perpetrator had wrought, and the compensation he owed the victim or the victim's kin. The canonists also speculated the offender's interior disposition, and thereby made a lasting contribution to the Western tradition of jurisprudence:

> Medieval canonistic theories of culpability underlie the modern criminal law's concern with determining whether it was premeditated or impulsive, whether it was an isolated offense or part of a habitual pattern of behavior, whether the outcome of the offender's deeds resulted from deliberate, purposeful action or was accidental and unforeseen.[128]

Of course, a premeditated crime should be punished more severely than an impulsive one, and a repeat offender deserves a greater penalty than someone who commits an isolated offense.

The penitential literature of the early Middle Ages inspired this jurisprudence. The penitentials were first written in the monasteries of sixth-century Ireland. The penitentials listed sins, and recommended penances for those sins. They also distinguished between accidental and purposeful malefactions, as in the *Penitential of Finnian* (c. 550 AD):

> If any cleric commits murder and kills his neighbor and he is dead, he must become an exile for ten years and do penance seven years in another region . . . but if he killed him suddenly and not from hatred . . . through an inadvertence, he shall do penance for three years.[129]

Penitentials enjoyed great popularity everywhere in Latin Christendom during the early Middle Ages. They served to popularize Christ's teaching, as in the Gospel of Matthew:

> It is not what goes into a man's mouth that makes him impure; it is what comes out of his mouth." His disciples approached him and said, "Do you realize the Pharisees were scandalized when they heard your pronouncement?" "Every planting not put down by my heavenly Father will be uprooted," he replied. "Let them go their way; they are blind leaders of the blind. If one blind man leads another, both will end in a pit." Then Peter spoke up to say, "Explain the parable to us." "Are you, too, still incapable of understanding?" he asked. "Do you not see that everything that enters the mouth passes into the stomach and is discharged into the latrine, but what comes out of the mouth originates in the mind? It is things like these that make a man impure. *From the mind* stem evil designs—murder, adultery, fornication, stealing, false witness, blasphemy. These are the things that make a man impure." (Mt 15.10–20).

Modern legal theories of culpability, then, ultimately derive from the canonists' appropriation of their inherited tradition of Christian textual authorities.

International Law

Historians have sometimes discussed a medieval "expansion" of Europe, by which they meant that Latin Christians left their homeland to trade or fight *in partibus infidelibus*, "in the lands of the nonbelievers." For medieval Latin Christians the nonbelievers—the infidels—meant either the Jews, who lived among them, or the Muslims, who dwelt beyond Christendom's frontiers. Were they subject to the law of the church and were non-Christian governments licit? To answer these questions, the canonists relied on several sources. They employed the authority of the scriptural texts that described a universal, human brotherhood. Roman natural law theory, with its insistence on rationality, was also useful, as was Augustine's teaching on just war, which said: "A just war is wont to be described as one that avenges wrongs, when a nation or state has to be punished, for refusing to make amends for the wrongs inflicted by its subjects, or to restore what it has seized unjustly." Augustine also argued that war must be made to restore peace (not for loot, for instance), and with right intentions, not hatred.[130] Throughout his thoughts, Augustine assumed all human beings shared basic convictions about just order, and that neighboring nations could coexist peacefully if they agreed on their mutual interest.

In general, the canonists agreed that canon law did not pertain to unbaptized persons, although there were exceptions, in that Christ came to save all mankind, and the pope was His vicar on Earth. But, since the Jews and the Muslims rejected Christ, should they be subjected to Christian rulers, whether secular or religious? Innocent IV, the most influential author on this topic, argued that infidels possessed their lands licitly, both by the *ius naturale* and the *ius gentium*:

> Is it licit to invade the lands of the infidels? . . . In truth the earth belongs to God . . . for God is the creator of all things, and he subjected everything to the rational creature for whom he made all these things as in Genesis, 1. In the beginning, therefore, all things were common until, by the usage of our first parents, it was introduced that lands should be divided and delimited and appropriated. . . . Now this was not bad but good, for common ownership gives rise to discord and common possessions are often neglected. Thus in the beginning all things and possessions belonged to no one except God and they were conceded to the first occupier. . . . But once they had been occupied it was not licit for anyone else to occupy them. This was forbidden by the law of nature which tells everyone not to do to another what he does not want done to himself. . . . No one had ownership of men as slaves before the introduction of the Law of Nations, because by nature all men are free.[131]

God had created all the world's goods for mankind in common, but the Fall of Adam and Eve created the need for division of lands. Common property gave way before private possessions because a fallen humanity neglected its stewardship over common goods.

The Fall of the first parents also created the need for government and jurisdiction. Since human beings sometimes harm one another, the wielders of jurisdiction limit the violence that vengeance begets:

I read of just and lawful jurisdiction where the sword given for vengeance is mentioned above at X 1.33.6. But how this jurisdiction first began I do not know unless perhaps God assigned some person or persons to do justice to criminals or unless in the beginning the father of a family had complete juris-diction over his family by the law of nature, though now he has it only in a few minor matters. . . . This at any rate is certain, that God himself exercised ju-risdiction at the beginning as is noted above at X 2.2.10 (*Licet*).[132]

Innocent thus entertained the idea that governments may have developed nat-urally among peoples, regardless of Original Sin, according to the model of the nuclear family. Just as parents preside over their children, larger communities needed authorities to protect them and to institute the order necessary for pros-perity. Thus, for Innocent, infidel and Christian governments are *both legitimate*:

I maintain, therefore, the lordship, possession and jurisdiction can belong to infidels licitly and without sin, for these things were made not only for the faithful but for every rational creature as has been said. For *he makes his sun to rise on the just and the wicked and he feeds the birds of the air* (Matthew c. 5, c .6). Accordingly, we say that it is not licit for the pope or the faithful to take away from infidels their belongings or their lordships or jurisdictions because they possess them without sin.[133]

Still, said the pope, the authority of the Vicar of Christ extends to all of hu-manity, even though he may choose not to wield it:

Nevertheless, we do certainly believe that the pope, who is vicar of Jesus Christ, has power not only over Christians but also over all infidels, for Christ had power over all, whence it is said in the psalm, *Give to the king thy judgment, O God* (Psalm 71), and he would not seem to have been a careful father unless he had committed full power over all to his vicar whom he left on earth. Again, he gave the keys of the kingdom of heaven to Peter and his successors and said, *Whatsoever you shall bind*, etc. (Matthew 16). And again, elsewhere, *Feed my sheep*, etc. (John 21). . . . But all men, faithful and infidels, are Christ's sheep by creation even though they are not of the fold of the church and thus from the foregoing it is clear that the pope has jurisdiction and power over all *de iure* though not *de facto*.[134]

Perhaps Innocent was referring to a sacramental authority? In which case, the exercise of his authority would be inefficacious, but could be exercised should conversions to Christianity take place.

Innocent's ideas reappeared in the proceedings of the Council of Con-stance. The Polish-Lithuanian monarchy brought a complaint there through

Paul Vladimir, a Polish canonist, against the Teutonic Knights.[135] For years, the Knights, claiming that they were defending Christendom's eastern frontiers, had made war upon the pagan Lithuanians. The Lithuanians, however, had converted to Catholicism in the fourteenth century, and the crowns of Poland and Lithuania united through a dynastic marriage. The Teutonic Knights continued to attack the Lithuanians. Paul Vladimir argued that the Council, which by *Haec sancta* claimed to be the government of the church, should instruct the Knights to cease attacking the Lithuanians on two grounds. First, the Knights had no reason to attack a Christian monarchy. Second, even if the Lithuanians were yet pagan, Pope Innocent IV had taught that their government and territory was inviolate, unless the Lithuanians had attacked the Knights without just cause, an argument that no one had made.

Together then, Innocent and Paul Vladimir, with Augustine as their guide, laid the foundations for the first concern of international law, namely, limitation on war. Regardless of religion, no Christian state could attack any other state without just cause. That a ruler or a people or a government professed a religion other than Christianity was no justification for initiating hostilities.

The Jurisprudence of St. Thomas Aquinas

Thomas Aquinas (c. 1224–1274) was, of course, one of the great minds of the Middle Ages, indeed, of any era. While many of his contemporaries found his synthesis of faith and reason problematic, Aquinas's writings on the state and law influenced jurisprudence and political theory in both his own lifetime and down to the present day. His legal theory joined together a theory of moral acts with the competence of the law and law-making. In his initial reflections on the nature of law, Aquinas agreed with the Roman jurists that the law was rational and arguable but he also added that the aim of the law was the benefit of the commonwealth: "[law] is nothing else than an ordnance of reason promulgated by the ruler for the common good."[136] Since the law was directed to the ends of justice and the welfare of the community, it ushered forth from the reason, whose task was to discern both the final end desired and the intermediate ends whereby it could be reached. Aquinas also agreed with the Roman jurists insofar as he taught that the law applied to external actions, and so served as "a rule and measure of human acts," as opposed to thoughts or emotions. Consequently, the law was the concern of the practical, rather than speculative, reason. Nonetheless, Aquinas believed the working of the will, which desired and sought the best, was likewise essential to proper law-making.[137] Aquinas's thinking, furthermore, reflects the larger trend of medieval legal history which invested the public authority alone with law-making power, since only that authority was empowered to ordain the good of the whole state.

Like the Roman jurists, Aquinas enumerated the kinds of law. He believed in a fundamental order in reality that reflected the Intelligence that had brought that reality into being. Every thing had not only being but essence (*quidditas*), which gave that thing a character and purpose of its own. Since the rational order existed in God, the cosmos had been created according to an "idea of the government of things in God the Ruler of the universe."[138] Thus did Aquinas think of reality itself as a perfect community that obeyed the rule of law. Like other polities, the universe has a Ruler, and the law originates in His mind, who then promulgates and imposes it on His community. The law of the universe, said Aquinas, was the Divine Wisdom.[139] Furthermore, that law, since it exists in the mind of the eternal God, is the eternal law. The eternal law, then, may be known only to "the blessed who see God in His essence."[140]

The sophistication of Aquinas's teaching on natural law exceeded that of the Roman jurists. He crafted that teaching with the human person's relation to God in mind. "Law, being a rule and a measure, can be in a person in two ways: in one way, as in him that rules and measures; in another way, as in that which is ruled and measured." Now all things "are ruled and measured by the eternal law," the law in the mind of God and imprinted in His creation. Human beings, argued Aquinas, especially bear the imprint of the eternal law since they are made in the image and likeness of the Creator and so are "subject to divine Providence in the most excellent way." The natural law, then, is "nothing other than the rational creature's participation in the eternal law." The natural law permits men and women to distinguish between good and evil.[141] The first precept of the natural law (corroborated by the Scriptures) is that good is to be done and evil avoided. The human person, argued Aquinas, pursues those goods which agree with the essence of humanity, namely, the preservation of individual and communal life (because of innate sociability), sexual intercourse and the education of offspring (for the survival of the species), the knowledge of God and the rejection of ignorance (because of the rational faculty).[142] Furthermore, since human beings are made for perfection and beatitude, they seek to live in accordance with the virtues. In so far as the natural law enjoins virtue on the human person, that law also constitutes a habit in the virtuous.[143] To live otherwise corrupts human nature and dignity.[144] Thus, dispensations from the human law are permitted but not from the natural law.[145]

Unlike the Roman jurists, Aquinas said little about the *ius gentium*. He had much to say, however, about human law (*lex humana*). This law was statute or positive law—the law that legislators actually promulgated and which citizens were expected to abide. Aquinas tied human law much more closely to the natural law than had the Roman jurists: "Every human law has just so much of the nature of law as it is derived from the law of nature."[146] The derivation of the human law from the natural law should resemble the speculative intellect's reaching of conclusions from indemonstrable first principles: "We conclude that just as, in the speculative reason, from naturally known indemonstrable principles we draw the conclusions of the various sciences, the knowledge of which is not imparted to us by nature, but acquired by the efforts of reason; so, too, it is from the precepts of the natural law, as from general and indemonstrable principles, that the human reason needs to proceed to the more particular determination of certain matters. These particular determinations, devised by human reason, are called human laws."[147] Only in this way could human laws be crafted with the confidence that they were faithful to justice: "The practical reason is concerned with practical matters, which are singular and contingent, but not with necessary things, with which the speculative reason is concerned. Wherefore human laws cannot have that inerrancy that belongs to the demonstrated conclusions of sciences."[148] Indeed, human legislation that was not derived from the natural law resembled violence more than law, and could not bind the conscience.[149]

Aquinas was convinced that human law, like natural law, aids in the cultivation of virtue. Indeed, the law's innate power teaches virtue. Although the human person is made for it, virtue must nonetheless be learned from a teacher through practice. The law is especially vital for persons whose temperament disposes them to vice: "A man needs to receive this training from another, whereby to arrive at the perfection of virtue. And as to those young people who are inclined to acts of virtue, by their good natural disposition, or by custom, or rather by the gift of God, paternal training suffices . . . but since some are found to be depraved and prone to vice, and not easily amenable to words, it was necessary for such to be restrained from evil by force . . . this kind of training which compels through fear of punishment is the discipline of laws."[150] For some persons, the virtues were simply harder to inculcate. For them, the law remedied the defects in their moral constitution by instruction in doing good.

In Romano-canonical jurisprudence, of course, the opinions of the jurists formed a source of law. Aquinas, however, argued that legislators, not judges, crafted the best laws. He agreed with Aristotle that since legislators deliberated with general goals in mind, in contrast to judges, who considered individual cases, legislators made better laws, which in turn taught the citizens moral excellence:

> Those who make laws consider long beforehand what laws to make, whereas judgement on each single case has to be pronounced as soon as it arises; and it is easier for man to see what is right by taking many instances into consideration than by considering one solitary fact. . . . lawgivers judge in the abstract and of future events, whereas those who sit in judgement judge of things present, toward which they are affected by love, hatred, or some kind of cupidity; wherefore their judgment is perverted."[151]

Aquinas believed, with Aristotle, that a mixed constitution, with elements of monarchy, aristocracy, and popular rule, did the best legislating: "For this is the best form of polity, being partly kingdom, since there is one at the head of all; partly aristocracy, in so far as a number of persons are set in authority; partly democracy, i.e., government by the people, in so far as the rulers can be chosen from the people and the people have the right to choose their rulers."[152]

The legislator's responsibility, then, was to get the law right in the main, for "in contingent matters, such as natural and human things, it is enough for a thing to be certain, as being true in the greater number of instances, though at times and less frequently it fail."[153] While the law prescribes every kind of virtue, it could not proscribe every vice, for every rule and measure must be proportionate to what is ruled and measured.[154] Since human beings are imperfect, whatever rules and measures them will also be imperfect: "Human law is framed for a number of human beings, the majority of whom are not perfect in virtue. Wherefore human laws do not forbid all vices from which the virtuous abstain, but only the more grievous vices from which it is possible for the majority to abstain . . . thus human law prohibits murder, theft, and suchlike."[155] Aquinas reasoned that the law must have gentleness and lenience, since "the purpose of human law is to lead men to virtue, not suddenly, but gradually. Wherefore it does not lay upon the multitude of imperfect men the burdens of those who are already virtuous . . . otherwise these imperfect ones, being unable to bear such precepts, would break out into yet greater evils."[156] Simple common sense well served the legislator.

While Aquinas emphasized that legislators and the laws they handed down must serve the common good, he also affirmed that citizens play an important part in law and order. Aquinas argued for what might be called radical civic-mindedness: "Since one man is a part of the community, each man, *in all that he is and has*, belongs to the community." Thus, the citizen must obey duly enacted civil laws: "Laws framed by man are either just or unjust. If they be just, they have the power of binding in conscience, from the eternal law from which they are derived."[157] Aquinas also taught that citizens and subjects must obey government officials, for "it is not competent for everyone to expound what is useful and what is not useful to the state; those alone can do this who are in authority."[158] Magistrates must be heeded or chaos ensues.

Customary law was still very much in force in the thirteenth century, and so Aquinas discussed the relation between custom and law. For him custom often made the best law, since it was akin to virtue, having become deeply imbedded in civic life. Whereas governments imposed statutes, custom resided within the very being of each citizen: "If they are free and able to make their own laws, the consent of the whole people expressed by a custom counts far more in favor of a particular observance than does the authority of the sovereign."[159] Ancient laws, then, should be changed with great caution, because "the mere change of law is of itself prejudicial to the common good because custom avails much for the observance of the laws, seeing that what is done contrary to general custom, even in slight matters, is looked upon as grave . . . when a law is changed, the binding power of the law is diminished in so far as custom is abolished."[160] The power of the government and of custom is in many instances quite limited, as the frequency of crime makes clear. The legislator's art, to say nothing of his challenge, is to craft laws that will commit the citizenry to law and order without much coercion or compulsion, such that the citizens are law-abiding because they are virtuous, rather than terrorized. This conclusion also serves as Aquinas's commentary on Rm 13.1: "A man is said to be subject to a law as the coerced is subject to the coercer. In this way the virtuous and righteous are not subject to the law, but only the wicked. Because coercion and violence are contrary to the will, but the will of the good is in harmony with the law, whereas the will of the wicked is discordant from it. Wherefore in this sense the good are not subject to the law, but only the wicked."[161] The virtuous citizen does right without having even to convince himself of it: "In so far as he does what he ought spontaneously and readily . . . this is to act virtuously."[162]

The chief virtue that the law teaches, of course, is justice, which Aquinas defined in Aristotle's terms: "Justice is a habit whereby a man renders to each one his due by a constant and perpetual will." Justice was by its nature a virtue directed to public intercourse, because the just man respects the rights of fellow citizens. Justice is also a voluntary acceptance of the equality of all citizens, as the commonwealth owes each citizen his due.[163] Families illustrate this idea very well, for justice is likelier to exist between husbands and wives, who are equals, than between parents and children, who are less nearly so.[164] Justice, in particular, disciplines the will since it concerns actions towards others, for "justice is first of all and more commonly exercised in voluntary exchanges of things, such as buying and selling."[165] Aquinas distinguished between two kinds of justice: moral virtue, which inheres in individual citizens, and legal justice, which is enacted through the laws. Hence, justice was the greatest of the cardinal virtues because it well orders both individuals and community.[166]

Aquinas appreciated well, however, the limits of justice. Since some citizens would always have a limited capacity for virtue, justice would also have limits. Furthermore, men and women were called to be members of another, more sublime community, whose purpose exceeded civil order and proceeded to beatitude. Since that last end of humankind—eternal happiness—exceeded the ability of human reason to grasp it, God Himself gave the Divine Law to the community of the blessed:

> Because it is by law that man is directed how to perform his proper acts in view of his last end . . . if man were ordained to no other end than that which is proportionate to his natural faculty, there would be no need for man to have any further direction on the part of his reason besides the natural and human law which is derived from it. But since man is ordained to an end of eternal happiness, which is disproportionate to man's natural faculty . . . therefore it was necessary that, besides the natural and the human law, man should be directed to his end by a law given by God.

The divine law, however, served as a general aid to the legislator and the jurist:

> On account of the uncertainty of human judgment, especially on contingent and particular matters, different people form different judgments on human acts; whence also different and contrary laws result. In order, therefore, that man may know without any doubt what he ought to do and what he ought to avoid, it was necessary for man to be directed in his proper acts by a law given by God, for it is certain that such a law cannot err.[167]

The divine law, then, perfected the human law, for disagreements could exist between reasonable people. But that meant, at the same time, that some might follow a course contrary to God's design, even though they believed themselves perfectly rational in following that design. The divine law permits humans to adopt the right course even if their reason has gone astray.

Whereas the Roman law paid scant attention to the motivations that underlaid human acts, the principal concern of the *secunda secundae* of Aquinas's *Summa*, the divine law's scope, and the reason for its necessity, extended to human motivations and dispositions. The civil law failed to measure or judge confidently the souls of men. Since interior disposition preceded exterior action, the Divine Law helped the cultivation of virtue: "Man is not competent to judge of interior movements that are hidden, but only of exterior acts which appear; and yet for the perfection of virtue it is necessary for man to conduct himself aright in both kinds of acts. Consequently, human law could not sufficiently curb and direct interior acts, and it was necessary for this purpose that a divine law should supervene."[168] Indeed, the civil law should not prohibit many of the malefactions which usher forth from these evil dispositions, yet their perpetration endangers the salvation of souls. Thus the Divine Law prohibits the commission of certain acts that the human law does not: "Human law cannot punish or forbid all evil deeds; since while aiming at doing away with all evils, it would do away with many good things, and would hinder the advance of the common good, which is necessary for human intercourse. In order, therefore, that no evil might remain unforbidden and unpunished, it was necessary for the divine law to supervene, whereby all sins are forbidden."[169]

Aquinas equated Divine Law with the Scriptures. God had given to humankind two divine laws—the Old and the New Testaments. The Old Testament Aquinas characterized as an ordination of sensible and earthly goods, as for instance the Israelites' occupation of the land of Canaan. The New Testament, in contrast, set in order the intelligible and heavenly goods, that is, the opening of the gates of Heaven, for the essence of Christ's ministry was to herald the Kingdom of Heaven. The Old Law, argued Aquinas, measured exterior acts. The New Law ruled interior dispositions. The Old Law threatened men and women with the fear of punishment. The authority of the New Law rested upon love.[170] Clearly, in Thomist jurisprudence, as in the thought of Augustine, fear and coercion are sometimes necessary for the *tranquillitas ordinis*, but ultimately love is the foundation of authority in the Christian commonwealth. A favorite metaphor on this score, and one perfectly in line with the Scriptures, was paternal authority.[171] Fathers encourage their small children to do the right thing out of fear of punishment or the hope of reward but as the children grow and mature, they teach them to act rightly for love of self, and then love of neighbor, and finally love of God. By their adulthood, good dispositions and acts have become virtues, such that the coercion of the father's "law" yields to love—the desire for the good of others and for the good works that provide for their welfare.

English Common Law

The legal system that regulates life in the United States (except for that of the state of Louisiana) originated as the common law of the kingdom of England. Some of its essential features had been laid down during the Anglo-

Saxon period but in the main English common law began to take shape during the reign of King Henry II (1154–1189) and was mostly established by the death of Henry III (1216–1272). The essential feature of the common law were courts beholden to the king, such that whatever rulings were handed down by these courts were "common" to the whole realm, whereas the jurisdiction of the manor or hundred courts could extend to no more than a single estate. Furthermore, the decisions of royal judges influenced the development of the common law in a way impossible in Romano-canonical jurisprudence. There are many criticisms today in the United States of judges who, by their decisions, "legislate" rather than "interpret" the law. The merits or demerits of these arguments notwithstanding, such decisions have been a part of the common law tradition from its origins.

The kingdom of England came into existence in the ninth century. Britain had been a province of the Roman Empire from 43 til 405 AD. The legions were recalled from the island in the latter year, in order to buttress the defense of Italy, and the Romano-British were left to fend for themselves. In the 440s, three Germanic nations began migrating to the island, the Angles, the Saxons, and the Jutes. They attacked the British, and forced many into Scotland, Wales, Cornwall, and Brittany. The British often fought among themselves as well. The ordinariness of slavery in fifth-century Britain testifies to the ongoing violence there. As the Germans extended their control over the island, they founded seven independent, often antagonistic kingdoms known as the Heptarchy. As the epic poem *Beowulf* indicates, the Anglo-Saxons long remembered their ancestors in Scandinavia, and England entered into a North Sea concert of kingdoms.

In the late eighth century, another set of Germanic invaders attacked England—the Vikings, mostly from Denmark. They raided England and established an area of settlement that came to be called the Danelaw—the place where Danish law was observed—which at its height composed more than one-half of England. Viking attacks devastated England as much as they did northern Frankland. The king of Wessex, Alfred the Great (871–899), unified much of England, drove the Danes back to the north and east, and reduced the Danelaw. Alfred also aimed to improve the defense of his kingdom. He built the first English navy, reorganized the army, and constructed a line of fortifications. A scholar of sorts himself, Alfred feared that the Danish occupation had degraded English learning. Anglo-Saxon England had been the intellectual capital of Latin Europe prior to the Viking attacks but the destruction of a number of monasteries, in particular that of Jarrow and Wearmouth, had markedly reduced the number of scholars and libraries. Alfred encouraged a broader-based literacy and founded schools. He himself translated *The Pastoral Care* of Pope St. Gregory I into Old English. He organized England's local government into shires and maintained a presence in each shire through an officer known as the shire-reeve (sheriff). Other important developments characterized the reigns of Alfred's successors. By the tenth century, shire courts and state prosecution of crime had emerged. A panel of the sheriff, the ealdormen (local nobles), and the bishop heard and judged most cases, even those subject to high justice. The kings of England maintained a royal chancery for the drafting and writing of royal documents, known as writs. Writs, documents wherein the king commanded that a judicial procedure be applied to a given case, were written in Old English, not Latin. Thus, in late Anglo-Saxon England documentation and the written vernacular language assumed an importance in legal matters unknown anywhere else in Latin Christendom.

The conquest of England in 1066 by William the Conqueror (1066–1087) introduced Norman administrative methods into England. At the same time, many Anglo-Saxon traditions survived, such as the office of sheriff and the reliance on written documents, and were made to serve the new regime. Unlike many feudal barons, who struggled to maintain control of their nobles, the dukes of Normandy had consolidated a centralized principality—they were in solid control of the nobility of the duchy. William's royal regime in England, furthermore, had the advantage of starting in many senses from scratch, so unlike the kings of France, or the German emperors, he could more effectively subject the English landed magnates, whether native Anglo-Saxons or Norman French, to his rule. Of course, he rewarded his soldiers with estates. Anglo-Saxon nobles had to recognize William's lordship to keep their lands; rebels were ruthlessly eradicated. Whether the magnates were English or Norman, their holdings were scattered about the kingdom, which made the consolidation of resources very difficult, and so made the prospects of rebellion against him uncertain at best. The famous *Domesday Book*, commissioned in 1089, recorded the terms of tenure of virtually every holding in England. The purpose of this survey, as its name suggests, was to serve as a reference for inheritance of real property, that is, to whom a holding would belong after its possessor had met the day of his "doom." The survey, then, was another important legal innovation whereby the English crown tracked possession of virtually every landed property throughout England.

Under the reign of Henry I (1100–1135) another set of developments important for the common law took place. To increase his authority over the kingdom, Henry appointed royal justices whose responsibility was to travel about the realm and to hear serious criminal cases. Criminal cases were said to be "pleas of the crown"; that is, criminals disturbed the king's peace. The first list of pleas of the crown may be found in Henry I's *Leges Henrici Primi* (1115) and included murder, robbery, rape, counterfeiting, and treason.[172] Thus, Henry assumed responsibility for maintaining the public peace, which mostly meant making violent acts by his subjects unlawful. In this, Henry was part of a larger twelfth-century trend, which on the continent of Europe surfaced as the Truce of God movement against "feudal" warfare. Unlike the king of France or the German emperor, Henry was powerful enough in England to suppress private violence. Henry also reformed the office of sheriff. In the past, local barons had often been named as sheriffs. Henry named men of lower ranks to these offices, so that they would be dependant upon the crown. His justices and sheriffs owed whatever power and rank they enjoyed in English society to royal favor, so their loyalty was more reliable. Finally, Henry created the office of coroner in 1100, and ever since an officer of the crown has investigated suspicious deaths in England. Many inquisitions *post mortem* have survived and they are some of the saddest historical records in existence. Most concern the accidental death of children, usually by drowning or fire.

While Henry seems to have sowed his oats all over England and Normandy, he had but two legitimate children, a son named William and a daughter Matilda. When William was still a young man, he and some noble friends drank themselves into oblivion, and then took a joyride on a ship, whose captain and crew were equally inebriated. A storm blew up and all were lost, leaving Matilda as Henry's heir. Matilda was the widow of Emperor Henry V of the German Empire, and the wife of Geoffrey Plantagenet, the powerful count of Anjou. Henry compelled the barons and prelates to swear loyalty to Matilda as queen.

Henry's only other living relatives were his sister's two sons. Thibaut was count of Blois and Stephen (who had landed in England after hearing the news of Henry's death) was count of Boulogne. While the barons of England had sworn loyalty to Matilda, they had little enthusiasm for a woman ruler and found her husband, Geoffrey of Anjou, a dominating annoyance. Stephen was believed more civilized, better liked, and more easily manipulated, so most of the barons supported him. Geoffrey invaded Normandy and Matilda crossed over into England and attacked Stephen, whose entire reign (1135–1154) was embroiled in civil war. The barons took advantage of the chaos to increase their own power at the expense of the crown. The conflict ended when Stephen reached an agreement with Henry, Matilda's son. The agreement stipulated that Stephen would rule and be succeeded upon his death by Henry. When Henry became king in 1154, he was by dynastic right already count of Anjou, Maine, and Touraine, as well as duke of Normandy.

Through his marriage to the heiress Eleanor, he also became duke of Aquitaine, and thus ruled an empire that stretched from the Mediterranean to the Firth of Forth. He was by far the strongest ruler in western Europe.

Henry understood very well that the civil wars had badly damaged royal power, as both Stephen and Matilda gave lands and privileges (which could not easily be recovered) to gain supporters. He was eager to restore what he imagined to be the condition of the crown during the reign of his grandfather Henry I. He largely restored the power of the crown through several brilliant initiatives, among which was a reform of the courts. Henry's legal reforms depended both on English traditions and the canon law. Since the king and his loyalists had been dispossessed of land, Henry invoked the canonical principle of *spoliatus ante omnia restituendus* (from the ninth-century Pseudo-Isidorian decretals): Whatever had been seized must be restored before any litigation could begin. Another principle from the Pseudo-Isidorian decretals was that no one could be made to plead in court while disseised. Seisin meant possession, so to be disseised meant to have been stripped of property. A disseised party would then have the disadvantage of litigating while deprived of income; furthermore, to allow such disseisins amounted to assuming guilt rather than innocence. In 1166, Henry issued writs of the crown that ordered sheriffs to have lands thus disputed viewed by a jury of twelve local freemen. These twelve would swear before royal justices whether the land was unjustly disseised. If so, then the legal remedy called *assize of novel disseisin* was granted, which returned the land to the dispossessed and fined the violator of the land. If the plaintiff was shown to be in error, he would be fined:

> The king to the sheriff, health. N. has complained to me that R. has, unjustly and without judgement, disseised him of his free tenement in such a vill, since my last voyage to Normandy; and, therefore, I therefore command you, that if the aforesaid N. should make you secure of prosecuting his claim, then, you cause the tenement to be reseised, with the chattels taken on it, and that you cause him with his chattels to be in peace, until the Pentecost; and, in the mean time, you cause twelve free and lawful men of the neighborhood to view the land, and their names to be imbreviated; and summon them, by good summoners, that they be then before me, or my justices, prepared to make the recognition; and put, by gage and safe pledges, the aforesaid R., or his bailiff, if he be not found, that he be then there to hear such recognition, and have there, etc. Witness, etc.[173]

Through this initiative, Henry placed all land in England under the protection of the crown. Note also that the process required documentation, in keeping with English traditions. In time, preference for documentation, rather than oral testimony, became a feature of civil litigation in common law courts. Finally, Henry here relied on another canonical principle, namely, that endless litigation compromised the common good, so he fixed a definite time for the legal action.

Henry's *Assize of Northampton*, held in 1176, clarified issues related to the inheritance of land. First, heirs of deceased tenants should remain in seisin and perform all services for the land:

> If any freeholder dies let his heirs remain in such seisin as their father had of his fee on the day of his death, and let them have his chattels out of which they shall execute the will of the deceased: and afterwards they shall seek out their lord and pay him a relief and the other things which they ought to pay him from their fee.[174]

Second, the *Assize* stipulated that heirs who were minors should be held in wardship. If the lord refused seisin to the heir, and a jury stated before the royal justices that his father was lawfully seised of the tenement on the day of his death, then the remedy of *assize mort d'ancestor* was granted, and the seisin handed over to the heir, as in the following case from Normandy:

> The assize came to inquire if Simon son of Thomas, father of Richard son of Simon who is under age, was seised in his demesne and of fee of half a virgate of land with appurtenances in Brinton on the day on which he died, etc., and if etc., which land Gunnora of Britain held, who came and called Richard of Brinton to warrant it, who came warranted it to her and said . . . and since Richard is under age it was judged that he is not able to answer to this and so the assize proceeds. The jurors say that the said Simon died so seised as the writ says and that Richard is next heir of that same land which Gunnora held, concerning which she called to warrant the said Richard, whether there was more or less than half a virgate there.[175]

These laws, of course, had several purposes, first to reduce violence and litigation over property, second to protect the rights of children to their parents' patrimony.[176]

Finally, in England as on the continent, a layman's right of presentment accompanied just about every diocesan benefice. A plaintiff who won a jury's recognition that he had presented the last priest to a parish then received an *assize of darrein presentment*, which enabled its possessor to present another candidate to the office:

> It is judged that Alan de Av. have seisin of the presentation of the church of Av., since Henry de Al. who disseised the same Alan of this is unwilling to submit to a recognition according to the usages and customs of Normandy as to

who presented the last parson deceased to that church, and the same Henry is in mercy.[177]

Together, the *assize of novel disseisin*, the *assize mort d'ancestor*, and the *assize of darrein presentment* formed what were called the possessory assizes. With this system of writs and assizes, King Henry II is generally said to have founded the common law of England, for the crown assumed protection of all lands in England. Furthermore, the king invited all freemen to make their pleas in the king's courts. Henry's reforms made litigation in manor, hundredal, and shire courts less attractive, dominated as they were by local great nobles. Royal courts, on the other hand, enjoyed a greater reputation for impartiality.

Henry also reformed the criminal law of the realm. Prior to Henry, criminal cases in England were initiated much like civil cases; that is, a criminal case could be brought into court through formal accusation by a private party, generally a relative or friend of the victim. Unless some benefactor championed the victim, the crime would go unprosecuted. Henry II restored the spirit of Henry I's reforms, naming criminal cases as "pleas of the crown." Henry introduced a new criminal procedure at the *Assize of Clarendon* in 1166, which contained twenty-two chapters of instructions for the indictment, apprehension, and punishment of criminals. The king ordered that twelve men from every hundred and four from each township should appear before either his justices or the sheriff and state on oath whether they suspected anyone of a crime. Any named suspects were to be arrested and brought before the king's itinerant justices, in the case of a hundred, or before the sheriff, in the case of a vill:

> King Henry, with the consent of all his barons, for the preservation of the peace and the keeping of justice, has enacted that inquiry should be made through the several counties and through the several hundreds, by twelve of the most legal men of the hundred and by four of the most legal men of each vill, upon their oath that they will tell the truth, whether there is in their hundred or in their vill, any man who has been accused or publicly suspected of himself being a robber, or murderer, or thief, or of being a receiver of robbers, or murderers, or thieves.[178]

Essentially, what Henry enacted here was the grand jury, whose job was to issue an indictment of suspected criminals. The accused was then subjected to the ordeal of water. Convicted defendants were exiled.[179] At the Assize of Clarendon, then, the crown assumed the responsibility for maintaining law and order. The king's servants investigated, tried, and punished criminals.

Henry also gave to his judiciary a new texture. Sheriffs, for instance, had once been powerful local magnates but Henry I had mostly replaced them with humbler men. Likewise, justices had originally been barons but Henry II appointed justices from lesser families. Henry thus relied on able servants such as Ranulf de Glanville (d. 1190), whose treatise *On the Laws and Customs of England* forms one of the most important sources for Henry's reforms. Ranulf came from a landowning family in Suffolk, although not one of the greatest, yet served his sovereign as sheriff of Yorkshire, judge, and chief justiciar.[180] That reliance, in turn, meant that the officers of the royal courts increasingly became highly trained, professional experts, in contrast to the amateurs of earlier eras.[181] Henry also established several different courts. The justices who traveled with the monarch were named the King's Bench. These judges heard pleas *coram regis* (in the presence of the king). Henry appointed other itinerant royal judges as well. Henry also installed a permanent royal court at Westminster, which came to be known the *court of common pleas*.

In all English courts, laymen and clerics served as justices. Consequently, innovations in canon law deeply affected the history of the common law.[182] For instance, canon law encouraged the rationalization of justice in England. In 1215, Lateran IV forbade clerics to participate in trial by ordeal. No longer could a cleric bless the water or red-hot iron used in ordeals. Thus, Lateran IV temporarily paralyzed the entire English judiciary.[183] English courts then replaced trial by ordeal with trial by jury, wherein compurgation was the procedure. The defendant pleaded innocence and presented compurgators who swore to his innocence and good character.

Canon law also introduced into England the ban on double jeopardy. This ban, enshrined more familiarly in the Fifth Amendment of the American Bill of Rights, resulted from the famous dispute between Henry II and Thomas Becket, the Archbishop of Canterbury.[184] The two men quarreled over the liberties of the church. Thomas Becket opposed the judicial procedure Henry intended to institute for criminous clerks. They were first to be degraded by an ecclesiastical court and then tried by a secular court. Becket argued that such a procedure punished the accused twice for the same crime. All England was outraged when Henry's thugs murdered the beloved bishop, which meant that the king would have to acquiesce in Becket's wishes. Ever since, no one in England could be tried twice for the same offense.

The long reign of Henry III (1216–1272) constituted the next formative era in the history of the English common law. Most of these developments survive in the works of the great jurist Henry de Bracton (d. c. 1268), a royal judge whose *De legibus et consuetudinibus Angliae* (*On the Laws and Customs of England*) was written about 1260. Bracton's work makes clear that the characteristic development of Henry III's reign was the continued development of the common law through the decisions and innovations of royal judges, working in tandem with the royal chancery, rather than legal reforms of the king, as under Henry II. One very important innovation of Henry III's reign was the writ of entry, which initiated proceedings for land which had been pledged for debt in prior years.[185] If the debt had been paid, the heir could petition for a writ of entry, which began the proceedings whereby the possession of land was traced over the generations. In that writs of entry were introduced to allow heirs to repossess lands that had not been taken illegally, they represented an important complement to the original possessory assizes.

Constitutional law was also an interest of Bracton's, who insisted that the king had no equal in the whole realm:

> The king has no equal within his realm, subjects cannot be the equals of the ruler, because he would thereby lose his rule, since equal can have no authority over equal, nor *a fortiori* a superior, because he would then be subject to those subject to him.[186]

At the same time, Bracton believed that the king was subject to the law: "The king must not be under man but under God and under the law, because law makes the king."[187] For Bracton, the king's will was not the sole source of legislation: "Whatever has been rightly decided and approved with the counsel and consent of the magnates and the general agreement of the *res publica*, the authority of the king or prince having first been added thereto, has the force of law."[188] Indeed, the king who ruled solely according to his own will perverted his own legitimacy: "There is no king where will rules rather than law."[189]

Still, royal statutes continued to be important in the thirteenth century, no less so than the famous Magna Carta of 1216, conceded by King John I (1199–1216) after a baronial uprising. In this famous document, the king pledged to abide certain, coveted rights, such as the right of earls to bequeath their property to their heirs without interference from the crown.[190] Magna Carta also confirmed the liberties enjoyed by the city of London.[191] Due process of law was guaranteed to all free subjects of the English crown: "No free man shall be taken or imprisoned or dispossessed, or outlawed, or banished, or in any way destroyed, nor will we go upon him, nor send upon him, except by legal judgment of his peers or by the law of the land."[192] Finally, Magna Carta also formally separated the court of common pleas from the King's Bench. The court of common pleas remained at Westminster, while the King's Bench continued to accompany the monarch as he journeyed about his realm.[193] New statutes, such as the Statute of Merton (1236), revised the original possessory assizes. The Statute of Merton granted legal remedies to widows whose dowries had been withheld from them after the death of their husbands. The statute also provided for the imprisonment of those who redesseised tenants after an assize had restored seisin. The Statute of Marlborough (1267), a consequence of the baronial uprising of 1258–1267, provided for penalties on lords who had compelled tenants to sue for an ancestor's property, that is, had forced them to seek an *assize mort d'ancestor*.

Over time, the business of the royal courts, both civil and criminal, increased dramatically, a development the kings eagerly encouraged. Judicial fines contributed to the royal coffers, as did the confiscation of the property of convicted criminals. The writs required for such cases became law, until the barons insisted in the late thirteenth century that law could only be made with the consent of the barons as expressed in a statute of the King-in-Parliament. Henry's reign put all the essential pieces of the common law into existence. In a century's time, justices had become full-time professionals, as did lawyers who defended clients, a corps of which formed around the court of common pleas. From the 1230s, the court of common pleas, the King's Bench, and the Exchequer (where the king's revenue cases were heard) continually heard and judged cases. The Exchequer and the King's Bench served as courts of appeal. The King's Bench heard appeals from the court of common pleas and the itinerant justices, which after 1348 were no longer used. By 1300, all civil suits came to the court of common pleas.

Henry III's son and successor, Edward I (1272–1307), was a formidable ruler. He had proved his mettle during the rebellions against his father, having defeated and killed in battle the leader of the baronial opposition, Simon de Montfort. Yet, having defeated them, Edward coopted important nobles into his regime, by consulting them in frequent councils. Still, the royal power had to be recovered from the long years of rebellion under his father and Edward commanded that every lord who claimed a privilege or a franchise legally prove his right to it, generally with a royal charter. The whole exercise served to limit the powers that nobles could claim, although the crown suffered from no such handicap. Over the years, subinfeudation—the process of granting fiefs lower and lower down the aristocratic ladder—had far removed many estates from the control of the crown. Edward's statute *Quia emptores* allowed land to be bought or sold provided the buyer held it from the seller's lord, instead of the seller.[194] *Quia emptores* discouraged subinfeudation and increased royal authority over landed property.

Of course, the most important constitutional and legal developments of Edward's reign were the first regular meetings of the English Parliament. The first meeting of the Parliament took place in 1265. The baronial leader Simon de Montfort summoned two knights from every shire and two burgers from every borough to meet with the prelates and barons. During their rebellions against Henry III, the barons often named themselves the community of the realm, and so at this meeting, the first of the Parliaments, the barons spoke on behalf of all England, as well as themselves. Edward summoned a similar assembly in 1275 that passed legislation and granted the king new taxes. Edward had many expensive wars to fight. He found that the consent of Parliament made the collection of these revenues more certain and efficient. In 1295 the so-called Model Parliament met, which included lower clergy along with the secular and ecclesiastical lords. Thus, these late thirteenth-century meetings of Parliament included the great peers, commoners such as the "knights of the shire," and burgers; representatives of the shires and the towns were elected. In time, the great peers evolved into the Lords, on the one hand, and the knights of the shire and the burgers into the Commons, on the other. From the 1297 meeting forward, that the elected representatives of the realm must approve new taxes was taken for granted in England. The English Parliament also transacted a great deal of routine judicial business.

Edward III (1327–1377) enacted another series of reforms. Edward spent a good deal of his time fighting in France, and so new royal servants were needed to govern England in his absence. During his reign, all of Parliament, Lords and Commons alike, assumed a greater share of the responsibilities of government. Later in his reign, Edward's government grew confused. Parliament then assumed the power to impeach royal officials for the crime of malfeasance.[195]

Edward's reign also featured important judicial developments. First, new courts emerged. The House of Lords became the supreme court of the realm and the chancellor's court came into existence. According to common-law jurisprudence, justice was responsibility of the king. If an injustice had been committed that had no remedy in law, the king should, then, find some way to correct the injustice, which became the business of the chancellor's court. For example, the law had permitted suits for breach of contract, and violators could be fined but not compelled to fulfill the contract. The chancellor's court could command that violator to honor his part of the agreement. The chancellor's court was thus empowered to judge according to fair play, rather than the letter of the law, even to the point of enforcing oral agreements. The statute *Praemunire* also strengthened the jurisdiction of royal courts, as it forbade "cases cognizable in the king's court being taken abroad (i.e., to the Roman curia)."[196] *Praemunire* did not affect clearly spiritual cases (like marriage) but those involving church patronage.

In 1361 justices of the peace, with criminal jurisdiction, were established in all shires:

> In every county of England shall be assigned for the keeping of the peace, one lord, and with him three or four of the most worthy in the county, with some learned in the law, and they shall have power to restrain the offenders, rioters, and all other barrators, and to pursue, arrest, take, and chastise them according [to] their trespass or offence; and to cause them to be imprisoned and duly punished according to the laws and customs of the realm.[197]

The establishment of the justices of the peace capped several decades of judicial administrative developments. During the reign of Edward I, officials known as keepers of the peace were empowered to supervise sheriffs and coroners. In 1329, they were given the authority to try felony suspects, effectively making them justices of the peace. As guarantors of the peace, these justices were responsible for the goods of the king within their jurisdictions. In 1388, they were ordered to meet in the county seat four times each year—the beginning of the Quarter Sessions so important to the later English system of justice. Over time, justices of the peace assumed police powers that had once belonged to popular and franchise courts. Hundredal courts soon thereafter disappeared, and county courts retained only civil jurisdiction. Appointed by the king from the nobles and lesser landholders, justices of the peace became the chief power in local government. They were the last great development in the history of the medieval English common law, as justice in the realm foundered on the civil strife and dynastic instability that afflicted England after 1390.

Legal studies, then, flourished during the Middle Ages. New systems of law came into being, and old systems were rediscovered and reappropriated. Since judges, lawyers, and jurists studied almost all of them, these traditions were in conversation with each other, creating an extraordinarily rich legal environment. The rulers, judges, and jurists of the early modern period in European history relied heavily upon the achievements of their medieval predecessors.

Notes

1. *Lex Baiuvariorum*, prol. [Theodore John Rivers, trans., *Laws of the Alamans and Bavarians* (Philadelphia, PA: University of Pennsylvania Press, 1977), p. 110].

2. The most Germanic of these codes was the Frankish. The Lombard and Visigothic codes had the most Roman influence.

3. *Lex Gundobada*, 2.7 [Katherine Fischer Drew, trans., *The Burgundian Code* (Philadelphia, PA: University of Pennsylvania Press, p. 23].

4. *Lex Gundobada*, 2.7 [Drew, *Burgundian Code*, p. 24].

5. *Lex Gundobada*, 2.2 [Drew, *Burgundian Code*, p. 23].

6. *Lex Gundobada*, 2.3 [Drew, *Burgundian Code*, p. 23].

7. On early medieval ordeals, see Robert Bartlett, *Trial by Fire and Water: The Medieval Judicial Ordeal* (Oxford, UK: Clarendon Press, 1986).

8. *Lex Gundobada*, 20.2 [Drew, *Burgundian Code*, p. 38].

9. *Rothair's Edict*, 359 [Katherine Fischer Drew, trans., *The Lombard Laws* (Philadelphia, PA: University of Pennsylvania Press, 1973), p. 122].

10. *Pactus legis salicae*, 16.5 [Katherine Fischer Drew, trans., *The Laws of the Salian Franks* (Philadelphia, PA: University of Pennsylvania Press, 1991), pp. 81–82]: "If a Roman [inflicts arson] on another Roman and proof is not certain, he may clear himself with twenty oathhelpers, half of whom he has chosen. If he cannot find the oathhelpers, then he must go to the ordeal of boiling water. If he is judged guilty, he should pay twelve hundred denarii."

11. *Lex Gundobada*, 45.1 [Drew, *Burgundian Code*, p. 52].

12. *Lex Gundobada*, 14.3 [Drew, *Bugundian Code*, p. 32].

13. *Lex Gundobada*, 101.1 [Drew, *Burgundian Code*, pp. 85–86].

14. *Lex Gundobada*, 34.1–3 [Drew, *Burgundian Code*, pp. 45–46].

15. *Pactus legis salicae* 59.6 [Drew, *Laws of the Salian Franks*, p. 122]. Cf. *Lex Gundobada*, 1.2, 42.1, and 74.2 [Drew, *Burgundian Code*, pp. 22, 50, and 71].

16. F. L. Ganshof, *Feudalism*, trans. Philip Grierson (New York, NY: Harper & Row, 1961), p. 35.

7. Called *fief* in Old French, *feoff* or *fee* in Old English, and either *feodum* or *beneficium* in Latin.

18. G. Duby, *Rural Economy and Country Life in the Medieval West*, trans. Cynthia Postan (Columbia, SC: University of South Carolina Press, 1962), p. 373.

19. R. W. Southern, *The Making of the Middle Ages* (New Haven, CT: Yale University Press, 1953), pp. 98–99.

20. Harding, *Medieval Law and the Foundations of the State*, p. 109.

21. Philippe de Beaumanoir, *Coutumes de Beauvaisis*, 7.236 [F. R. P. Akehurst, trans., *The Coutumes de Beauvaisis of Philippe de Beaumanoir* (Philadelphia, PA: University of Pennsylvania Press, 1992), p. 92].

22. *Établissements de St. Louis*, 1.4 [F. R. P. Akehurst, *The Établissements de Saint Louis* (Philadelphia, PA: University of Pennsylvania Press, 1996), p. 11].

23. *Établissements de St. Louis*, 1.1 [Akehurst, pp. 8–9], and *Sachsenspiegel*, 2.22 and 4.26 [Maria Dobozy, trans. *The Saxon Mirror: A Sachsenspiegel of the Fourteenth Century* (Philadelphia, PA: University of Pennsylvania Press, 1999), pp. 99–100 and 152].

24. *Établissements de St. Louis*, 1.4 [Akehurst, p. 11–12].

25. Beaumanoir, *Coutumes*, 7.246 and 67.1915 [Akehurst, pp. 96 and 700–701].

26. *Établissements*, 1.52 and 1.156 [Akehurst, pp. 36 and 99].

27. *Établissements*, 1.53 [Akehurst, p. 36].

28. *Établissements*, 1.158 [Akehurst, p. 99].

29. Fredegar, *Chronicle*, 4.58 [J. M. Wallace-Hadrill, trans. *The Fourth Book of the Chronicle of Fredegar with its Continuations* (London, UK: Thomas Nelson and Sons Ltd, 1960), p. 48].

30. Stein, *Roman Law*, p. 53.

31. Stein, *Roman Law*, p. 61.

32. For a general discussion of *ius commune*, see Manlio Bellomo, *The Common Legal Past of Europe, 1000–1800*, trans. Lydia G. Cochrane (Washington, DC: Catholic University of America Press, 1995).

33. Stein, *Roman Law*, p. 48.

34. Harding, *Medieval Law and the Foundations of the State*, p. 285.

35. R. H. Helmholz, *The Spirit of Classical Canon Law* (Athens, GA: University of Georgia Press, 1996), p. 30.

36. D. 54 c. 1 [*Corpus iuris*, 1:206].

37. D. 54 c. 2 (decree of the council of Turrecremata, 895 [*Corpus iuris*, 1:207]).

38. X 1.17.1 (decree of the council of Poitiers, 1087 [*Corpus iuris*, 2:135]).

39. X 1.20.1-7 [*Corpus iuris*, 2:144–146], and C. 23 q. 4 c. 47 [*Corpus iuris*, 1:899–900].

40. D. 62 c. 3 [*Corpus iuris*, 1:234].

41. D. 62. c. 1 [*Corpus iuris*, 1:234].

42. D. 63 c. 12 [*Corpus iuris*, 1:238], and D. 62 c. 2 [*Corpus iuris*, 1:234].

43. D. 63 c. 19 [*Corpus iuris*, 1:240].

44. X 1.6.1 [*Corpus iuris*, 2:48]. "Canons" in the sense of the diocesan priests who lived as monks, usually as companions of the bishop.

45. C. 1 q. 7 c. 7 [*Corpus iuris*, 1:430].

46. D. 23 c. 1 [*Crisis of Church and State*, p. 42 (*Corpus iuris*, 1:77)].

47. X 1.6.6 [Tanner and Alberigo, *Decrees*, 1:211 (*Corpus iuris*, 2:51)].

48. D. 22 c. 1, addressed to the people of the city of Milan [*Corpus iuris*, 1:73].

49. D. 40 c. 6 [*Corpus iuris*, 1:146].

50. C. 23 q. 5 c. 3 [*Corpus iuris*, 1:930], D. 45 c. 5 [*Corpus iuris*, 1:161–162], and X 5.6.9 [*Corpus iuris*, 2:774].

51. Cod. Theo. 16.6.6 [Pharr, p. 465]: "If someone shall be found to rebaptize a person of the catholic faith, he commits a crime as does one who makes an idolatrous offering." Some North African heretics had demanded that Christians who had renounced the faith under the compulsion of persecution must be rebaptized if they should desire to return to the church. The orthodox teaching, upheld here by the emperors, was that baptism could be conferred only once, unlike all the other sacraments except for confirmation and holy orders. (Cod., 1.6.2).

52. X 3.42.3 [*Corpus iuris*, 2:644–646].

53. De cons. D. 4 c. 31 [*Corpus iuris*, 1:1371].

54. C. 1 q. 7 c. 11 [*Corpus iuris*, 1:432].

55. Helmholz, *Spirit of Classical Canon Law*, pp. 211–222.

56. C. 30 q. 5 c. 3 [David Herlihy, *Medieval Households* (Cambridge, MA: Harvard University Press, 1985), pp. 73–74].

57. X 4.1.29 [*Corpus iuris*, 2:671–672], and C. 31 q. 2 c. 1 [*Corpus iuris*, 1:1113].

58. X 4.4.3 [*Corpus iuris*, 2:681].

59. X 4.1.15 [*Crisis of Church and State* (*Corpus iuris*, 2:666–667)].

60. David Herlihy, *Medieval Households*, pp. 81–82.

61. C. 27 q. 2 c. 21 and X 3.32.1 [*Corpus iuris*, 2:579].

62. Helmholz, *Spirit of Classical Canon Law*, pp. 240–241.

63. *The Rule of St. Benedict*, c. 58, called for a novitiate of ten months [Anthony C. Meisel and M. L. del Mastro, trans. and eds. (New York, NY: Doubleday, 1975), pp. 93–95].

64. X 3.31.1 [*Corpus iuris*, 2:569] and C. 20 q. 3 c. 4 [*Corpus iuris*, 1:850]: "Let no one be subjected to monastic discipline unwillingly."

65. X 3.31.15 [*Corpus iuris*, 2:574].

66. X 1.6.34 [*Crisis of Church and State*, pp. 133–134 (*Corpus iuris*, 2:80)].

67. X 2.1.13 [*Crisis of Church and State*, pp. 134–135 (*Corpus iuris*, 2:243)].

68. X 4.17.13 [*Crisis of Church and State*, p. 136 (*Corpus iuris*, 2:714–715)].

69. X 2.2.10 [*Crisis of Church and State*, p. 138 (*Corpus iuris*, 2:251)].

70. *Catechism of the Catholic Church*, nos. 1883–1885, p. 460.

71. Nov. 77.1 [Krueger and Mommsen, 3:424–425].

72. X 2.2.10 [*Crisis of Church and State*, p. 138 (*Corpus iuris*, 2:251)] and X 2.2.15 [*Corpus iuris*, 2:252–253].

73. See the discussion in Helmholz, *Spirit of Classical Canon Law*, pp. 121–136.

74. Ignatius of Antioch, *Letter to Polycarp*, c. 4 [Maxwell Staniforth, trans., *Early Christian Writings* (New York: Penguin Books, 1968), p. 110]. Polycarp was bishop of Smyrna in Asia Minor.

75. C. 24 q. 3 c. 25 [*Corpus iuris*, 1:997].

76. D. 87 c. 1 [*Corpus iuris*, 1:304]; C. 23 q. 5 c. 23 [*Corpus iuris*, 1:937]; C. 24 q. 3 c. 21 [*Corpus iuris*, 1:996]; C. 23 q. 5 c. 26 [*Corpus iuris*, 1:938].

77. D. 86 c. 26 [*Corpus iuris*, 1:304].

78. X 1.29.38 [*Corpus iuris*, 2:181].

79. Azo, *Summa codicis*, ad Cod. 3.14.1, cited in Helmholz, *Spirit of Classical Canon Law*, p. 129.

80. Helmholz, *Spirit of Classical Canon Law*, pp. 129–130.

81. Joannes Andreae, *Commentaria*, ad X 1.29.38, cited in Helmholz, *Spirit of Classical Canon Law*, pp. 132–134.

82. For what follows, I am indebted to Brian Tierney, *Medieval Poor Law* (Los Angeles, CA: University of California Press, 1959).

83. Ambrose, *De officiis*, 1.149 [Ivor J. Davidson, ed. and trans., *Ambrose: De officiis* (Oxford, UK: Oxford University Press, 2001), p. 203].

84. C. 12 q. 2 c. 23, 26–31 [*Corpus iuris*, 1:694–695, 696–698].

85. D. 82 c. 1 [Orleans I (511), canon 16 (*Corpus iuris*, 1:289)].

86. D. 84 c. 1 [Gregory I, *The Letters of Gregory the Great*, John R. C. Martyn, trans. (Toronto, ON: Pontifical Institute of Medieval Studies, 2004), 3:846].

87. Glos. ord. ad D. 82 ante c. 1 [Tierney, *Medieval Poor Law*, p. 58].

88. Walter Daniel, *Life of Ailred of Rievaulx*, chap. 5 [F. M. Powicke, trans., *Walter Daniel: The Life of Aelred of Rievaulx and the Letter to Maurice* (Kalamazoo, MI: Cistercian Publications, 1994), p. 97].

89. Francis of Assisi, *Testament*, c. 20–21 [Regis J. Armstrong, O. F. M Cap., and Ignatius C. Brady, O. F. M., trans. *Francis and Clare: The Complete Works* (New York, NY: Paulist Press, 1982), p. 155].

90. Thomas More, *Utopia*, Robert M. Adams, ed. and trans. (New York, NY: W. W. Norton & Company, 1975), p. 24.

91. Dig. 48.2.10 [Watson, 4:798].

92. Glos. ord. ad C. 2 q. 1 c. 14 [Tierney, *Medieval Poor Law*, p. 13].

93. Glos. ord. ad VI 1.3.11 [Tierney, *Medieval Poor Law*, p. 12].

94. X 5.5.1 [Tanner and Alberigo, *Decrees*, 1:220 (*Corpus iuris*, 2:768–769].

95. X 5.5.4 [Tanner and Alberigo, *Decrees*, 1:240 (*Corpus iuris*, 2:770)].

96. X 1.32.1 [*Corpus iuris*, 2:194–195].

97. D. 47 c. 8 [Tierney, *Medieval Poor Law*, p. 34 (*Corpus iuris*, 1:171–172)].

98. Guido de Baysio, *Rosarium*, ad D. 47 c. 8 [Tierney, *Medieval Poor Law*, p. 36].

99. Tierney, *Medieval Poor Law*, p. 38.

100. Thomas Aquinas, *Summa theologiae*, II-II.66.7 [*Political Ideas*, p. 138].

101. Rufinus, *Summa*, ad D. 86 d. p. c. 5 [Tierney, *Medieval Poor Law*, p. 52].

102. Ambrose, *De officiis*, 1.150 [Davidson, p. 205] and Augustine, *De civitate dei*, 19.14 [Henry Bettenson, trans., *City of God* (New York, NY: Penguin Books, 1972), p. 873].

103. C. 1 q. 1 c. 27 [*Corpus iuris*, 1:369–370]; C. 14 q. 5 c. 3 [*Corpus iuris*, 1:739]; C. 24 q. 1 c. 28 [*Corpus iuris*, 1:977].

104. Glos. ord. ad D. 45 c. 13 [Tierney, *Medieval Poor Law*, p. 53].

105. D. 86 c. 9 [*Corpus iuris*, 1:300].

106. D. 86 c. 14, 16–17 [*Corpus iuris*, 1:300–301, 301].

107. Tierney, *Medieval Poor Law*, p. 62.

108. Glos. ord. ad D. 86 c. 19.

109. Rufinus, *Summa*, ad D. 42 ante c. 1 [Tierney, *Medieval Poor Law*, p. 59].

110. Much of what follows is inspired by Brian Tierney, *Foundations of the Conciliar Theory* (Cambridge, UK: Cambridge University Press, 1955).

111. X 1.41.1 [*Corpus iuris*, 2:222–223].

112. Alberigo and Tanner, *Decrees*, 1:409. (*Haec sancta*)

113. Bernard of Clairvaux, *De consideratione*, 1.4 [John D. Anderson and Elizabeth T. Kennan, trans., *Five Books on Consideration: Advice to a Pope* (Kalamazoo, MI: Cistercian Publications, 1976), p. 29].

114. James A. Brundage, *Medieval Canon Law* (New York, NY: Longman, 1995), p. 142, and Edward Peters, *Torture*, 2nd ed. (Philadelphia, PA: University of Pennsylvania Press, 1996), p. 41. Biblical authorities were Dt 19.15, Mt 18.16, and 2 Cor 13.1.

115. Innocent IV, *Commentaria*, ad X 2.22.15, as cited in Brundage, *Medieval Canon Law*, p. 133, n. 18.

116. X 5.3.31 [*Corpus iuris*, 2:760–761] and X 5.1.24, (Tanner and Alberigo, *Decrees*, 1:237–239 [*Corpus iuris*, 2:745–747]).

117. Brundage, *Medieval Canon Law*, p. 148.

118. Huguccio, *Summa decretorum*, D. 4 d. p. c. 3, cited in Kenneth Pennington, *Pope and Bishops: The Papal Monarchy in the Twelfth and Thirteenth Centuries* (Philadelphia, PA: University of Pennsylvania Press, 1984), pp. 21–22.

119. Hostiensis, *Summa aurea*, 5.56 [(Lyons: Jacob Giunta, 1537), 289rb].

120. Brundage, *Medieval Canon Law*, p. 157.

121. D. 11 c. 4 [Augustine Thompson, O. P., and James Gordley, trans., *Gratian: The Treatise on Laws with the Ordinary Gloss* (Washington, DC: Catholic University of America Press, 1993), p. 38 (*Corpus iuris*, 1:23–24)] and D. 12 c. 1 [Thompson, *Treatise on Laws*, p. 42 (*Corpus iuris*, 1:27)].

122. X 5.40.8 [*Corpus iuris*, 2:913–914]. Cf. *Dig.*, 1.3.24 [Watson, 1:13].

123. VI 5.12.30 [*Corpus iuris*, 2:1122]. Cf. *Dig.*, 50.17.9 [Watson, 4:957].

124. C. 1 q. 1 c. 41 [*Corpus iuris*, 1:374].

125. No *ex post facto*. Cod. 1.14.7 [Krueger and Mommsen, 2:68].

126. X 1.2.13 [*Corpus iuris*, 2:16].

127. Paulus, *Opinions*, 5.24 [Naphtali Lewis and Meyer Reinhold, eds., *Roman Civilization* (New York, NY: Harper & Row, 2:549].

128. Brundage, *Medieval Canon Law*, p. 172.

129. John T. McNeill and Helena M. Gamer, eds. and trans., *Medieval Handbooks of Penance* (New York, NY: Columbia University Press, 1990), p. 91.

130. Augustine, *Quaestionum in Heptateuchum libri vii*, 10 *super Josue* (CCSL 33:319) [I. Fraipont, ed. (Turnhont, Belgium: Brepols, 1955)]); *De civitate dei*, 19.12–13 [Henry Bettenson, pp. 866–872]; *Letter* 189.6 [E. M. Adkins and R. J. Dodaro, eds., *Augustine: Political Writings* (Cambridge, UK: Cambridge University Press, 2001) p. 217; C. 23 q. 1 c. 6 [*Corpus iuris*, 1:893–894].

131. Innocent IV, *Commentaria ad* X 3.34.8 [Tierney and Scott, *Western Societies*, p. 295].

132. Innocent IV, *Commentaria ad* X 3.34.8 [Tierney and Scott, *Western Societies*, p. 295].

133. Innocent IV, *Commentaria ad* X 3.34.8 [Tierney and Scott, *Western Societies*, p. 296].

134. Innocent IV, *Commentaria ad* X 3.34.8 [Tierney and Scott, *Western Societies*, p. 256].

135. For this story, see W. Brandmüller, *Das Konzil von Konstanz* (Paderborn, Germany: Ferdinand Schöningh, 1997), 2:150–175.

136. Thomas Aquinas, *Summa theologiae*, I-II.90.4 [*Political Ideas*, p. 9].

137. *Summa theologiae*, I-II.90.1. ad 3 [*Political Ideas*, p. 3].

138. *Summa theologiae*, I-II.91.1 [*Political Ideas*, p. 12].

139. *Summa theologiae*, I-II.93.1 [*Political Ideas*, p. 30].

140. *Summa theologiae*, I-II.93.2 [*Political Ideas*, p. 32].

141. *Summa theologiae*, I-II.91.2 [*Political Ideas*, pp. 13–14]. Cf. *Summa theologiae*, I-II.93.2 [*Political Ideas*, p. 32].

142. *Summa theologiae*, I-II.94.2 [*Political Ideas*, p. 45].

143. *Summa theologiae*, I-II.94.1 [*Political Ideas*, p. 43].

144. *Summa theologiae*, I-II.94.3 [*Political Ideas*, p. 61].

145. *Summa theologiae*, I-II.97.4.ad 3 [*Political Ideas*, 85].

146. *Summa theologiae*, I-II.95.2 [*Political Ideas*, p. 58].

147. *Summa theologiae*, I-II.91.3 [*Political Ideas*, p. 15].

148. *Summa theologiae*, I-II.91.3.ad 3 [*Political Ideas*, p. 16].

149. *Summa theologiae*, I-II.96.4 [*Political Ideas*, p. 72].

150. *Summa theologiae*, I-II.95.1 [*Political Ideas*, p. 56].

151. *Summa theologiae*, I-II.95.1.ad 2 [*Political Ideas*, p. 57]. Cf. Aristotle, *Ethics*, 1103b: "Legislators make the citizens good by forming habits in them [McKeon, p. 952].

152. *Summa theologiae*, I-II.105.1 [*Political Ideas*, p. 88].

153. *Summa theologiae*, I-II.96.1.ad 3 [*Political Ideas*, p. 67].

154. *Summa theologiae*, I-II.96.3 [*Political Ideas*, pp. 69–70].

155. *Summa theologiae*, I-II.96.2 [*Political Ideas*, p. 68].

156. *Summa theologiae*, I-II.96.2.ad 2 [*Political Ideas*, p. 68].

157. *Summa theologiae*, I-II.96.4 [*Political Ideas*, p. 71].

158. *Summa theologiae*, I-II.96.6 [*Political Ideas*, p. 76].

159. *Summa theologiae*, I-II.97.3.ad 3 [*Political Ideas*, p. 83].

160. *Summa theologiae*, I-II.97.2 [*Political Ideas*, p. 81].

161. *Summa theologiae*, I-II.96.5.5 [*Political Ideas*, p. 73]. The reference to St. Paul includes the orthodox teaching on Paul's alleged antinomianism. The Great Church did not take St. Paul to mean that the faithful ignore moral teaching, indeed, they could not, but that there comes a point in their ongoing perfection whereby they cease to do right from fear, and come to do it from love.

162. *Summa theologiae*, II-II.58.3. ad 1 [*Political Ideas*, p. 111].

163. *Summa theologiae*, II-II.58.1 [*Political Ideas*, p. 106].

164. *Summa theologiae*, II-II.57.4 [*Political Ideas*, p. 103].

165. *Summa theologiae*, II-II.58.11. ad 3 [*Political Ideas*, p. 124].

166. *Summa theologiae*, II-II.58.12 [*Political Ideas*, pp. 125–126].

167. *Summa theologiae*, I-II.91.4 [*Political Ideas*, p. 17].

168. *Summa theologiae*, I-II.91.4 [*Political Ideas*, p. 17].

169. *Summa theologiae*, I-II.91.4 [*Political Ideas*, pp. 17–18].

170. *Summa theologiae*, I-II.91.5 [*Political Ideas*, 19–20].

171. See Robert W. Shaffern, "*Mater et magistra*: Gendered Images and Church Authority in the Thought of Pope Innocent III," *Logos* 4 (2001), 65–88.

172. *Leges Henrici Primi*, 10.1 [L. J. Downer, ed. and trans. (Oxford, UK: Clarendon Press, 1972), pp. 108–109].

173. Ralph de Glanville, A *Treatise on the Laws and Customs of the Kingdom of England*, 13.33 [John Beames, trans., A *Translation of Glanville* (Littleton, CO: Fred B.

Rothman & Co., 1980, repr. 1812), pp. 335–336]. Civil remedy is one meaning of assize. Another is a meeting of a high royal council, and another still a law issued by that high royal council, as in the Assize of Clarendon, below.

174. *English Constitutional History*, p. 21.

175. *English Constitutional History*, p. 38.

176. Glanville, 13.2 [Beames, p. 305].

177. *English Constitutional History*, p. 3; Glanville, 13.20 [Beames, trans., pp. 325–326].

178. *English Constitutional History*, pp. 14–15.

179. *English Constitutional History*, p. 16.

180. Frederick Pollock and Frederic William Maitland, *The History of English Law before the Time of Edward I* (Cambridge, UK: Cambridge University Press, 1895), 1:141–142.

181. Pollock and Maitland, 1:139.

182. For the standard treatment, see R. H. Helmholz, *Canon Law and the Law of England* (London, UK: Hambledon Press, 1987).

183. X 3.50.9 [Alberigo and Tanner, *Decrees*, 1:244 (*Corpus iuris*, 2:659–660)]: "No cleric may be put in command of mercenaries or crossbowmen or suchlike men of blood; nor may a subdeacon, deacon or priest practise the art of surgery, which involves cauterizing and making incisions; nor may anyone confer a rite of blessing or consecration on a purgation by ordeal of boiling or cold water or of the red-hot iron, saving nevertheless the previously promulgated prohibitions regarding single combats and duels."

184. Ibid.: " . . . nor shall any person be subject for the same offence to be twice put in jeopardy of life or limb."

185. George Woodbine, ed., *Bracton: On the Laws and Customs of England*, Samuel D. Thorne, trans. (Buffalo, NY: William S. Hein & Co., 1997, repr. 1968), 4:21–22.

186. *Bracton*, 2:33.

187. *Bracton*, ibid.

188. *Bracton*, 2:19.

189. *Bracton*, 2:33.

190. *Magna Carta*, c. 2 [Brian Tierney and Joan Scott, eds., *Western Societies: A Documentary History* (New York, NY: Alfred A. Knopf, Inc., 1984), 1:275].

191. *Magna Carta*, c. 13 [Tierney and Scott, 1:276].

192. *Magna Carta*, c. 39 [Tierney and Scott, 1:277].

193. *Magna Carta*, c. 17 [Tierney and Scott, 1:276].

194. *English Constitutional History*, pp. 81–82.

195. *English Constitutional History*, pp. 132–135.

196. W. A. Pantin, *The English Church in the Fourteenth Century* (Toronto, CA: University of Toronto Press, 1955, repr. 1980), p. 85. Text of *Praemunire* may be found in *English Constitutional History*, pp. 123–124.

197. *English Constitutional History*, pp. 127–128.

PART IV

The Early Modern Era

Great changes were afoot in Europe at the close of the medieval period, and beyond. In western and central Europe, rulers consolidated their power, and often employed Roman law unto their purposes. In many regions, social upheaval dissolved ancient legal bonds tying elites to their dependants. The Protestant Reformation sundered the unity of Latin Christendom. The Enlightenment of the eighteenth century challenged the beliefs of Christianity, and rejected Europe's ancestral social organization and its legal heritage.

The Dissolution of Legal Ties of Dependence

European civilization entered another transitional era at about the turn of the fourteenth century, such that medieval historians call the period from 1300 to 1500 the Late Middle Ages. Whereas economic prosperity and demographic expansion characterized the social history of the High Middle Ages (1000–1300), economic dislocation and population decline were the stories of the next two centuries. The high medieval growth in population was quite unprecedented for a premodern civilization. The population in both cities and countryside grew, although emigrants from the countryside accounted for most of the urban growth. The overall population seems to have increased at least fourfold between 900 and 1250. In some regions the growth may have been even greater. A great deforestation of the continent accompanied the population increase, as more land needed to be brought under the plow, to feed the greater number of mouths. These newly cleared lands, called assarts, benefited the cultivators in two ways. First, because customary law fixed the dues owed to lords, the crops grown on assarts were duty-free. Second, more crops could be grown.

A number of factors probably contributed to the cessation of assarting by 1200, and the contraction of the population by the first quarter of the fourteenth century. The rate of demographic growth had perhaps begun to decrease. Fertility maintenance of what had once been forest was difficult and so these plots exhausted themselves faster than other soils. The climate of Europe, which had been relatively warm and dry from around 800 and therefore more conducive to agriculture, seems to have rather abruptly grown cold and wet around the turn of the fourteenth century. The new conditions subjected both crops in the fields and in storage to greater risk of rot. The change in climate seems to have spiked the frequency and magnitude of crop failures between 1311 and 1323. By the end of the 1320s, much of the population of Europe was undernourished. The aged and the young were especially vulnerable to disease. In 1347, the terrible Black Death struck a population already in decline and seriously weakened. Over the next three years, between one-fourth and one-third of Christian Europe perished.

This demographic contraction dissolved ancient social networks and the laws that supported them. Medieval agricultural villages were cooperative ventures. Families farmed their own fields and helped others in the village as well. In this way, they could reduce their costs—instead of each family acquiring a plowteam (which included a plow, draft animal, and crew), several families would share one. Cooperative cultivation meant, however, that these villages were fragile. Any reduction in the number of villagers—let alone a large, sudden reduction—would make the villagers unable to support themselves. Archaeological studies of fourteenth-century England, in particular, have unearthed numerous abandoned villages; their residents either fled the plague, or sought out new, viable homesteads. Fourteenth-century peasants moved about the countryside more than their immediate ancestors. Obviously, in the course of only a few years, the overall number of laborers declined precipitously.

In many regions of western Europe, the new mobility and bargaining power of laborers ended personal bonds of legal dependence, or serfdom, between lords and peasants. Up to the middle of the thirteenth century, lords had increasingly been inclined to commute labor dues into money payments or rents. Both parties benefited from such commutations. Peasants could spend more time on the plots they worked the hardest, and the lords' paid laborers worked better than resentful, *corvée* peasants. Lords had even been inclined to rent, rather than cultivate, their own plots, called *demesne*, which consisted of strips of land interspersed among those belonging to the peasantry. By 1250, the population increase had placed lords in a favorable position relative to peasants and most seem to have chosen to once again demand labor dues, and to directly cultivate more of their *demesnes*.

By 1350, that relationship reversed. Laborers now used their competitive advantage in the labor market to obtain their personal freedom and better wages. Some lords tried to manage their manors as before and demanded labor services. The policies of other lords, however, who offered peasants personal freedom and higher wages to emigrate to their lands, undermined other, more authoritarian lords. Some lords opted for labor-saving enterprises such as converting arable into pastoral lands—fewer hands were needed to raise sheep than crops, particularly if grazing could be enclosed by some sort of fence. These lords ejected the peasants from their manors, and created terrible suffering and widespread resentment. In his *Utopia*, Thomas More complained about the same policies at the beginning of the sixteenth century:

> They leave no land free for the plow: they enclose every acre for pasture; they destroy houses and abolish towns, keeping only the churches, and those for sheep-barns . . . there is no need for farm labor . . . when there is no land left to be plowed. One herdsman or shepherd can look after a flock of beasts large enough to stock an area that would require many hands if it were plowed and harvested.[1]

By the end of the sixteenth century, legions of paupers, wandering the countryside with no means of support, filled the English countryside. Many of these poor folk sought better conditions in towns and cities, where many became thieves to survive. In England, the medieval system of poor relief simply collapsed and would not be replaced until 1601 with the enactment of the Elizabethan Poor Law Act. This legislation retained the distinction between the deserving and undeserving poor but relegated the deserving poor to the poorhouses and workhouses made famous in Dickens's novels. The idle poor were to be imprisoned; indeed, the Elizabethan law entrusted the administration of poor relief to parish officials called overseers of the poor, who in turn worked under the supervision of the justices of the peace, whose first responsibility was the capture, trial, and sentencing of criminals.

All over Christian Europe, the intensity of peasant and worker resentments grew. The first in a long series of European peasant rebellions broke out in Flanders in 1325. Count Louis I of Nevers (r. 1322–1346) had levied an unpopular new tax and drove rustics under the leadership of a prosperous peasant named Nicholas Zannekin into sedition. Nicholas and his men successfully defied the count for three years, until King Philip VI of France

(1328–1350), eager to assert his sovereignty over Flanders, intervened on the count's behalf.

The famous widespread rebellion of the Jacquerie in France broke out in 1358 over anger at the royal conduct of the Hundred Years' War. New exactions to pay for the war greatly angered the peasants. Those exactions, however, constituted only one source of discontent. French politics had virtually disintegrated after the defeat at the Battle of Poitiers (1356), where King John I (1350–1364) himself had been taken prisoner. The *dauphin* (heir to the French throne) Charles, his cousin Charles the Bad of Navarre, and a commoner named Étienne Marcel, a leading merchant of Paris, all contested for power. As authority crumbled, unemployed bands of mercenaries pillaged the countryside. The nobles failed to restore order, but continued to demand dues from the peasants. In May, 1358, not far from Paris, villagers attacked a company of soldiers and killed nine of them. This incident released the frustrations of other peasants and much of France erupted in violence. The Jacquerie mainly targeted the nobles, rather than the king, since most peasants believed that the monarch, a more distant figure, protected them against the confiscations of the nobles, on whose estates they lived and from whose rapacity they were likelier to suffer. The number of nobles who lost their lives to the Jacquerie was probably rather small, however, since many fled at the news of approaching mobs. The peasants looted and burned many a chateau. For a time, Etienne Marcel joined his fellow commoners against the nobles. The warriors of Charles the Bad brutally crushed the Jacquerie by mid-June.

In 1378, Florentine cloth workers rebelled against merchant oligarchs. The rebellion of the Ciompi resulted from much the same complaints as those of peasant-laborers in other parts of Europe. In the thirteenth century, a remarkable heterogeneity characterized the neighborhoods of Florence. Like the villages of the countryside, rich and poor resided near one another, and socialized civilly, if not warmly. From the street, the houses of the wealthy would have been scarcely distinguishable from the poor. Workers often sought out elite godparents for their children. Through godparentage, poor folks received valuable gifts and became the clients of the powerful. Elite families extended their network of social dependants. After the Black Death, however, Florentine oligarchs struggled to maintain their supremacy over the city. They built great palace-fortresses, whose very appearance suggested power, influence, and intimidation. They, too, sponsored legislation aimed at limiting wages. The Ciompi managed to win power in the city for about eighteen months but were then driven from power. The oligarchs successfully prevented any other disturbances for more than a century.

English peasants likewise had their complaints. In an effort to limit wages in the wake of the Black Death, nobles passed the Statute of Laborers through Parliament in 1351. The Statute of Laborers stipulated that "carters, ploughmen, drivers of the plough, shepherds, swineherds, dairy maids, and all other servants, shall take liveries and wages, accustomed the said twentieth year, or four years before," that is to say that the workers thus enumerated must take the wages they were paid in the twentieth year of King Edward III's reign, which was 1347! The statute declared that other workers must do likewise, lest they contribute "to the great damage of the great men." The statute attributed increased wages to "the malice of the said servants."[2] Peasants deeply resented the statute, along with the nobility's renewed insistence on collecting labor dues. A new tax in 1377 further angered peasants. In the past, most new taxes in England had been collected on movable property, which fell more heavily upon the wealthy, and so were regarded as mainly fair to all. The 1377 tax, however, was a head tax, and therefore regressive. Another head tax was imposed in 1380 at the outrageous level of twelve pence per household member over the age of fifteen. Many peasants refused to pay. The government sent out commissioners to collect the tax, with brutality if necessary. In May 1381, peasants in Essex attacked tax commissioners and within a few days rebellion spread throughout the shire. Thus began Wat Tyler's Rebellion, named for the yeoman (free peasant) and veteran of the Hundred Years' War who became its leader. Rather better organized than the rebellion of the Jacquerie, English peasants chafed neither at the king nor at the nobility but at certain royal agents; like the Jacquerie, they stressed their loyalty to the fourteen-year-old king (Richard II, 1377–1399). Wat Tyler's men attacked the homes of royal servants they believed were oppressing simple folk. They demanded fairness in taxation and the rule of traditional English law, by which they meant that new exactions should be canceled. They also demanded that serfdom be eliminated. Richard decided to negotiate with the rebels. An agreement was reached between the king and the rebels, who nonetheless continued their slayings of hated government officials. Another meeting was held on June 15, during which Wat Tyler was killed. Leaderless and discouraged, the peasants obeyed the king's order to go home. After tensions had settled down, the government arrested and executed some of the rebellion's leaders, but fewer English peasants died than had French in 1358.

Other peasant uprisings broke out for the rest of the fourteenth and fifteenth centuries. The last and most widespread of these rebellions was the Peasant War of 1525, which broke out in southern Germany. As elsewhere, the late fifteenth-century German Empire teemed with the disaffected. Peasant uprisings had erupted in Würzburg (1474), Switzerland (1513–1515), Württemberg (1514), the Upper Rhine (1517), and Stühlingen (1524). As in fourteenth-century England and France, the weakness of the central authority contributed to social tensions. The *Reichsrittern* (imperial knights who were small estate owners) rebelled in 1522–1523 against territorial lords who demanded they serve themselves rather than the emperor. Two years later, south German peasants again erupted in rebellion. In March 1525, a band of Swabian peasants enumerated their demands in the so-called Twelve Articles, a list of grievances against the aristocracy:

1. It is our humble petition and desire . . . that in the future . . . each community should choose and appoint a pastor, and that we should have the right to depose him should he conduct himself improperly. . . .
2. We are ready and willing to pay the fair tithe of grain. . . . The small tithes [of cattle], whether to ecclesiastical or lay lords, we will not pay at all, for the Lord God created cattle for the free use of man.
3. We . . . take it for granted that you will release us from serfdom as true Christians, unless it should be shown us from the Gospel that we are serfs.
4. It has been the custom heretofore that no poor man should be allowed to catch venison or wildfowl or fish in flowing water, which seems to us quite unseemly and unbrotherly as well as selfish and not agreeable to the Word of God. . . .
5. We are aggrieved in the matter of woodcutting, for the noblemen have appropriated all the woods to themselves. . . .
6. In regard to the excessive services demanded of us *which are increased from day to day*, we ask that this matter be properly looked into so that we shall not continue to be oppressed in this way. . . .
7. We will not hereafter *allow ourselves to be further oppressed by our lords*, but will let them demand only what is just and proper according to the word of agreement between the lord and the peasant. *The lord should no longer try to force more services or other dues from the peasant without payment.* . . .
8. We are greatly burdened because our holdings cannot support the rent exacted from them. . . . We ask that the lords may appoint persons of honor to inspect these holdings and fix a rent in accordance with justice. . . .
9. *We are burdened with a great evil in the constant making of new laws.* . . . In our opinion we should be judged according to our old written law. . . .

10. *We are aggrieved by the appropriation . . . of meadows and fields which at one time belonged to the community as a whole.* These we will again take into our own hands. . . .

11. We will entirely abolish the due called *Todfall* ["death tax," by which the lord received the best horse, cow, or garment of a family upon the death of a serf] and will no longer endure it, nor allow widows and orphans to be thus shamefully robbed against God's will, and in violation of justice and right. . . .

12. It is our conclusion and final resolution, that if any one or more of the articles here set forth should not be in agreement with the Word of God, as we think they are, such article we will willingly retract.[3]

As the ninth of the articles makes clear, these demands amounted to a call for the restoration of traditional dues and customary law, which Emperor Charles V (1519–1556) was then replacing with Roman law.

The aristocracy refused to consider the Twelve Articles and in April the peasants resorted to violence. The unrest soon spread to Austria, Thuringia, and Saxony. Bavaria would likewise have been embroiled in the anarchy but for the skillful intervention of its duke, whose meetings with both peasants and nobles reduced animosity. Like the other late medieval rebellions, the peasants, although fairly well-organized, could not contend with the professional warriors of the nobility. The princes of Hesse, Brunswick, and Saxony met the peasant army at Frankenhausen on May 15, 1525. The peasants were defeated, although not massacred. The rebellion ended with the battle.

The catastrophes of the Late Middle Ages had many legal and juristic ramifications. With increasing frequency did criminal trials impose more severe sentences that were likelier to be carried out. The sentences of high medieval criminal trials, in contrast, were generally quite lenient. In many cases they were completely ignored. The relative isolation of many medieval settlements meant that vendetta might well be the fallout from criminal proceedings. While medieval peasants felt more acutely than had their ancestors the presence of the government, in the ordinary course of events most villages self-governed on the basis of kinship; most landlords were more interested in exploiting rather than ruling their dependant peasants. Indeed, time and space limited the power of even the closest castellan. Furthermore, the cooperative nature of cultivation demanded that villagers stay on civil terms with each other. Thus, instead of terminating conflict between plaintiffs and defendants, judicial procedures might intensify them. Most high medieval trials, then, amounted to an admission that injury had been done and a promise that compensation would be made. Anything more severe would have created more tension than they released in the village, as the kin of the defendant might vow vengeance.[4]

The governing classes of the later medieval period, in contrast, responded to the social unrest with increasingly severe and certain court sentences. In more and more cases, execution replaced restitution. In *Utopia* Thomas More complained: "This way of punishing thieves [hanging] goes beyond the call for justice, and is not, in any case, for the public good. The penalty is too harsh in itself."[5] More argued that the traditional penalty, namely restitution, should be the penalty for theft.[6] In the past, severe punishments were more probably imposed upon the sociopath—the highwaymen and outcasts who lived like animals in the forest, and who preyed on respectable, sedentary rural villagers or travelers. These people, who in the past could expect lighter punishments for crimes, now found themselves subject to the same harsh justice as the traditionally marginalized. Such proceedings aroused resentment toward the local nobles who administered justice.

Thus, elites attempted to maintain their supremacy over society through the law, with mixed results. In the long term, the pressures of the labor market overcame wage ceilings and servile labor dues, for not only were landowners and manufacturers negotiating for wages and working conditions with laborers, but they also competed against each other. That competition undermined the efficacy of repressive legislation. On the other hand, nobilities dominated European society until the early twentieth century. Nobility continued to be an either acquired or (more usually) inherited legal status that entitled its bearers to certain privileges, in particular, remission from paying certain taxes and protection from cruel criminal punishments.

The relationship between nobles and commoners, however, much altered during the early modern period. The superiority of elites then was rather less personal than in the High Middle Ages. To be a serf meant to be tied legally and personally to a lord. High medieval lords lived among their inferiors, and as often as possible appeared among their serfs and free tenants. Lords needed to be seen to be respected and feared. No doubt both parties discussed issues pertinent to their relationship during these encounters. Manor houses were generally close to villages. Similar relationships could be found in medieval towns. During the High Middle Ages, heterogeneity characterized the neighborhoods of most medieval towns and cities. The wealthy lived among the humble; indeed, from the street their houses would have been scarcely distinguishable (although the interiors, of course, would have been very different!). After the tumult of the last two medieval centuries, the legal bonds of serfdom had almost completely disappeared in western Europe, and retreated from the rest of society. Nobles built great, manor houses within fenced estates. Through chivalry and heraldry, medieval nobles had cultivated a lifestyle that differed from tillers of the soil, craftsmen, and merchants. The early modern nobility intensified that otherness.

The Dissolution of Latin Christendom

Religious conflict contributed to the social upheaval after the outbreak of the Protestant Reformation in 1517. Religious dissent, of course, had been a feature of medieval civilization since the eleventh century. The issue of dissent in the medieval centuries was more complex than is usually understood. Dissent generally took two forms: error and heresy. Error simply referred to a mistaken notion of church teaching, and was a kind of ecclesiastical misdemeanor. Church authorities usually dismissed with a lenient penance anyone who came before them convicted of error. Heresy was a more serious ecclesiastical crime. According to the law of the church, heresy (from the Greek verb, *heresein*, "to choose one's own way") was a stubborn and public rejection of the teaching of the church; that is, the heretic had both a mistaken idea of church teaching, had made that teaching known to others, and had refused before church authorities to accept the correct teaching. All heresy procedures began with the assumption that the accused was guilty only of error. No matter how wrong, anyone who would submit to the teaching authority of the church was not guilty of heresy.

Most medieval heresies, however, concerned either church authority or the problem of evil. In the twelfth century, the southern French Waldensians and Albigensians formed the two largest and most alarming groups of dissenters. The Waldensians took their name from their leader, a prosperous merchant of Lyons named Peter Waldo, who had a conversion experience, sold off his belongings, and desired to live in evangelical poverty while preaching the Gospel. The problem was that church law forbade laymen from preaching (one had to be at least a deacon). Furthermore, Waldo had commissioned a translation of the Bible from Latin into French without first seeking the permission of church authorities. The archbishop of Lyons approved of Waldo's motivations, and encouraged his adoption of poverty and good works. The archbishop, however, commanded that Waldo refrain from preaching. Waldo first agreed to the archbishop's commands, but later disregarded them. Thus, Waldensianism mostly amounted to a refusal to recognize church authority, but also came to espouse an antisacramentalism. Like the Donatists of the fifth century, Waldensians denied the efficacy of the sacraments because worldly and sinful clerics often administered them.

In contrast, the Albigensians, or Cathars (the "pure," derived from Greek *kathairein*, "to purify") as they were also known, were scarcely recognizable as Christians, owing to their radical dualism. This sect taught that only spiritual realities were truly good and created by the ultimate good principle. An ultimate evil principle, however, had created all corporeal reality, which was likewise deemed evil. This dualist metaphysic accompanied an extreme asceticism, for the point of the good life was to liberate the soul from its prison, the body. The Albigensians thus likewise denounced procreation, since having children merely imprisoned more souls. The Albigensians had a church organization parallel to that of the Catholics, and some of their religious leaders, called *perfecti*, were indeed expected to starve themselves to death, so as to free the soul from the body.

In keeping with canon law, church authorities first confronted these dissenters with preaching and persuasion. Pope Lucius III (1181–1185) promulgated the bull *Ad abolendam*, which handed down rules for dealing with heretics. The pope ordered the bishops to investigate religious dissent.

> Every archbishop or bishop, by himself, or his archdeacon, or by other trustworthy and fit persons, shall twice, or once, in the year go around any parish in which it shall have been reported that heretics reside; and there call upon three or more persons of good credit, or, if it seem expedient, on the whole neighborhood, to take an oath that if anyone shall know that there are heretics in the place or any persons holding secret conventicles or differing in life and manners from the common conversation of the faithful, he will make it his business to point them out to the bishop or archdeacon. Moreover, the bishop or archdeacon shall cite the accused to appear before him, who, unless they shall clear themselves from the charges brought against them to their satisfaction . . . they shall be punished by the judgment of the bishop. . . .
>
> Moreover, we ordain that counts, barons, rectors, consuls of cities and other places, being called upon by the archbishops and bishops, shall bind themselves with an oath that in all matters aforesaid, they will stoutly and effectually aid the Church against heretics.[7]

Innocent III repeated the substance of this decree at Lateran IV and provincial councils followed suit.[8]

Patience on both sides wore thin, however, as persuasion had little effect. After the murder of the papal legate Peter of Castelnau in 1209, Pope Innocent III decided that force must be employed, so as to protect the orthodox from the heretics. He would have preferred that one of Christendom's kings lead an army against the heretics, but all of them were in trouble with the pope for one reason or another and so the task of humbling the dissenters fell to an army of northern French barons. The pope elevated the military campaign to a crusade, whose warriors enjoyed all the appurtenant benefits. The Albigensian Crusade, which was actually a series of bloody campaigns fought between 1209 and 1229, mostly aimed at destroying the power of the barons who sheltered heretics, so that the bishops could investigate and punish heretics without interference.

In 1231, Pope Gregory IX decided that the efforts of south French bishops had failed to produce the desired results, and promulgated the decree *Ille humani generis*, which provided for inquisitorial tribunals directly subject to the pope:

> We seek, urge, and exhort your wisdom . . . that you be sent as judges into different districts to preach where it seems useful to you to the clergy and people assembled together, using for this purpose other discreet people known to you, and to seek out diligently those who are heretics or are infamed by heresy. If you should discover heretics or people infamed by heresy, unless they should be willing, upon examination, to obey the commands of the church, you are to proceed against them according to our statutes against heresy recently promulgated. . . . If any heretic, having abjured, wishes to return to the unity of the Church, you may receive him according to the Church's formula of absolution, and lay upon him the burden that it is customary to lay upon such people. . . .
>
> You may exercise the office thus given to you freely and efficaciously, concerning this and all of the things which we have mentioned above, and all in particular places who are swayed by your preaching [may be accepted thus back into the Church] within twenty days.[9]

Gregory has often been said to have founded the papal Inquisition with this decree. Instead, he established the *office* of inquisitor. The pope founded no department of the church, but a new official that could be appointed as necessary or useful. Inquisitors were itinerant, and traveled in teams of two members.

Once arrived in their jurisdictions, letters of the pope explaining their mission were read publicly. Inquisitors also preached sermons that encouraged confession of errors of faith, and accusation of suspects. The inquisitors would then interrogate suspects in private. According to a manual for the inquisitors of the south French town of Carcassone, inquisitors were just as interested in discovering the associates of a suspect as they were in finding errors of belief: "Thereafter, the person is diligently questioned about whether he saw a heretic or Waldensian, where and when, how often and with whom, and about others who were present; whether he listened to their preaching or exhortation and whether he gave them lodging or arranged shelter for them."[10] Inquisitors generally worked in areas where heresy was common, and where secular and diocesan authorities had done little about them. Both canon and civil law agreed that cases of heresy should be investigated by the church, but punished by secular authority, as in a law of Swabia, in southwest Germany (1235): "Where persons are believed to be heretics, they shall be accused before the spiritual court, for they should in the first place be tried by ecclesiastics. When they are convicted they shall be taken in hand by the secular court, which shall sentence them as is right; that is to say, they shall be burned at the stake."[11] Authorities imposed the death sentence only upon the third conviction, which meant that a condemned heretic had already lapsed twice, as in these comments from Aquinas:

> With regard to heretics two points must be observed: one, on their own side; the other, on the side of the Church. On their own side there is the sin, whereby they deserve not only to be separated from the Church by excommunication, but also to be severed from the world by death. For it is a much graver matter to corrupt the faith which quickens the soul than to forge money, which supports temporal life. Wherefore if forgers of money and other evildoers are forthwith condemned to death by the secular authority, much more reason is there for heretics . . . to be not only excommunicated but even put to death.
>
> On the part of the Church, however, there is mercy which looks to the conversion of the wanderer, wherefore she condemns not at once, but after the "first and second admonition" . . . after that, if he is yet stubborn, the Church no longer hoping for his conversion, looks to the salvation of others, by excommunicating him and separating him from the Church, and furthermore delivers him to the secular tribunal to be exterminated thereby.[12]

Aquinas here typified medieval thinking about heresy and punishment. Heretics publicly and stubbornly rejected the teaching of the church. They led others to perdition, and so if the mercy of the church had been exhausted, they must be destroyed lest they threaten the salvation of their neighbors.

The Spanish Inquisition

In fifteenth-century Spain, King Ferdinand the Catholic established the most famous of all heresy courts, the Spanish Inquisition, which was from the start a royal, not papal, institution, as well as a unique development in Spain's history.[13] For centuries, Spain was the most religiously diverse region in western Europe. In 711, Muslim invaders crossed the Straits of Gibraltar and subdued most of the Iberian peninsula. The remnants of Christian Spain almost immediately began the work of recovering what had been seized. By 1085, the *Reconquista* had won for Christendom about half of Spain, including the important city of Toledo. The great Christian victory at Las Navas de Tolosa in 1212 delivered most of Spain into Christian hands. Of course, as territory changed hands, Christians, Muslims, and Jews exchanged Muslim for Christian rulers. Christian Spain was finally united in 1474, when Queen Isabella of Castile (the most powerful Iberian kingdom) wedded King Ferdinand of Aragon.

Jews and Christians, of course, had lived in the Iberian peninsula since Roman times and the Muslim conquest meant that the adherents of three religions dwelt closely together there. Relations were often civil but uneasy. Generally, when the Christians won more territory, the terms of surrender guaranteed Muslim and Jewish properties and places of worship.

The social tensions which had caused peasant rebellions in northern Europe contributed to the establishment of the Inquisition in Spain. The crown feared that the often-tense relations between "Old Christians," Jews and *conversos* (Jewish converts to Christianity) fostered violence and disorder in Spain. In particular, the monarchs worried that *conversos* who had converted to conform to royal dictate actually undermined the faith of others. In addition, Old Christians often disdained New Christians. Cervantes's Sancho Panza boasted to Don Quixote: "Though I am poor I am an Old Christian, and I don't owe anybody anything."[14] New Christians rivaled Old Christians for preferment in state and church.

In 1480, Ferdinand sought and received permission from Pope Sixtus IV for an inquisition to be established in Spain. The control by the crown meant that from its inception the Spanish Inquisition served royal as well as ecclesiastical policy. Indeed, the church scarcely differed from the crown, so closely did the monarchs control the church. The Spanish Inquisition targeted the *conversos*, converts from Judaism who often observed Jewish practices and honored Jewish beliefs. The Inquisition also monitored *moriscos*, converts from Islam suspected of secretly clinging to their former religion. Thus, Ferdinand and Isabella founded the Inquisition primarily for religious conformity. Furthermore, like any other religious court, the Spanish Inquisition wielded jurisdiction over *baptized Christians alone*. Consequently, English and Dutch Protestants doing business in Spain sometimes found themselves before its tribunals as well.

Like other inquisitions, the Spanish began as an itinerant court. Its reach was felt less acutely in remote regions. Once newly-arrived in a town, the inquisitors (mostly Jesuits by 1600) would preach a sermon that invited heretics to be reconciled to the church. They generally announced an initial grace period of forty days, during which light penalties would be imposed. An admission of offense during the grace period would not be taken as legal heresy. Like other courts of the day, accusations generally came from private individuals, and so sometimes gave villagers the chance to settle scores with their enemies. Accusers may well have approached the Inquisition more boldly than other courts of the early modern period, since the accused were examined in secret, and the names of informants kept from the accused, so as to impede recriminations.

Once accused, suspects were arrested and imprisoned pending trial. The Inquisition inventoried their belongings, and sales of their property were used to pay for room and board while in jail, since the Inquisition lacked a regular source of income. Most of the jails of the Inquisition were in good condition; the jailers usually left the prisoners alone. Most prisoners who died in jail perished from disease rather than starvation or beatings. Many prisoners never came before the tribunal, for as in Roman law, trials presumed the guilt of the accused because enough evidence of guilt had already been collected. Without this evidence, prisoners could be set free with a warning, as in the famous instance of Ignatius Loyola, whom the Inquisition first detained and then warned to stay out of ecclesiastical trouble; Ignatius was then released and became one of the storied figures of early modern Catholicism. Generally, the inquisitorial tribunals attended to their tasks speedily, lest the accused's money run out, and the inquisitors' jobs made impossible through lack of funds.

Once a trial began, the inquisitors' goal was to get a confession from the accused, thereby confirming other evidence already compiled. The tribunal, then, served as both judge and jury. Defendants were handed a copy of the prosecution's case, so as to be given the opportunity to rebut it. They did have the right to counsel but defense lawyers worked for the Inquisition. Prisoners could discredit witnesses or claim extenuating circumstances, such as drunkenness, insanity, or youthfulness. Tribunals usually employed impressive critical methods to establish the truth. While other courts of the day accepted the existence of witchcraft, for instance, the Spanish Inquisition almost always took it to be a form of insanity. Still, since the burden of proof fell on the defense, and not the prosecution, acquittals were unusual.

Only a minority of all the cases that came before the Inquisition involved heresy. The great majority of procedures were for lesser ecclesiastical crimes, especially error, forgery of church documents, blasphemy, or usury. Inquisitors also investigated observance of traditionally Jewish or Muslim practices, not in themselves heretical, by converts to Catholicism. Some combination of fine and penance served as the punishments for these infractions of church law. More serious crimes, such as bigamy or sodomy, might send the convicted to the galleys of the Spanish Empire. The most serious crime, of course, was heresy. The Spanish Inquisition regarded heresy much as its medieval predecessor; that is, only relapsed or unrepentant heretics got into serious trouble. Defendants convicted of heresy for the third time could be sentenced to death by burning. Like many other medieval court sentences, however, many burnings were never carried out. A good number of burnings were by effigy, because the convicted had either died in the meantime or had fled the country (easy enough to do by bribing the jailers). Executioners often strangled the condemned who repented on the pyre and so delivered them from a rather more agonizing death by burning. Despite the historiographical and literary hysterics, the Spanish Inquisition condemned, on average, about three convicts a year, in an empire that stretched from the Pyrenees to Patagonia, far fewer than any other court of its era.

The Protestant Reformation

In the sixteenth century, the law and the jurists confronted for the first time the problem of permanent, national religious dissent. The orthodox church had in earlier eras eliminated all dissenters, from the Arians to the Albigensians. The sixteenth-century divisions in Latin Christendom, however, proved permanent. The Protestant Reformation began as the protest of academic elites, like Martin Luther, John Calvin, and Huldrych Zwingli, against the traditional understanding of Christian justification. Luther in particular also detested the Catholic Church's preoccupations with canon law, and presented his own version of antinomianism (the belief that grace liberates from law). In its implementation, the Reformation became a movement of political elites. Protestantism enjoyed most success where princes and monarchs imposed the break with Roman Catholicism (Germany, England, Scandinavia). In every case, the replacement of the old church by the new served to enhance the power of the ruler. Of course, the Catholic Church's land tenures and jurisdiction ended wherever the rulers established Protestantism. Marriage, which had since the twelfth century been solely under the jurisdiction of ecclesiastical courts, fell under the supervision of secular courts. Whereas one of the goals of the medieval reform movement was the removal of the priesthood from secular society (through the imposition of celibacy, for example), Protestant reformers aimed to restore Christian ministry to the old arrangement whereby ministers lived much like everyone else, that is, took wives and raised families. The Protestants reversed the monasticization of the diocesan clergy that eleventh-century reformers initiated. They also restored the early medieval relation between the church and state, especially in the cases of the Lutheran and Anglican churches, whereby the princes dominated the church.

Initially, both sides wanted to restore unity without violence. Religious war did break out, however, in both Germany and France, as persuasion proved unable to eliminate religious divisions. In the case of Germany, the weakness of the emperor enabled religious discord. Emperor Charles V took very seriously his role as chief layman of Christendom, and loathed heretics and their doctrines, but failed to prevent powerful territorial lords from embracing the Reformation. Charles inherited costly wars with the French Valois dynasty that preoccupied the first decades of his reign. The French allied with the Ottoman Turks and forced Charles to fight a two-front war. By the 1540s, however, he had defeated the French and turned his attention to the heretics of northern Germany. Charles took the field against an alliance of northern Protestant German princes known as the Schmalkald League. He was decisively victorious in the first war against them but he was stalemated in the second. All sides having exhausted themselves, the only reasonable course was to enshrine religious toleration in imperial law. In 1555, the Peace of Augsburg established the principle in German imperial law of *cuius regio, eius religio*; that is, each prince could select the religion—either Catholicism or Lutheranism, but not Calvinism—for his principality:

> In order to bring peace into the holy empire of the Germanic Nation, between the Roman imperial majesty and the Electors, princes, and estates: let neither his imperial majesty nor the Electors, princes, etc., do any violence or harm to any estate of the empire on account of the Augsburg [Lutheran] Confession, but let them enjoy their religious belief, liturgy and ceremonies as well as their estates and other rights and privileges in peace. . . . Likewise the Estates espousing the Augsburg Confession shall let all the estates and princes who cling to the old religion live in absolute peace and in the enjoyment of all their estates, rights, and privileges.[15]

Both denominations were to be licit in the imperial free cities, so that "the burghers and inhabitants of these Free and Imperial towns, whether spiritual persons or secular, shall live together quietly and peacefully."[16] Charles V here initiated a general trend in early modern European civilization, namely, the establishment in law of religious toleration. For fifty years, the Peace of Augsburg gave Germany freedom from religious war.

In France, the Wars of Religion which broke out in 1562 destroyed the Valois dynasty. Religious combat combined with dynastic ambitions to produce a quarter-century of civil war wherein an estimated one million Frenchmen died from the famine, disease, and violence for which wandering companies of soldiers were responsible. By 1589, all but one of the great religio-political faction leaders was dead. In that year, assassination ended the life of the last Valois, Henry III (1574–1589), leaving his cousin Henry of Navarre—a decidedly lukewarm Protestant—king by dynastic right.

Catholic Paris defied Henry of Navarre and so he agreed to become a Catholic monarch for a country whose great majority was still Catholic. No reasonable grounds for opposition to his coronation could be presented after his conversion to Catholicism. As king, Henry IV (1589–1614) proclaimed the Edict of Nantes (1598), which permitted "those of the so-called Reformed religion to live and dwell in all the towns and districts of this our kingdom and the countries under our rule, without being annoyed, disturbed, molested or constrained to do anything against their conscience . . . we also permit those of the aforesaid religion to carry out and continue its practice in the towns and districts under our rule, where it was established and carried out publicly several distinct times in the year 1597." The edict granted Calvinists the right to serve in the government and forbade schools and universities to deny them admission for study. The edict limited their ability to proselytize.[17] Another precedent for religious toleration had been established.

In England, royal weakness also contributed to religious dissent. The Tudor Henry VIII (1509–1547) worried about the continuation of his dynasty. Only one child of Henry and his Queen Catherine of Aragon survived into early childhood, a daughter named Mary. As only the second of his line, and with only the unhappy twelfth-century precedent of Queen Matilda, Henry feared for the future of his dynasty, and determined to divorce Catherine for a woman he thought could bear a healthy boy. Henry had required a dispensation to marry Catherine in 1509. She had first been married to his elder brother Arthur (d. 1502), who had died before he could succeed their father Henry VII (1485–1509). The Tudors wished to continue the Spanish alliance, and petitioned the pope for a dispensation from the impediment of affinity (in-law marriage, as suggested by Leviticus). The pope granted the dispensation and Henry and Catherine were wedded.

Catherine had had a number of pregnancies by Henry, but aside from Mary, the children were either miscarried or still-born. In addition to his dynastic anxieties, Henry honestly wondered whether their union was cursed because he had married his brother's widow, in violation of the usual rules governing marriage. He sent his chancellor, the unscrupulous Cardinal Wolsey (1471/1474–1530), to petition Rome for a divorce, on the grounds that the dispensation that Henry sought in 1509 was unlawful! The prospective divorce created scandal at home. Furthermore, Catherine enjoyed the support of influential men like Thomas More. In the end, Wolsey failed to get a divorce because the armies of Emperor Charles V had virtually imprisoned Pope Clement VII in the Castel Sant Angelo in Rome. The pope had double-crossed Charles in war and the emperor avenged his honor with an invasion of Italy as well as the famous *Sacco di Roma* (sack of Rome) of 1527. Catherine, moreover, was Charles's aunt. Because he was the prisoner of her nephew, Clement could not grant Henry the divorce. Henry would have executed Wolsey for his failure in such an important mission but Wolsey died before the king could exercise his wrath. More was named to succeed him.

Wolsey's secretary, Thomas Cromwell (c. 1485–1540), now began to urge Henry to imitate continental Reformers and break with the Catholic Church. Henry should name himself head of the Christian church in England, which is essentially what territorial princes in Germany were doing. Henry was persuaded but also determined to garner widespread support for such an epochal step. He determined that Parliament should approve the split with the Catholic Church through an act of the King-in-Parliament, the highest legislation in English law. In 1532, the Act of Supremacy ended papal, and enacted royal, authority over the Christian church in England:

> Albeit the King's Majesty justly and rightfully is and ought to be the Supreme Head of the Church of England, and so is recognized by the clergy of this realm in their Convocations; yet nevertheless for corroboration and confirmation thereof, and for increase of virtue in Christ's religion within this realm of England, and to repress and extirp all errors, heresies, and other enormities and abuses heretofore used in the same, Be it enacted by authority of this present Parliament that the King our Sovereign Lord, his heirs and successors kings of this realm, shall be taken, accepted, and reputed the only Supreme Head in earth of the Church of England.[18]

Henry advanced the Reformation in England with another act of the King-in-Parliament, the Act of Dissolution (1536), whereby the government confiscated monastic lands. Henry retained some of these lands in royal hands but redistributed others to influential peers, who then had a stake in Henry's religious reconfiguration of the kingdom. Still, when Henry died in 1546, most Englishmen remained Catholic in their religious temperament. The "Henrician Reformation," after all, largely amounted to a Catholicism without the pope. In his will, Henry had made provision for numerous masses to be said for the salvation of his soul!

Henry's daughter Queen Elizabeth I (1558–1603) initiated the final victory of Protestantism in England with another Act of Supremacy (1559), as well as with her Act of Uniformity (1559), which made Archbishop Cranmer's *Book of Common Prayer* the only lawful liturgical text in the realm. Both were acts of the Queen-in-Parliament. No previous monarchs had so aggressively involved Parliament in legislation as the Tudors; indeed, prior to Henry VIII,

Parliament served as an advisory body to the king and its speaker was one of the king's highest subordinates. The Tudors' impressment of the Parliament into the Reformation invested it with new constitutional authority.

The Jurisprudence of Hugo Grotius

By the 1600s, religious and political tensions within the German Empire were growing once again. New developments were straining the peace afforded the empire by the Augsburg settlement. First, Calvinism, which was not recognized as legal by the Peace of Augsburg, had made important gains in Germany; in particular, Frederick V, the Elector of the Palatinate, was a militant Calvinist, and, determined to establish a legitimate presence for Calvinism in the empire. Second, the Protestant princes of the empire feared the accession of Ferdinand II (1618–1637). Educated by Jesuits, Ferdinand was militantly Catholic, and like many Lutheran princes, disturbed by the growing Calvinist presence in the empire. Frederick's militancy especially vexed the young emperor. Ferdinand also inherited the crown of Bohemia, which had a large Protestant population. He could well be expected to re-Catholicize that kingdom in cooperation with his Jesuit advisors. All these tensions came to war in 1618, when the Elector Palatine Frederick V raised an army against Ferdinand. The ensuing war, known as the Thirty Years' War (1618–1648), may well be considered the first European world war, for by its end virtually every state in Europe had entered or been drawn into the war. Both the Austrian and Spanish branches of the Habsburg family suffered defeat in the war, while the Bourbons gained important territories on France's eastern frontier. France thus superseded Spain as the great power on the continent of Europe. The Thirty Years' War capped the collapse of the medieval German Empire. In the Peace of Westphalia (1648), which ended the war, the emperor conceded to the German territorial princes the power to pursue their own foreign policies. The war both ended the Habsburg aspiration to unite Christendom under imperial authority and began the early modern concert of European nation-states.

The time was ripe, then, for a new theory of government, international order, and law. The theorist of the new order was the Dutch humanist scholar Hugo Grotius (1583–1645).[19] Grotius was a true Renaissance man—a jurist, poet, historian, and theologian (of the Arminian sort). His ideas on international law may be found in his two treatises *De iure praedae* (*On the law of capture*), written in 1604–1605, but not published until discovered among his papers in 1864, and *De iure belli et pacis* (*On the law of war and peace*), written in 1625, while the Habsburg cause in the Thirty Years' War was still ascendant.

In the midst of war's carnage, Grotius yet insisted that war required its own code of law, rooted in human nature:

> Fully convinced, by the considerations which I have advanced, that there is a common law among nations, which is valid alike for war and in war, I have had many and weighty reasons for undertaking to write upon this subject. Throughout the Christian world I observed a lack of restraint in relation to war, such as even barbarous races should be ashamed of; I observed that men rush to arms for slight causes, or no cause at all, and that when arms have once been taken up there is no longer any respect for law, divine or human.[20]

Grotius rejected absolutely any notion that war might be without law or morality: "Least of all should that be admitted which some people imagine, that in war all laws are in abeyance. On the contrary war ought not to be undertaken except for the enforcement of rights; when once undertaken it should be carried on only within the bounds of law and good faith."[21] Just as Augustine had argued that no evil could erase the divine image and likeness within every human being, Grotius insisted that war, no matter how horrible, was still a moral enterprise, because human beings waged it: "Between enemies . . . unwritten laws are in force, that is, those which nature prescribes, or the agreement of nations has established."[22] Just war may be fought in "defence, recovery of property, and punishment."[23] War was permitted to preserve life and limb but Grotius counseled caution against waging preemptive war out of the fear of being attacked, since "the danger, again, must be immediate and imminent in point of time . . . those who accept fear of any sort as justifying anticipatory slaying are themselves greatly deceived, and deceive others."[24]

For Grotius, just war fought in recovery of property meant that international law must govern commerce. In particular, the nature of intercontinental commerce suggested utter freedom of the seas. The very vastnesses of the oceans meant that they could be owned or claimed by no government nor any nation.[25] Wars fought in defense of trade, and laws against piracy, were licit because "no one, in fact, has the right to hinder any nation from carrying on commerce with any other nation at a distance."[26]

Grotius linked licit war-making to the new system of national states just then maturing in Europe. Natural law reserves to monarchs the right of war-making—"this [royal] power is understood to have been ordained by the approval of the will of God"—since right reason commands self-preservation in the face of unjust aggression.[27] Grotius argued that the horrors of war could be best limited by confining licit war to the business of nation-states that recognized protocols for its conduct. He drew a distinction between two types of war—formal and less formal. Of the two, Grotius believed that formal war better limited the violence, since it required that "on both sides it be waged under the authority of the one who holds the sovereign power in the state; then, that formalities be observed."[28] The formalities of war, indeed, derive from the *ius gentium*: "A definite formality in the conduct of war was introduced by the law of nations, and that particular effects follow wars waged in accordance with such formality under the law of nations."[29] Less formal war lacks these formalities, and threatens either escalation or unending war.[30]

Grotius thus crafted a system of international law with natural law theory as its foundation. He was convinced that the basis of natural law was human nature, "the mother of natural law,"[31] and that such a jurisprudence served the purpose of a stable, peaceful concert of nations. Grotius, however, also depended on arguments of the Schoolmen, who "when they agree on a point of morals, it rarely happens that they are wrong." Grotius took insights from the Schoolmen and then refashioned them according to humanist principles, with illustrations from the literature of ancient Greece and Rome.[32] Although Grotius upheld most of medieval jurisprudence, his humanist style convinced many that he was a great innovator. The greatest difference between himself and the Schoolmen, however, was that he assumed a system of national monarchies, rather than a universal, Christian empire. He also rejected the papacy as an arbiter for international conflicts:

> Grotius envisaged a world made up of free sovereign states, Christian and non-Christian, owing allegiance to no external superior. It was a world in which commercial rivalries as well as religious conflicts had become a major cause of wars. A degree of order and harmony in such a world could be maintained, Grotius thought, not by an appeal to an overriding spiritual authority, but by the common consent of all nations to the code of international conduct that he had diligently worked out for them.[33]

For all his humanist training, Grotius defined law in conventionally scholastic language: "Natural law is a dictate of right reason indicating that an act, on account of its conformity or lack of moral turpitude or moral necessity, and that consequently such an act is either commanded or prohibited by God, the Author of Nature."[34]

Like the Schoolmen, Grotius combined ideas that later thinkers understood to be contradictory. In Scholastic thought, voluntarism and rationalism, nature and history, love of self and love of neighbor all found place settings at the same intellectual table, since each in its turn was a part of the human experience. In terms of law, the Scholastics had emphasized both "individual rights and the common good as complementary rather than conflicting aspects of the human condition."[35] In his system, Grotius argued that individual rights flourished only within a well-ordered society, and at the same time

> A society could flourish only if the individual members cared, not only for their own well-being, but that of their fellow members and the whole community. Grotius does not confront us with isolated individuals facing an omnipotent state but with human persons sociable by nature, bound by ties of friendship and mutual support.[36]

Thus did Grotius appropriate the tradition of the *ius commune*. Like Innocent IV, he argued that the story of Adam and Eve teaches that regardless of religion all human beings are brothers and sisters and so must be treated with human dignity.[37] He insisted that Christians could make treaties with non-Christians and that, once agreed to, Christians must honor those treaties.[38] He also accepted, however, the tradition of the canon law which said that the New Testament bound only Christians.[39] Grotius reaffirmed the traditional view that war could not be used to spread the Christian faith.[40] He rejected absolutely the justice of wars against heretics.[41] The respective competencies of faith and reason, then, influenced Grotius's jurisprudence. Human nature dictated law to all men and women but the mysteries of the faith were revealed to Christians alone. The articles of the Christian faith could not be proved but could be believed through an extension of God's grace. Compulsion had no place in the Christian church.

At the very least, the law commands that each leave to each life and property.[42] Thus, the law of nations is simply those humane rules by which peoples have lived since the dawn of history.[43] The law grants to each person the right to defend hearth and home, for, as Cicero remarked, the first principle of nature is the instinct to self-preservation.[44] Consequently, just as any individuals who break the law lose the advantages of civil society, so do nations that violate the peace and territory of others lose theirs.[45] War, then, may well be a moral enterprise if it abide the principle of self-preservation.[46] Like Augustine and Aquinas, Grotius argued that we are not enjoined to love all equally, but have especial obligations to defend families and neighbors.[47] Not even the Gospels absolutely forbid the use of force or violence; otherwise, widows and children would be abused and deprived of their goods, and evildoers not be restrained.[48] Rather, the injunction to "turn the other cheek" was addressed to individual persons, not magistrates or others entrusted with the common good.[49] The example of Christ should not be taken as a general rule, "but in accordance with a special promise and covenant, as it were, made with the Father."[50] Grotius did insist, however, that violence was best reserved to the ruler, lest vengeance replace justice.[51] A royal monopoly on violence protects the commonwealth from vengeance-violence that escalates, and protects the wrong-doer from excessive punishments.[52]

Grotius envisioned a system of Christian monarchies at peace with each other and their non-Christian neighbors. He was confident that that peace could rest upon a foundation of natural law, and so he may be counted among the early modern intellectuals for whom the tradition of Roman law held great promise. That legal tradition should also govern the intercontinental commercial system then just coming into being. For Grotius, freedom of the seas best served the growth of such commerce. Unfortunately, the ambitions of rulers ruined the pacific vision of Grotius. Even after the great bloodletting of the Thirty Years' War, armed conflict broke out again and again in seventeenth-century Europe, particularly after the expansionist French monarch Louis XIV (1643–1715) embarked upon his wars of territorial aggrandizement. A lengthy series of colonial wars lasted until the defeat of Napoleon in 1815.

Reform of Criminal Law

South German peasants had complained in 1525 that they had been subjected to "new laws." The laws that so dismayed them, and which were rapidly replacing customary law, were Roman criminal law and procedure. Roman law had figured more and more prominently since its "rediscovery" in the eleventh century but this process had been much slower in Germany than elsewhere in continental Europe. The general conviction throughout sixteenth-century Germany that crime had become far too commonplace hastened the adoption and spread of Romano-canonical jurisprudence.[53]

Between 1480 and 1550 governments throughout Christendom promulgated new criminal legal procedures based on Roman jurisprudence. These criminal law codes were in force until the eighteenth century. The governments of Germany (1532), France (1539), and Holland (1570) enacted new, lengthy codes of criminal procedure. In Germany the new procedures meant that a foreign system, with which few people were familiar, eclipsed traditional laws, customs, and courts (Schöffen).[54] Furthermore, Romano-canonical jurisprudence could be taken as arbitrary, for unlike customary law, wherein ancient use magnified the power of law, the legislative theory of classical

Roman law meant that the ruler could change law at his pleasure. Old law ceased to be good or efficacious law. The adoption of Roman law, however, enabled German territorial princes to consolidate power over their subjects. Indeed, the legal reforms of the sixteenth century both required and amplified the power of the state, for older criminal systems based on ordeal and compurgation could only be replaced when a practical alternative had developed. The reforms of Lateran IV virtually nullified ordeal; for rulers and their servants, the problem with compurgation was that the government needed to consult and cooperate with compurgators, which rulers disliked as a limitation on the power of government.

Roman law served the interests of the princes. Apart from its academic prestige, the rationalism of Roman jurisprudence called for the introduction of either testamentary or documentary evidence. Roman law also amplified the power of the ruler, since feudal and customary law curtailed the ruler's power by holding him to reciprocal obligations. Roman law stressed the vastness of the ruler's power, with the limitations imposed by reason and the common good.[55] Furthermore, neither feudal nor customary law were systematic, and Roman jurisprudence was increasingly relied upon to sort out the difficulties in those "systems": "Gradually, the Roman civil law was permeating all legal culture; it provided the categories, the methods of legal reasoning and the forms of argumentation, which was essential for anyone who wished to be considered a jurist."[56] Elements of the feudal and customary law survived, but were organized and interpreted according to Romano-canonical jurisprudence.

The German Emperor Maximilian I (1493–1519) committed the empire to a thorough implementation of Romano-canonical jurisprudence and procedure by imperial decree (*Reichskammergericht*) in 1495. Of course, Roman law had existed in the empire since the twelfth century, although it had little influence in either civil or criminal matters. Because of university instruction Roman jurisprudence had become well-known in academic circles by the mid-thirteenth century, even though the empire itself had no university until the foundation of the University of Prague in 1356. By 1500 Roman law was also studied in Cologne (1388), Louvain (1425), and Basel (1459). Law faculties argued that since the empire had been transferred from the Romans to the Germans, Roman law should follow suit. Torture had become a more common feature of German legal procedures between 1350 and 1400. Still, the breakdown in German political institutions following the death of Frederick II in 1250 inhibited the development of the inquisitorial process in the empire.

The Emperor Charles V (1519–1558) further refined Romano-canonical criminal procedure in the *Constitutio criminalis carolina* of 1523. Perhaps of all the early modern German emperors, only Charles could have so thoroughly reformed the law. By dynastic right he held several great titles. Sovereign of the German Empire, he ruled also as king of Spain (which included Sicily and southern Italy, to say nothing of Spain's increasingly great possessions in the New World), and the lord of both the Netherlands and the Franché-Comté. Charles was the most powerful Christian ruler of the first half of the sixteenth century, even though his power in Germany could be successfully challenged by the great German territorial princes, especially if they received aid from their French and Ottoman allies. Of all the criminal law codes promulgated in sixteenth-century Europe, Charles's *Carolina* was the longest.

The *Carolina* systematized what had been growing up haphazardly in German legal history during the previous century and a half. Particularly desirable were guidelines for the employment of torture. The 1498 *Wörmser Reformation* was an earlier attempt to assist investigators in its application:

> Although a general rule for what is sufficient to justify torture is impossible, illustrations can be given . . . for example, when someone of wanton character is found with stolen goods; when the accused is found with the bloody dagger and the victim has been stabbed.[57]

The concern here, as in the classical Roman law, was that the use of torture be limited. The *Carolina* also regulated the employment of torture, for many believed that torture was used as a punishment, and that its employment had been excessive, and, in too many cases, lethal.

The *Carolina* had also didactic purposes, for unlike the professionalized and bureaucratized judiciaries of France and England, amateurs in need of help from professional and learned experts still presided over many German courts: "Most criminal courts are staffed with persons who have not studied, had experience with, or exercised our imperial law."[58] Thus, the *Carolina* orders that judicial experts be brought into cases where the application of torture was probable: "When something is doubtful in these matters, those responsible for ordering and conducting examination under torture shall seek advice from the legally knowledgeable."[59] The *Carolina*, then, provided benchmarks for decision making to men with little legal education. The *Carolina* thus includes *Indizienlehre*, a set of rules "taken over from Roman-canon procedure establishing preconditions for examination under torture," in other words, probable cause for torture.[60] Essentially, the *Carolina* calls for investigators to weigh fairly the evidence in the case:

> When, in consequence it is decided that the weight of suspicion is greater than the weight of exculpation, then torture may be employed. When, however, the

grounds of exculpation have higher regard and attention than some lesser suspicions which have been made out, then examination under torture shall not be employed.[61]

The *Carolina* also offered guidelines for interrogations under torture; for instance, questioning should elicit details, not supply them: "We want nothing to be put to the accused before or during examination."[62] It also contained criteria for the evaluation of the confessions obtained. They should be more than admissions of guilt; the accused should also be able to provide details of how the crime was committed. When murder had been confessed,

> [The accused] shall be asked the reason he did the crime, on which day, at what hour, and at what place, whether anyone helped him to it and who; also where he buried or put the dead man, with what weapons the said murder was committed, how and what sort of blows or wounds he gave or inflicted upon the dead man, or how otherwise he killed him, what the murdered person had upon him by way of money or other things, and what he took from him, where he put this, or sold, dispersed, parted with, or hid it.[63]

The *Carolina* here called for elocution as well as confession.

Such details needed to be provided because many innocent persons did not know how to exculpate themselves. The law should help these people:

> When . . . the accused denies the crime under consideration, then it shall be assiduously inquired of him whether he can show that he is innocent of the alleged crime, and the prisoner shall in particular be asked to remember whether he can prove and establish that at the time the crime under consideration was committed he was with people or at a place or location whereby it can be recognized that he cannot have done the crime of which he is suspected. And such exhortation is thus needed because many a person out of simpleness or fright, even when he is quite innocent, does not know how he should proceed to exculpate himself of the thing. And when the prisoner in this manner or in like-serving way indicates his innocence, then the judge shall as quickly as possible investigate the exculpation proffered.[64]

The pressures on criminal courts in Germany were quite extraordinary. The Romano-canonical procedure required a brutal standard of proof for conviction, and thus made great demands on investigators and judges. Unlike English jury trials, whose standard was reasonable doubt, the Romano-canonical procedure demanded certainty, which, in the absence of most other forms of proof, meant that in criminal cases confession was indispensable. Thus, authorities invested a great deal of their time and effort dealing with criminal cases. This standard of proof, combined with Germany's constitutional fragmentation, prevented the development of appellate jurisdictions.[65]

A similar reform of the criminal law took place in France but within a rather different historical and political context. Of course, the Capetian reconstruction of royal authority between 1150 and 1250 was crucial. A professionalized, learned bureaucracy had since the thirteenth century served the king of France, and by 1450 the kings of France commanded local courts to record royal laws in writing, which in turn demanded the cooperation of professional lawyers, royal servants, and the mass of the king's subjects.[66] While Romano-canonical criminal procedure trickled into Germany through the church and university-trained legal experts, in France the crown aggressively spread and employed Roman jurisprudence: "The history of criminal procedure in France in the late Middle Ages is essentially the history of the criminal procedure of the royal courts."[67] Furthermore, the south of France long preserved vestiges of Roman law.

The Capetian royal recovery of power, however, postdated the English by a century. The breakdown of royal authority in the tenth and eleventh centuries meant that many courts remained in ducal, comital, and baronial hands. The Capetians thus built a judiciary virtually from scratch. Like all medieval rulers, the Capetians claimed a monopoly on the use of violence, so most of their legal initiatives involved criminal rather than civil law. Those legal initiatives, moreover, depended on experts and bureaucrats. By 1190, the *baillis* of Philip II Augustus (1180–1223) held monthly assizes, recorded and collected fines, and made an accounting to Paris. Whereas the collapse of the monarchy prevented the emergence of a criminal appellate court in Germany, the position of the *Parlement* of Paris in the French legal system was assured. Indeed, these appellate courts generally disdained the decisions and procedure of lower courts as unprofessional and irrational. The *Parlements* often insisted on examining cases *de novo* using Romano-canonical procedure.[68] By 1302, the office of royal prosecutor (*procureur du roi*) had been established. Initially, this official had duties in civil litigation but by 1500 he was empowered to initiate the criminal process when there was no private complainant.[69]

In 1539 King Francis I capped this series of developments with his promulgation of the *Ordonnance royale*, commonly known as the Ordinance of Villers-Cotterets, after the place of its issuance. In contrast to the didactic purposes of the *Carolina*, the *Ordonnance* reflects the strong monarchy and tradition of Roman law characteristic of France. The *Ordonnance* mentions no untrained authorities in court; rather, it assumes a professional class of lawyers, judges, and jurists trained in Romano-canonical criminal procedure.

While Germany possessed no government prosecutors in the sixteenth century, France did. Furthermore, while the *Ordonnance* retained a role for criminal accusations from private subjects, especially in the initial stages of investigation, the *Ordonnance* understood criminal offenses as assaults against the king and his commonwealth, to be investigated and prosecuted by royal officers.[70] Indeed, the king's peace, rather than the guilt or innocence of the accused, was the central preoccupation of the *Ordonnance*, for judicial procedure exists to "find out the truth about the said crimes, lesser offences, and transgressions from the mouth[s] of the accused persons if possible."[71] The *Ordonnance*, then, lacked the explicit concern found in the *Carolina* about fearful innocents incriminating themselves, although the more advanced state of Romano-canonical jurisprudence in France may explain the difference. Still, the *Ordonnance* offered defendants little aid. If the *procureur's* case lacked what was considered full proof, he could resort to judicial examination by torture. Accused criminals could deny the jurisdiction of the court, based on either feudal or ecclesiastical privilege, but such denials were available to few people.[72] The accused could also object to the testimony of witnesses on the basis of conflict of interest.[73] Otherwise, defendants had to rely on the failure of the evidence introduced against them. If the investigation produced two witnesses against them, they were lost.[74] The *Ordonnance royale's* secondary concern was that criminal proceedings in France take as little time as possible: "We make known to all men living and to those yet unborn, that in order to provide in some measure for the good of our legal system, for the shortening of proceedings, and for the relief of our subjects, we have by perpetual and irrevocable edict established and decreed, and we do establish and decree, the following things . . ."[75] Since the officers involved were royal servants, the government paid the costs of criminal procedures. Speedy trials saved the crown money.[76]

Still, French Romano-canonical procedure may well have been more humane than the German, since "it is difficult to sense how important torture was to the French system, how prevalent the tortured confession really was. It was obvious from the *Carolina* that torture was almost the first and only resort of the German investigating magistrate. The French system appears to treat examination under torture more exceptionally."[77] The later *Ordonnance criminelle* of Louis XIV (1670) also suggests that French officials employed torture more reluctantly, since in that document the king reminded judges that they can resort to it in capital cases where a good deal of evidence against the defendant has been compiled, and to get defendants to identify their accomplices.[78] The *Ordonnance criminelle* at least envisioned a very limited application of torture. The *Ordonnance royale*, then, may reflect a more benign, because more mature, Romano-canonical procedure.

The Enlightenment

The Enlightenment marks the next great movement in European thought and culture. The great figures of the Enlightenment mostly argued for reform of Europe's ancestral institutions. The scientific revolution served as the model for their ideas. That great intellectual upheaval began with Nicholas Copernicus (1473–1543), a Polish priest and astronomer. Copernicus argued that the tables of planetary motion, contained in the *Almagest* of the ancient astronomer Ptolemy of Alexandria (c. 83–161 AD), suggested that the Earth and the planets revolved around the sun. Ptolemy, among many others, believed that the Earth was at the center of the universe. Copernicus's groundbreaking reinterpretation of Ptolemy's work prompted other intellectuals to study what modern physicists call mechanics—the principles whereby things move and alter. The synthetic genius of the scientific revolution was the Englishman Sir Isaac Newton (1643–1727), who proposed an entirely new system of mechanics, which rested upon his famous laws of motion. He said that the operations of the universe resembled those of a clock—God had put the springs and coils into place, wound the stem, and movement came to the universe. Thus, Newton was the first in a series of mechanistic thinkers like Charles Darwin (1809–1882), Karl Marx (1818–1883), and Sigmund Freud (1856–1939), who all contributed to modern thinking. The Enlightenment thinkers wanted to use Newton's mechanistic approach for solving the problems of government, law, and political economy—find the foundational principles governing their operation, and institute reforms based on those principles. Just as Newton had found the "lever" that put the universe into motion, they sought the lever whereby law, politics, and economy operated. Enlightenment thinkers applied the mechanistic metaphors of the scientific revolution to jurisprudence: "The lawgiver is the engineer who invents the machine; the prince is merely the mechanic who sets it up and operates it."[79]

Enlightenment thinkers, of course, had much to say about the law and jurisprudence. In the main, Enlightenment thinkers, sometimes called *philosophes*, rejected the cultural heritage of Europe. They had particularly little use for the legal tradition. Indeed, they were convinced that the legal and juridical inheritance stood in the way of justice and civility: "What makes the task of the lawgiver so difficult," said Jean-Jacques Rousseau (1712–1778), "is less what has to be established than what has to be destroyed."[80] The influential political thinker Montesquieu (1689–1755), for instance, found the laws of the thirteenth-century king of France, St. Louis, absolutely confounding: "What is this compilation then which goes at present under the name of St. Louis's Institution? What is this obscure, confused, and ambiguous code, where the French law is continually mixed with the Roman . . . there was an intrinsic defect in this compilation; it formed an amphibious code, in which the French and Roman laws were mixed, and where things were joined that were in no relation, but often contradictory to each other."[81] .

Montesquieu rejected the tradition of the *ius commune* as ancient and obsolete. That tradition instituted much the same jurisprudence in every kingdom. A more rational and just society required that laws be framed for particular societies:

> Law in general is human reason, inasmuch as it governs all the inhabitants of the earth: the political and civil laws of each nation ought to be only the particular cases in which human reason is applied. They should be adapted in such a manner *to the people for whom they are framed* that it should be a great chance if those of one nation suit another. They should be in relation to the nature and principle of each government: whether they form it, as may be said of politic laws; or whether they support it, as in the case of civil institutions. They should be in relation to the climate of each country, to the quality of its soil, to its situation and extent, to the principal occupation of the natives, whether husbandmen, huntsmen, or shepherds: they should have relation to the degree of liberty which the constitution will bear; to the religion of the inhabitants, to their inclinations, riches, numbers, commerce, manners, and customs. *In fine*, they have relations to each other, as also to their origin, to the intent of the legislator, and to the order of things on which they are established; in all of which different lights they ought to be considered . . . all these together constitute what I call the spirit of the laws.[82]

Rousseau argued similarly: "Freedom is not a fruit of every climate, and it is not therefore within the capacity of every people."[83] Thus, Enlightenment jurisprudence advocated the codification of the laws, such that one legal system should prevail everywhere in a nation-state. Codification would unify the realm (thereby making commerce more profitable), and limit the independence of the courts.[84]

A number of *philosophes* had little use for monarchy. Montesquieu believed that, since they preserved legal distinctions between persons, monarchies created legal chaos. Law under monarchy proliferated and became contradictory, confused, and unjust. Rousseau rejected the idea of the monarch as either the chief or sole source of legislation. Being only one man, he has only a private, rather than public, interest.[85] The Prussian monarchy served as a good example of the proliferation of laws under that form of government. In Prussia nearly every able-bodied young man was subject to both military and civil law. Because of military conscription, Prussian young men were subject to military law even when inactive.[86] Equally problematic, aristocratic domination of the judiciaries of Europe meant that court decisions protected the narrow interests of the nobility.[87] The complexity of the jurisdiction of the courts created confusion as to where cases should be pleaded and heard.

The Enlightenment thinkers largely agreed that traditional systems of law were too harsh, and deprived the people of their "natural" state of liberty. "Man was born free, and he is everywhere in chains."[88] The legal distinctions between persons created "misunderstanding and confusion," and "destroyed natural freedom for all time, established the law of property and inequality, changed a clever usurpation into an irrevocable right, and for the profit of a few ambitious men henceforth subjected the whole human race to work, servitude, and misery."[89] Thus, the erection of most laws and political institutions were, contrary to classical thought, not for the enhancement of human life, but for its degradation. Long years of decay and decadence had produced eighteenth-century European society, manners, and government. In general, most laws originated in fear for security: "Why did they give themselves superiors if not to defend themselves against oppression, and to protect their goods, their freedoms, and their lives, which are, so to speak, the constituent elements of their being?"[90] Still, since the body politic had originated as a "contract between the people and the chiefs it chooses for itself," then the people could change the regime and its laws, if they were inclined.[91] "In these various governments, all magistracies were at first elective; and when wealth did not prevail, preference was accorded to merit."[92]

The savagery of the old regime's punishments disgusted the *philosophes*. In particular, methods of execution horrified them, and their condemnation of eighteenth-century society and politics often pointed out the inhumanity of death sentences. Traditionally, most of the condemned were hanged. Most hangings of the old regime did not employ the trapdoor made famous by American western movies but rather deployed a rope and a strong tree branch. The condemned's neck might not break. Instead, the criminal spent the last minutes of life choking for air. Other methods of execution were even more brutal. Murderers and traitors were sometimes "broken on the wheel," a particularly cruel form of execution inherited from the early medieval Germans. After the condemned was tied to a wheel, the executioner broke arms and legs with a heavy metal club. The condemned's shattered limbs were then interwoven into the spokes of the wheel, and the wheel hoisted up on a tree branch, where the criminal was left to die of thirst while in extraordinary pain. Executioners sometimes did extend mercy to the condemned, however, by either first beheading or bludgeoning the condemned. In 1788, French onlookers were so outraged at a sentence of breaking on the wheel that they attacked the executioner, freed the condemned, and destroyed the wheel. Soon thereafter, King Louis XVI (1774–1793) banned the wheel altogether. In central and eastern Europe, executioners impaled traitors. Heretics and witches were burned at the stake. The most humane form of execution was beheading—quick and believed to be relatively painless. Most Englishmen considered Henry VIII's commutation of Thomas More's death sentence from disembowelment (the original sentence for the crime of treason by a commoner) to beheading an act of mercy. According to the law of persons, nobles were generally immune from cruel forms of execution, which created great resentments. Thus the revolutionary National Assembly proclaimed on October 6, 1791 that all executions in France would henceforth take place by beheading. Of course, the Revolution shortly thereafter adopted the guillotine, named for its inventor Joseph-Ignace Guillotin, since it excluded the gruesome possibility of the executioner's error with either ax or sword.

The disgust of Enlightenment figures at most executions also led to their denunciation of the Romano-canonical criminal procedure, which depended for convictions on confessions often obtained either through the threat or application of torture. That procedure also called for a "vastly greater investigative-prosecutorial organization because it effectively resolved all issues in the preliminary process"; that is, guilt had generally been determined even before formal judicial proceedings had begun.[93] Instead, just as they usually upheld as their model English political institutions, the Enlightenment thinkers argued for a criminal procedure more like that of English common law, with its trial by jury. In that system, of course, the burden of proof was on the prosecution rather than the defense. While Romano-canonical tradition relied heavily upon it, English prosecutors could convict without confession. Furthermore, common law procedure was more consultative, in that prosecutors had to convince a jury of the accused's guilt.[94]

Of all the ancestral European institutions, the Enlightenment thinkers probably most despised the Christian, especially the Catholic, church. In their view, the church hampered the establishment of rational and just society for three main reasons. First of all, the church spread superstition; indeed, her fundamental teachings violated the laws of reason. Virgins, they said, bear no children nor do the dead come back to life. Second, the power of the church amplified the harm of her superstitious doctrines. While the Christian church taught that sin had damaged every human being, the *philosophes* argued that the only sin was ignorance, which in turn caused human suffering and misery. Finally, the Christian churches generally upheld strong monarchy as the best form of government. Enlightenment figures preferred limited monarchy, like that of Great Britain after the Glorious Revolution of 1689.

The *philosophes*, then, denied any religious justification for the laws: "All power comes from God, I agree; but so does every disease, and no one forbids us to summon a physician."[95] Especially odious were laws that punished heresy and witchcraft, for crimes against religion pertained to private conscience, not public tranquillity: "We must honor the Deity and leave him to avenge his own cause."[96] Witchcraft trials endangered liberty, since the accusations required to initiate the legal inquiries generally arose because of ignorant people seeking to settle scores rather than seeking justice.[97]

Voltaire, for instance, established himself as an international celebrity through his investigation of the famous Calas affair. Jean Calas was a French Calvinist whose son was discovered dead. Rumor said that the lad, who seems to have suffered from depression, loved a Catholic girl, and that his father murdered the boy to prevent his conversion to Catholicism. The trial for the murder, conducted by the *parlement* of Toulouse, convicted the sixty-year-old Jean Calas, and he was executed by breaking on the wheel. This convergence of law and religion aroused Voltaire's suspicions. He investigated the trial and the evidence produced to secure Calas's conviction. In a series of articles, Voltaire convinced many, though not all, that Calas was in fact innocent; his son had committed suicide. Voltaire's arguments also denounced the traditional interweaving of religious and criminal law.

The Reforms of Cesare Beccaria

The most influential Enlightenment writer on the law was Cesare Beccaria (1738–1794), a Jesuit-educated, Milanese nobleman. He studied law at the University of Parma, where he became acquainted with Pietro Verri, a fellow Milanese noble from whom he learned Enlightenment ideas. Beccaria spent most of his life in the Austrian bureaucracy, teaching young aspirants to the imperial civil service. Rather than a traditional jurist, Beccaria was an advocate for penal reform whose enterprise was a rational exposition of the law.

Beccaria's most famous composition was a short treatise, *Dei delitti e delle pene* (*On Crimes and Punishments*), published in 1764, wherein he argued for reforms of European penal systems. Renaissance political thought, liberal autonomy, and utilitarianism buttressed the penal reforms Beccaria advocated. Like Thomas More and Machiavelli, Beccaria believed that necessity should be the criterion by which punishments should be imposed: "Even if punishments produce a happy result, they are not always therefore just, for, in order to be just, they must be necessary."[98] In Beccaria's thought, like that of the political philosopher John Locke and the economist Adam Smith, necessity meant minimalism, lest the government become tyranny, for government only came into existence when men yielded some of their liberty.[99] That minimalism extended most famously into his discussion of capital punishment, which he opposed in almost every instance. "The death of a citizen cannot be deemed necessary except for two reasons. First, if he still has sufficient connections and such power that he can threaten the security of the nation even though he be deprived of his liberty . . . I see no necessity whatever for destroying a citizen. The sole exception would be if his death were the one and only deterrent to dissuade others from committing crimes. This is the second reason for believing that capital punishment could be just and necessary."[100]

Beccaria was convinced that punishments were chiefly useful as deterrents to crime. Thus, punishment was primarily directed at the mind of the prospective criminal, rather than his body:

> The purpose of punishment, then, is nothing other than to dissuade the criminal from doing fresh harm to his compatriots and to keep other people from doing the same. Therefore, punishments and the method of inflicting them should be chosen that, mindful of the proportion between crime and punishment, will make the most effective and lasting impression on men's minds and inflict the least torment on the body of the criminal.[101]

Beccaria did not think of punishment as a "leveling of the scales," nor did he much advocate retributive justice. Instead, a desirable or useful outcome should be the chief criterion for the imposition of judicial punishment. The certainty, rather than the severity, of punishment better served society's good: "The more prompt the punishment is and the sooner it follows the crime, the more just and useful it will be."[102] Consequently, one of the Enlightenment's most important contributions to subsequent thinking about crime and the law was the growth in the frequency of imprisonment. Imprisonment was a penalty that could be imposed on everyone. In the past, those who could afford it only paid fines, while those who could not would be imprisoned. Imprisonment had thus reinforced social hierarchy. A rich man could injure another person and yet maintain his freedom. A poor man, who had committed the very same injury, would be imprisoned (or flogged). Beccaria also argued that imprisonment had the advantage of flexibility, as the length of term could be suited to the severity of the crime.[103]

Like other Enlightenment thinkers, Beccaria argued that the legal distinctions between persons (clergy, nobles, and commons), which constituted a fundamental and enduring source of injustices, should be eliminated. For instance, that clergymen are subject to the jurisdiction of relatively lenient canonistic, rather than secular, courts encouraged crime among priests and monks. The elimination of legal distinctions between persons also promised to simplify the criminal court system, which in turn should reduce the frequency of crime: "Do you want to prevent crimes? See to it that the laws are clear and simple, that the entire strength of the nation is concentrated in their defense, and that no portion of that strength is employed in their destruction. See to it that the law favors classes of men less than it favors men themselves."[104] The traditional legal framework of Europe, which gave privileges to some that it denied others, created resentments that likewise encouraged crime: "The majority of laws are only privileges, which is to say, a tribute by all to the conveniences of a few."[105] Whereas legal theorists from Cicero to Aquinas counseled cautious and incremental changes in the laws, Beccaria advocated much more radical reform, since "experience and reason have shown us that the probability and certainty of human traditions decline the farther removed they are from their sources."[106]

Beccaria's rebellion against the Roman law tradition extended to his ideas concerning criminal judicial procedure. He argued for the presumption of innocence instead of guilt. In the past, investigators obtained most evidence against the accused from relatives and neighbors. Beccaria insisted that the best testimony was the most disinterested: "The credibility of a witness, therefore, must diminish in proportion to the hatred or friendship or close relationship between himself and the accused." The testimony of witnesses ought to be considered all together, since "so long as the witness affirms the crime and the accused denies it, there is no certainty. What prevails in such a case is the right of everyone to be presumed innocent."[107] In weighing evidence, Beccaria preferred jury deliberations to the decisions of justices: "It is a most useful law that every man be judged by his peers, for, when the liberty and fortune of a citizen are at stake, those sentiments which inequality inspires should fall silent."[108] Of course, Beccaria denied that evidence obtained by torture had any validity whatsoever: "The sensitive innocent person will declare himself guilty if he believes that by so doing he can put an end to his torment."[109] Indeed, the outcry against torture formed a distinctive complaint of all Enlightenment jurists.

Like More, Beccaria analyzed the causes of crime and was also convinced that most criminal activity resulted from poverty: "ordinarily . . . theft is only the crime of misery and desperation."[110] Again, like More, he too protested the law's insensitivity to poverty: "Who made these laws? Rich and powerful men who have never deigned to visit the squalid hovels of the poor, who have never broken a moldy crust of bread among the innocent cries of their famished children and the tears of their wives."[111] Like other Enlightenment thinkers, Beccaria argued that ignorance and injustice generated criminal behavior: "Do you want to prevent crimes? See to it that enlightenment accompanies liberty. The evils that come from knowledge decline with its diffusion, and the benefits increase . . . in the face of widespread enlightenment in a nation, slanderous ignorance falls silent, and all authority not justified by sound reasons trembles."[112] Beccaria identified two eras in human history. During the first, priests propagated superstition, which was then necessary to wrest civil society from primeval barbarism. Beccaria believed that his own constituted a second era, which was characterized by a "difficult and terrible transition from error to truth, from the darkness of the unknown to light." Though painful, this historical transition permitted enlightened men to occupy the thrones of Europe. These rulers, unlike their predecessors, had the opportunity to ameliorate the condition of their subjects by promulgating rational policies. First, the Catholic Church must be disestablished; second, public education must be established.

The Results of Enlightenment

The reforms that Beccaria advocated bore most fruit in the central European monarchies of Prussia and Austria. Frederick II the Great of Prussia (1740–1786), recognized as an "enlightened despot," abolished torture in many criminal proceedings, and reduced the number of capital crimes in Prussia. He tried to eliminate corruption by increasing judges' salaries. His chancellor, Samuel von Cocceji (1679–1755), eliminated a number of courts and dismissed judges, thereby streamlining Prussian justice. He also required that judges study at university.[113] The Habsburg Emperor Joseph II (1780–1790) instituted even more comprehensive reforms. The Penal Code of 1787 and the Code of Criminal Procedure of 1788 abolished the legal distinction between persons, provided legal protections for defendants, and gave accused persons wider opportunities for appeal. They also restricted the application of the death penalty, and abolished many religious courts.[114]

Even in France, which most Enlightenment thinkers lamented as a lost cause, a kind of moral, if not formal, reform of criminal proceedings took place. The *baillages* and *sénéchaussées*, the royal courts of first instance (recall that the *parlement* of Toulouse carried out the barbarous execution of Calas) rarely imposed death sentences during the eighteenth century.[115] Of course, Enlightenment ideals inspired reform efforts during the first months of the French Revolution. The *cahiers de doléances* (list of grievances) presented to King Louis XVI (1774–1792) by the Third Estate at the meeting of the Estates-General in May 1789 called for the elimination of the legal distinctions between persons. The famous Declaration of the Rights of Man and of the Citizen, adopted by the National Assembly on August 27, 1789, stated that all French citizens were to be equal before the law: "All citizens, being equal in the eyes of the law, are equally eligible to all dignities and to all public positions and occupations, according to their abilities, and without distinction except that of their virtues and talents."[116]

Other Enlightenment legal reforms enhanced the authority of the monarch, for they further centralized the administration of justice. While Joseph II left the courts of first instance untouched, he did create a system of imperial oversight over their proceedings. The courts of second and third instance were entirely new and were regulated from the Imperial Supreme Court that Empress Maria Theresa (1740–1780) had established early in her reign. Knowledge of natural law and performance on state-administered exams formed the criteria for appointment to the Habsburg judiciary.[117]

Finally, calls for the codification of the law resounded in every quarter of eighteenth-century Europe. Such calls advocated the final replacement of customary law by written law, and the elimination of irrational and irregularly enforced laws. The first of these codes was the Prussian *Allgemeines Landrecht* (*General Landlaw*) of 1794. Written in German, instead of Latin, the vast *Allgemeines Landrecht* consisted of 19,000 articles that covered virtually every aspect of human endeavor. Of course, the most famous example of these codes was the *Code Napoléon* of 1804, which abolished France's traditional division between the northern *pays du droit coutumier* (land of the customary law) and the southern *pays du droit écrit* (land of the written, that is Roman, law). The *Code Napoléon* was itself mostly Roman law. Thus, the Enlightenment marked the final chapter in a longer story in Europe's legal history, namely, the final replacement of customary by Roman law. The medieval tradition of the *ius commune*, with its relatively weak central governments and parallel jurisprudences, yielded to the modern regime of increasingly powerful central governments and single codes of law.

Notes

1. Thomas More, *Utopia*, Robert M. Adams, ed. and trans. (New York, NY: W. W. Norton & Company, 1975), pp. 12–13.

2. Albert Beebe White and Wallace Notestein, eds., *Source Problems in English History* (New York, NY: Harper and Brothers Publishers, 1915).

3. From *Translations and Reprints from the Original Sources of European History* (Philadelphia, PA: University of Philadelphia Press, 1897), 2:113.

4. Michael R. Weisser, *Crime and Punishment in Early Modern Europe* (Atlantic Highlands, NJ: Humanities Press, Inc., 1979), p. 90.

5. More, *Utopia*, p. 9.

6. More, *Utopia*, p. 16.

7. X 5.7.9 [Edward Peters, ed., *Heresy and Authority in Medieval Europe* (Philadelphia, PA: University of Pennsylvania Press, 1980) p. 172 (*Corpus iuris*, 2:780–781)]. The call to secular officials ultimately depends on Cod. 1.4.8 [Krueger, 2:40].

8. X 5.7.13 [Tanner and Alberigo, 1:233–235 (*Corpus iuris*, 2:787–789)]. Council of Toulouse, c. 1 (1229), in Peters, *Heresy*, pp. 194–195.

9. Peters, *Heresy*, p. 197.

10. Peters, *Heresy*, p. 201.

11. Peters, *Heresy*, p. 209.

12. *Summa theologiae*, II-II.11.3 [Peters, *Heresy*, pp. 182-183].

13. For all of what follows on the Spanish Inquisition, I am indebted to Henry Kamen's magisterial *The Spanish Inquisition: A Historical Revision* (New Haven, CT: Yale University Press, 1997).

14. Miguel Cervantes, *Don Quixote*, 1.47 [Walter Starkie, trans. (New York, NY: New American Library, 1964), p. 476].

15. Tierney and Scott, *Western Societies*, pp. 414–415.

16. Sidney Z. Ehler and John B. Morrall, eds. and trans., *Church and State through the Centuries* (Westminter, MD: The Newman Press, 1954), pp. 170–171.

17. *Church and State*, pp. 184–188.

18. Gerald Bray, ed., *Documents of the English Reformation* (Minneapolis, MN: Fortress Press, 1994), pp. 113–114.

19. For what follows, I am indebted to Brian Tierney, *The Idea of Natural Rights: Studies on Natural Rights, Natural Law, and Church Law, 1150–1625*, Emory University Studies in Law and Religion 5 (Atlanta, GA: The Scholars Press, 1997), pp. 316–342.

20. Hugo Grotius, *De iure belli*, prol. 28 [Francis W. Kelsey, trans. (Oxford, UK: Clarendon Press, 1925), p. 20].

21. Grotius, *De iure belli*, prol. 25 [Kelsey, p. 18]. A revisitation of the traditional distinction between the *ius ad bellum*, the justification for war, and the *ius in bello*, the morality of war's conduct.

22. Grotius, *De iure belli*, prol. 26 [Kelsey, pp. 18–19].

23. Grotius, *De iure belli*, 2.1.2.2 [Kelsey, p. 171].

24. Grotius, *De iure belli*, 2.1.5.1 [Kelsey, p. 173].

25. Grotius, *De iure belli*, 2.2.3.1 [Kelsey, p. 190. See also Tierney, *Idea of Natural Rights*, p. 329].

26. Grotius, *De iure belli*, 2.2.13.5 [Kelsey, p. 199].

27. Grotius, *De iure belli*, 1.2.7.3 [Kelsey, p. 64] and 1.2.1.4 [Kelsey, pp. 52–53].

28. Grotius, *De iure belli*, 1.3.4.1 [Kelsey, p. 97].

29. Grotius, *De iure belli*, 1.2.4.2 [Kelsey, p. 57].

30. Grotius, *De iure belli*, 1.3.4.2 [Kelsey, pp. 97–98].

31. Grotius, *De iure belli*, prol.3 [Kelsey, pp. 9–10].

32. Grotius, *De iure belli*, prol. 52 [Kelsey, p. 28].

33. Tierney, *Idea of Natural Rights*, pp. 339–340.

34. Grotius, *De iure belli*, 1.1.10.1 [Kelsey, pp. 38–39].

35. Tierney, *Idea of Natural Rights*, p. 334.

36. Tierney, *Idea of Natural Rights*, p. 336.

37. Grotius, *De iure belli*, prol. 14 [Kelsey, p. 14]. That the basic humanity of non-believers was consistently upheld may also be found in the work of Francisco de Vitoria, O.P. (1483–1546), who argued (*American Indians*, q.1a.4 [in *From Irenaeus to Grotius: A Sourcebook in Christian Political Thought, 100–1625*, Oliver O'Donovan and Joan Lockwood O'Donovan, eds. (Grand Rapids, MI: William B. Eerdmans Publishing Company, 1999), p. 614]), that American Indians, even though they were barbarians, as human beings possessed *dominium*, possession of the goods of the earth. They could not be legally dispossessed of their property.

38. Grotius, *De iure belli*, 2.15.10.1 [Kelsey, p. 401].

39. Grotius, *De iure belli*, prol. 50 [Kelsey, p. 27].

40. Grotius, *De iure belli*, 2.20.48.1 [Kelsey, p. 516].

41. Grotius, *De iure belli*, 2.20.50.1 [Kelsey, pp. 518–519].

42. Grotius, *De iure belli*, prol. 10 [Kelsey, p. 13].

43. Grotius, *De iure belli*, 1.1.14.2 [Kelsey, p. 44].

44. Grotius, *De iure belli*, 1.2.1.1 [Kelsey, p. 51].

45. Grotius, *De iure belli*, prol. 18 [Kelsey, p. 16].

46. Grotius, *De iure belli*, 1.2.1.4 [Kelsey, pp. 52–53].

47. Grotius, *De iure belli*, 1.2.8.10 [Kelsey, p. 75].

48. Grotius, *De iure belli*, 1.3.2.2 [Kelsey, p. 92].

49. Grotius, *De iure belli*, 1.2.8.3–4 [Kelsey, pp. 71–72].

50. Grotius, *De iure belli*, 1.3.3.8 [Kelsey, p. 96].

51. Grotius, *De iure belli*, 1.2.8.13 [Kelsey, pp. 77–78].

52. Grotius, *De iure belli*, 2.20.9.1 [Kelsey, p. 475] and 2.20.8.1 [Kelsey, p. 472].

53. Weisser, *Crime and Punishment*, p. 1.

54. Stein, *Roman Law*, p. 89.

55. Stein, *Roman Law*, p. 61.

56. Stein, *Roman Law*, p. 64.

57. John H. Langbein, *Prosecuting Crime in the Renaissance: England, Germany, France* (Clark, NJ: The Lawbook Exchange, 2005, repr. 1974), p. 160.

58. *Carolina*, preamble [Langbein, p. 267].

59. *Carolina*, art. 28 [Langbein, p. 275].

60. Langbein, *Prosecuting Crime*, p. 179.

61. *Carolina*, art. 28 [Langbein, p. 275].

62. *Carolina*, art. 56.

63. *Carolina*, art. 48 [Langbein, p. 281].

64. *Carolina*, art. 47 [Langbein, p. 280].

65. Langbein, *Prosecuting Crime*, p. 202.

66. Stein, *Roman Law*, p. 83.

67. Langbein, *Prosecuting Crime*, p. 211.

68. Langbein, *Prosecuting Crime*, p. 214.

69. Langbein, *Prosecuting Crime*, p. 217.

70. Langbein, *Prosecuting Crime*, pp. 223–225.

71. *Ordonnance royale*, art. 146 [Langbein, p. 311].

72. Langbein, *Prosecuting Crime*, p. 229.

73. *Ordonnance royale*, art. 154 [Langbein, p. 312].

74. Langbein, *Prosecuting Crime*, pp. 237–238.

75. *Ordonnance royale*, pream. [Langbein, p. 310].

76. Langbein, *Prosecuting Crime*, p. 246.

77. Langbein, *Prosecuting Crime*, p. 241.

78. *Ordonnance criminelle du mois d'août 1670*, 19.1 and 19.3, www.ledroitcriminel .free.fr (accessed July 18, 2007).

79. Jean-Jacques Rousseau, *Le contrat sociale*, 2.7 [Maurice Cranston, trans., *The Social Contract* (New York, NY: Penguin, 1968), p. 84].

80. Rousseau, *Social Contract*, 2.10 [Cranston, p. 95].

81. Montesquieu, *L'esprit des lois*, 28.39 [Thomas Nugent, trans., *Montesquieu: The Spirit of the Laws* (New York, NY: Hafner Press, 1949), 2:145–146].

82. Montesquieu, *Spirit*, 1.3 [1:6–7].

83. Rousseau, *Social Contract*, 3.8 [Cranston, p. 124].

84. Stein, *Roman Law*, p. 110.

85. Rousseau, *Social Contract*, 1.5 [Cranston, pp. 58–59].

86. C. B. A. Behrens, *Society, Government, and the Enlightenment: The Experiences of Eighteenth-Century France and Prussia* (New York, NY: Harper & Row, 1985), p. 100.

87. Montesquieu, *Spirit*, 6.1 [1:71–72]. Rousseau, *Social Contract*, 2.9 [Cranston, p. 91]. Enlightenment figures especially despised the *parlements* of France.

88. Rousseau, *Social Contract*, 1.1 [Cranston, p. 49].

89. Rousseau, *Social Contract*, 2.9 [Cranston, p. 91]; and *First and Second Discourses*, Roger D. and Judith R. Masters, trans. (New York, NY: St. Martin's Press, 1964), p. 160.

90. Rousseau, *Discourses*, p. 163.

91. Rousseau, *Discourses*, p. 169.

92. Rousseau, *Discourses*, p. 171.

93. Langbein, *Prosecuting Crime*, p. 206.

94. Langbein, *Prosecuting Crime*, p. 209.

95. Rousseau, *Social Contract*, 1.3 [Cranston, p. 53].

96. Montesquieu, *Spirit*, 13.4 [1:185–186].

97. Montesquieu, *Spirit*, 11.5 [1:187]. Interestingly, the Spanish Inquisition generally dismissed witchcraft as a mental affliction, especially after 1526 (see Kamen, *The Spanish Inquisition*, pp. 270–272).

98. Beccaria, *Dei delitti* 25 [David Young, trans., *On Crimes and Punishments* (Indianapolis, IN: Hackett Publishing Co., 1986), p. 43].

99. Beccaria, *Dei delitti* 2 [Young, p. 8].

100. Beccaria, *Dei delitti* 28 [Young, p. 48].

101. Beccaria, *Dei delitti* 12 [Young, p. 23].

102. Beccaria, *Dei delitti* 19 [Young, p. 36].

103. Weisser, *Crime*, p. 135.

104. Beccaria, *Dei delitti* 41 [Young, p. 75].

105. Ibid.

106. Beccaria, *Dei delitti* 5 [Young, p. 13].

107. Beccaria, *Dei delitti* 13 [Young, p. 24].

108. Beccaria, *Dei delitti* 14 [Young, p. 26].

109. Beccaria, *Dei delitti* 15 [Young, p. 31].

110. Beccaria, *Dei delitti* 22 [Young, p. 39].

111. Beccaria, *Dei delitti* 28 [Young, p. 51].

112. Beccaria, *Dei delitti* 42 [Young, p. 76].

113. Behrens, *Society, Government, and the Enlightenment*, p. 103.

114. Leo Gershoy, *From Despotism to Revolution* (New York, NY: Harper & Brothers, 1944), p. 97.

115. Behrens, *Society, Government, and the Enlightenment*, p. 91.

116. *Declaration of the Rights of Man and of the Citizen*, article 6, www.constitution.org.fr (accessed July 27, 2007).

117. Gershoy, *From Despotism to Revolution*, pp. 96–97.

Bibliography

Part I

Primary Sources

Aeschylus, *The Oresteian Trilogy*. Translated by Vellacott, Philip. New York, NY: Penguin Books, 1956.

Aristotle, *The Athenian Constitution*. Translated by Rhodes, P. H. New York, NY: Penguin Books, 1984.

The *Code of Hammurabi*, www.wsu.edu/~dee/MESO/CODE.HTM (accessed December 16, 2004).

Grene, David, and Lattimore, Richmond, eds. *Greek Tragedies*, 2nd ed., 3 vols. Chicago, IL: University of Chicago Press, 1960.

Halliwell, Stephen, ed. and trans. *Aristophanes: Birds and Other Plays*. Oxford, UK: Oxford University Press, 1998.

Hamilton, Edith, and Cairns, Huntington, eds. *The Collected Dialogues of Plato*. Princeton, NJ: Princeton University Press, 1989.

Hesiod, *Works and Days*. Translated by Lombardo, Stanley. Indianapolis, IN: Hackett Publishing Co., 1993.

McKeon, Richard, ed. *The Basic Works of Aristotle*. New York, NY: Random House, 1941.

Thucydides, *The Peloponnesian War*. Translated by Warner, Rex. New York, NY: Penguin Books, 1954.

Xenophon, *Hellenica (History of My Times)*. Translated by Warner, Rex. New York, NY: Penguin Books, 1966.

Secondary Sources

Carmichael, Calum M., *The Spirit of Biblical Law*. Athens, GA: University of Georgia Press, 1996.

Finley, M. I., *Early Greece: The Bronze and Archaic Ages*. New York, NY: W. W. Norton and Co., 1970.

Todd, S. C., *The Shape of Athenian Law*. Oxford, UK: Oxford University Press, 1993.

Part II

Primary Sources

Birks, Peter, and McLeod, Grant, trans. *Justinian's Institutes*. Ithaca, NY: Cornell University Press, 1987.

Cicero, *The Republic and the Laws*. Translated by Rudd, Niall. Oxford, UK: Oxford University Press, 1998.

Eusebius of Nicomedia, *The History of the Church*. Translated by Williamson, G. A. New York, NY: Penguin Books, 1965.

———, *Life of Constantine*. Translated by Cameron, Averil, and Hall, Stuart G. Oxford, UK: Clarendon Press, 1999.

Gordon, W. M., and Robinson, O. F., trans. *The Institutes of Gaius*. Ithaca, NY: Cornell University Press, 1988.

Grubbs, Judith Evans, ed. *Women and the Law in the Roman Empire*. London, UK: Routledge, 2002.

Lewis, Naphtali, and Meyer, Reinhold, eds. *Roman Civilization*, 2 vols. New York, NY: Harper & Row, 1951.

Livy, *The Early History of Rome*. Translated by De Sélincourt, Aubrey. New York, NY: Penguin Books, 1960.

———, *Rome and Italy*. Translated by Radice, Betty. New York, NY: Penguin Books, 1982.

Scott, S. P., ed. *The Civil Law*, 17 vols. New York, NY: AMS Press, 1973.

Watson, Alan, trans. *The Digest of Justinian*, 4 vols. Philadelphia, PA: University of Pennsylvania Press, 1985.

Secondary Sources

Borkowski, Andrew, *Textbook on Roman Law*, 2nd ed. Oxford, UK: Oxford University Press, 1997.

Robinson, O. F., *The Criminal Law of Ancient Rome*. Baltimore, MD: Johns Hopkins University Press, 1995.

Watson, Alan, *The Spirit of Roman Law*. Athens, GA: University of Georgia Press, 1995.

Part III

Primary Sources

Akehurst, F. R. P., trans. *The Coutumes de Beauvaisis of Philippe de Beaumanoir*. Philadelphia, PA: University of Pennsylvania Press, 1992.

——, *The Établissements de Saint Louis*. Philadelphia, PA: University of Pennsylvania Press, 1996.

Drew, Katharine Fischer, trans. *The Burgundian Code*. Philadelphia, PA: University of Pennsylvania Press, 1949.

——, *The Laws of the Salian Franks*. Philadelphia, PA: University of Pennsylvania Press, 1991.

——, *The Lombard Laws*. Philadelphia, PA: University of Philadelphia Press, 1973.

Dobozy, Maria, trans. *The Saxon Mirror: A Sachsenspiegel of the Fourteenth Century*. Philadelphia, PA: University of Pennsylvania Press, 1999.

Downer, L. J., ed. and trans. *Leges Henrici Primi*. Oxford, UK: Clarendon Press, 1972.

Friedberg, Aemilianus, ed. *Corpus iuris canonici*, 2 vols. Leipzig, Germany: Bernard Tauchnitz, 1879–1891.

Ganshof, F. L. *Feudalism*. Translated by Grierson, Philip. New York, NY: Harper & Row, 1961.

Martyn, John R. C., trans. *The Letters of Gregory the Great*, 3 vols. Toronto, ON: Pontifical Institute of Mediaeval Studies, 2004.

McNeil, John T., and Gamer, Helena M., eds. *Medieval Handbooks of Penance*. New York, NY: Columbia University Press, 1990.

Rivers, Theodore John, trans. *Laws of the Alamans and Bavarians*. Philadelphia, PA: University of Pennsylvania Press, 1977.

Southern, R. W., *The Making of the Middle Ages*. New Haven, CT: Yale University Press, 1953.

Tierney, Brian, *The Crisis of Church and State, 1050–1300*. Toronto, ON: University of Toronto Press, 1988.

Wallace-Hadrill, J. M., trans. *The Fourth Book of the Chronicle of Fredegar with its Continuations*. London, UK: Thomas Nelson and Sons Ltd, 1960.

Secondary Sources

Bartlett, Robert, *Trial by Fire and Water: The Medieval Judicial Ordeal*. Oxford, UK: Clarendon Press, 1986.

Bellomo, Manlio, *The Common Legal Past of Europe, 1000–1800*. Translated by Cochrane, Lydia. Washington, DC: Catholic University of America Press, 1995.

Brandmüller, W., *Das Konzil von Konstanz*, 2 vols. Paderborn, Germany: Ferdinand Schöningh, 1991/1997.

Brundage, James, *Medieval Canon Law*. New York, NY: Longman, 1995.

Duby, Georges, *Rural Economy and Country Life in the Medieval West*. Translated by Posten, Cynthia. Columbia, SC: University of South Carolina Press, 1962.

Harding, Alan, *Medieval Law and the Foundations of the State*. Oxford, UK: Oxford University Press, 2002.

Helmholz, R. H., *Canon Law and the Law of England*. London, UK: Hambledon Press, 1987.

———, *The Spirit of Classical Canon Law*. Athens, GA: University of Georgia Press, 1996.

Herlihy, David, *Medieval Households*. Cambridge, MA: Harvard University Press, 1985.

Ganshof, F. L., *Feudalism*. Translated by Grierson, Philip. New York, NY: Harper & Row, 1961.

Pollack, Frederick, and Maitland, Frederic William, *History of English Law before the Time of Edward I*, 2 vols. Cambridge, UK: Cambridge University Press, 1895.

Pennington, Kenneth, *Pope and Bishops: The Papal Monarchy in the Twelfth and Thirteenth Centuries*. Philadelphia, PA: University of Pennsylvania Press, 1984.

Peters, Edward, *Torture*, 2nd ed. Philadelphia, PA: University of Pennsylvania Press, 1996.

Southern, R. W., *The Making of the Middle Ages*. New Haven, CT: Yale University Press, 1953.

Tierney, Brian, *Foundations of the Conciliar Theory*. Cambridge, UK: Cambridge University Press, 1955.

———, *Medieval Poor Law*. Berkeley, CA: University of California Press, 1959.

Part IV

Primary Sources

Beccaria, Cesare, *On Crimes and Punishments*. Translated by Young, David. Indianapolis, IN: Hackett Publishing Co., 1986.

Bray, Gerald, ed. *Documents of the English Reformation*. Minneapolis, MN: Fortress Press, 1994.

Declaration of the Rights of Man and of the Citizen, www.constitution.org.fr (accessed July 27, 2007).

Ehler, Sidney Z., and Morrall, John B., eds. and trans. *Church and State through the Centuries*. Westminster, MD: The Newman Press, 1954.

Grotius, Hugo, *De belli ac pacis libri tres*. Translated by Kelsey, Francis W. Oxford, UK: Clarendon Press, 1925.

Montesquieu, *The Spirit of the Laws*. Translated by Nugent, Thomas, 2 vols. New York, NY: Hafner Press, 1949.

Ordonnance criminelle du mois d'août 1670, www.ledroitcriminel.free.fr (accessed July 18, 2007).

Peters, Edward, ed. *Heresy and Authority in Medieval Europe*. Philadelphia, PA: University of Pennsylvania Press, 1980.

Rousseau, Jean-Jacques, *First and Second Discourses*. Translated by Masters, Roger D. and Judith R. New York, NY: St. Martin's Press, 1964.

———, *The Social Contract*. Translated by Cranston, Maurice. New York, NY: Penguin Books, 1968.

Translations and Reprints from the Original Sources of European History. Philadelphia, PA: University of Pennsylvania Press, 1897.

Secondary Sources

Behrens, C. B. A., *Society, Government, and the Enlightenment: The Experiences of Eighteenth-Century France and Prussia*. New York, NY: Harper & Row, 1985.

Gershoy, Leo, *From Despotism to Revolution*. New York, NY: Harper & Brothers, 1944.

Kamen, Henry, *The Spanish Inquisition: A Historical Revision*. New Haven, CT: Yale University Press, 1997.

Langbein, John H., *Prosecuting Crime in the Renaissance: England, Germany, France*. Clark, NJ: The Lawbook Exchange, 2005.

Tierney, Brian, *The Idea of Natural Rights: Studies on Natural Rights, Natural Law and Church Law, 1150–1625*, Emory Studies in Law and Religion 5. Atlanta, GA: Scholars Press, 1997.

Weisser, Michael R., *Crime and Punishment in Early Modern Europe*. Atlantic Highlands, NJ: Humanities Press, 1979.

White, Albert Beebe, and Notestein, Wallace, eds. *Source Problems in English History*. New York, NY: Harper and Brothers Publishers, 1915.

Index

About the Author

Robert W. Shaffern is professor of medieval history at the University of Scranton. His research interests lie in the fields of religious and intellectual history, with a particular focus on pastoral care and canon law. He is the author of *The Penitent's Treasury*, a study of indulgences from the twelfth through fourteenth centuries.